Day 1 – The adventure begins...

Land's End to Zennor – 16 miles

We were standing in our pants on the end of Britain. The sea chewed at the land around us, and the wind and rain attacked from all angles. We had the skin of freshly plucked turkeys. Cycling 1000 miles to the top of Scotland without any money, clothes, shoes, food or bikes, suddenly felt like a really stupid idea.

Land's End is frequented by three types of people; disillusioned holidaymakers who imagine that a trip to Britain's most south-westerly point is a rewarding experience, tourists who arrive there by mistake when they run out of road, and those who are starting or finishing the popular Land's End to John O'Groats expedition. We fell awkwardly into the latter category.

The plan was simple. We had three weeks to get from the bottom of England to the top of Scotland – by foot or by bike – without spending a single penny. Setting off in just a pair of Union Jack boxer shorts, we hoped to rely on the generosity of the British public to help us with everything from accommodation to food, clothes to shoes, and bikes to beer.

I was working as a photographer at the time. At least, that's what I told people. I quit my stable, easy and fairly well paid job a few years previously to become a full-time photographer. In truth, I spent my days doing unstable, mundane and badly paid temping jobs in order to pay the bills. The photography jobs did come in very occasionally and they provided me with enough credibility to convince those around me that the decision to leave my job was a wise one. I took a picture of a friend of a friend's dog the previous month and I had a bar mitzvah booking for the following year. Business was really booming, oh yeah.

My travelling companion was Ben. Ben worked as a composer and an actor, appearing in a number of Oscar-winning blockbusters such as Harry Potter, *The Phantom of the Opera and Lord of the Rings*. He had also appeared in countless TV shows including Eastenders, *The Bill and Casualty*. When I say 'actor', I mean 'extra', and you would have to be incredibly quick-fingered with the pause button to spot him in ANY of his roles. As I mentioned, he was also a composer. Specifically, he made music for film and television. Three seconds of his music once featured in a Taiwanese computer advert – shown only on the internet – and he was still reeling in the glory of

that moment. He spent his days watching Bargain Hunt and waiting for the advertising agency to phone back.

I asked Ben to join me on LEJOG (this is what those in the know call the Land's End to John O'Groats trip. It's an acronym, you see), because he was the only one of my friends that fitted the necessary criteria; he was a self-employed layabout like me who did not need permission to take three weeks off work at short notice.

We started early, at about 7.30am, in order to minimise the amount of people that would have to witness our scrawny bodies. The coastline around Land's End is impressive, but there is no sense whatsoever of being at the end of the country. Try standing there in your pants in the wind and rain, however, and it definitely heightens the experience.

The footpaths around the Land's End complex were not designed with the barefoot walker in mind, and the heavy gravel cut into our feet at every step. In fairness, it is unlikely that many visitors to that part of Cornwall come without shoes. Even the notorious 'Naked Rambler' wore a pair of walking boots. The cheating bastard. You can visit his boots – if you are really bored – in the 'End to End Experience' museum, which forms part of the Land's End complex. He is mentioned alongside Ian Botham, who has famously walked the route twice, and next to the story of a man who tried to push a pea with his nose the entire way. He got about two miles before he realised that it made his nose hurt.

We met up with Jemma – the End to End co-ordinator. Jemma had possibly the most enviable job in the world. Her working day involved sitting in a little office by a log fire, looking out to sea. She occasionally had to say 'Good Luck' to people like us who were setting off to John O'Groats, or 'Well-done' to those who had finished their journey. This, it seemed, was all she did. I was incredibly jealous.

We asked her if she had any interesting stories of fellow End to Enders, and she told us about a cyclist being hit by a car and killed, and another one concerning a group being robbed at gunpoint. These were not the inspirational, feel-good stories we were hoping for.

The idea of the penniless challenge was founded on the belief, that, as a nation, we have lost sight of the basic values of humanity and kinship. We tend to be very suspicious of those that we don't know, and of anything that falls outside the realms of normality. Britain is broken, or so we are led to believe, and every unfamiliar face masks an axe murderer or terrorist. We choose to close our doors and hide from the outside world.

I wanted to prove this notion wrong. I strongly believed that there was still a lot of good to be found in society, and that there lies within everyone, the desire to help others. By travelling without money and provisions, we were putting ourselves completely at the mercy of strangers, relying on their generosity to get us through.

The Land's End to John O'Groats challenge is an iconic British journey, and it seemed to tie in perfectly with the penniless format of the trip as it encapsulated the whole of Great Britain.

Clothes were a priority.

We stood little chance of getting food, accommodation or bikes with our pasty bodies on full show. Also, it was bloody freezing and we didn't want to become the first people to die at Land's End before crossing the official start line. Although, if we had, Jemma would have had another story to tell other End to Enders before they set off.

'Well if you make it past the visitor centre,' she would say, 'you'll have done better than George and Ben. They died right here in their pants.' It would have made her day.

We wandered aimlessly around Land's End not knowing what to do or how to begin the ridiculous challenge that we had set ourselves. After a few minutes of roaming we got talking to the only other weirdoes who had decided to visit Land's End at 7.30am on that unforgiving morning. They were Australian. We explained to them why we were standing there in our pants.

'Strewth, and we thought people back in Oz were mad,' said Bruce.

'Crikey,' said Sheila. 'Bruce, go and get that old t-shirt from the car for these fellas.'

'No worries, Sheila,' said Bruce. Bruce and Sheila were not their real names. Their actual names were lost in the wind somewhere.

Bruce and Sheila were halfway through their five-week world tour and had been in England just two days. Why they had decided to come to Land's End we had no idea. They were in their early forties and were travelling with another couple, Kylie and Jason, and the four of them were dressed like a mountain rescue team, as southern-hemisphere visitors to England tend to dress. Only a few square inches of their faces were exposed to the elements, but this was enough to see their kind and genuine smiles.

Bruce returned a few minutes later with the t-shirt. It was a momentous occasion; our first freebie and we hadn't even asked for it. The t-shirt itself was an XXXL made of silky white polyester, with a cigarette burn in the back and an inescapable scent of Australian body odour. I tried it on first, as Ben seemed more comfortable than me to prance around Land's End almost naked. It was ridiculously big and made me look like I was wearing a parachute.

The t-shirt did make a huge difference, however. Not only did it repel some of the icy temperatures that were being thrown at us, but it also transformed my confidence. I was instantly changed from a shivering fool in a pair of Union Jack boxer shorts, to someone that was about to cycle 1000 miles to the top of Scotland. The fact that I was still only half clothed and didn't have a bike was purely incidental.

We thanked Bruce, Sheila, Kylie and Jason and urged them not to judge England by Land's End, or the English by us. We decided to make our way to the Land's End Hotel, as it was the only place likely to be open so early. We had high hopes of raiding the lost property for some more clothes.

On our way to the hotel, Bruce's friend Jason caught us up.

'G'day again, guys. I got this for ya, too,' he panted and handed us another t-shirt. This one was cotton, clean, white, without cigarette burns and a cosy medium fit. I regretted hastily grabbing the first one. Ben gave me a smug grin.

The Land's End Hotel is a fairly ugly building, and is therefore in keeping with the surroundings. The interior, however, is rather posh and the reception area was crammed full of elderly American tourists who had been lulled there by the notion that it was a charming hotel perched on the edge of the country. There was an air of deep disappointment in the room. The conversations stopped and they all turned to watch as we entered the reception.

'WHATTA YA DOIN?' yelled one of the Americans who looked close to a hundred and spoke at twice the necessary volume.

'WE'RE ON OUR WAY TO JOHN O'GROATS AT THE TOP OF SCOTLAND,' said Ben, replying in a volume equal to the old man's.

'YOU'LL END UP IN HOSPITAL,' shouted the old man.

We both gave a nervous laugh and shuffled our way to the reception desk. The Americans shuffled out of the door through which we had just come, ready for their day of fun.

The hotel receptionist forced a smile when she saw us. She was in her late thirties and had the look of a supply teacher who would take no shit.

'Hello... Ruth,' I said, spotting her badge and dropping her name into conversation like a sleazy salesman, 'I wonder if you can help us.' Her smile disappeared and she began to look panicked. 'We're about to attempt to cycle to John O'Groats without spending a single penny...' Her face turned to mild bemusement as though she had just been told the punch line of a joke she didn't quite understand. '...and all of our food, accommodation, clothes and hopefully bikes will have to be acquired from the generosity of the British public,' I continued, sensing she was beginning to warm up, 'and we were wondering whether the hotel had any lost property that had not been reclaimed that we could possibly have?'

There was a long pause. A sense of relief passed over Ruth. My speech was over and she realised she wasn't being robbed, she wasn't going to have to sponsor us and we weren't asking her out on a date.

'Ok,' she said, 'I'll see what I can do.' She disappeared into the back office and we were left alone.

A middle-aged man and his wife arrived at reception to check out. He was dressed head to toe in Lycra and was wearing a pair of cycling gloves. He had a cycle helmet in one hand and a drinking bottle in the other. With some careful deliberation we guessed him to be a cyclist. Our suspicions were confirmed when we noticed that he was wheeling a bicycle.

'Are you going to John O'Groats?' asked Ben.

'I sure am,' said the cyclist.

'I'm his support crew,' said his wife.

'We're cycling to John O'Groats, too,' said Ben, standing shivering in a pair of damp boxers and an ill-fitting t-shirt.

'Really?' said the cyclist, who then gave a laugh as if to say 'you nearly had me there.'

Although our goal was the same, the differences between us could not have been further apart. He had at least £2000 worth of equipment, top-of the range Lycra cycling clothing, a lightweight Gortex jacket and a devoted support crew. We were unsupported, barely clothed and without any form of bike. Oh, how we longed for a couple of carbon-fibre racing bikes, waterproof jackets and a support crew. And the Lycra was strangely alluring, too.

The cyclist's name was John and he was about to begin his second End to End trip. He had completed the trip with a friend a few years previously and wanted to do it again alone, with his wife following behind in the car. He was aiming to finish the trip in ten days. We imagined we would probably still be in Cornwall in ten days. John explained that his Dad had been a professional medal-winning cyclist and that he had always lived in his shadow. Doing the Land's End to John O'Groats trip was his way of making his dad proud.

Once he understood that we were serious about our trip, he took a keen interest in how we were going to go about it.

'You'll need some shoes and socks,' he said. 'Hold on, I'll be right back.' His wife took hold of his bike and he scurried out of the door. He returned a minute later with a pair of trainers and a pair of socks.

'Take these,' he said, worryingly out of breath for someone about to cycle to Scotland. 'I brought way too many pairs of shoes and I never wear these anyway.' They were white leather trainers, slightly retro and a perfect fit for either of us. We thanked him gratefully and wished him luck for his bike ride. We had earned the respect of an End to End veteran and we had not even crossed the start line.

Ruth returned from the office holding a big box of lost property. She dropped it down on the reception desk in front of us and our eyes scoured eagerly over the contents like a couple of clothes perverts.

The first item that caught our eye was a pair of thick, woollen, pinstriped suit trousers. They were tailor-made to fit a big fat man. Ben decided I should have them, since I was the larger of the two of us. After trying them on, it was clear that there would have been room for both of us. Not only were they for a big fat man, but they were also previously owned by an extremely short fat man, or someone with a penchant for wearing their trousers at half-mast. The trousers hung halfway down my arse, and stopped halfway up my shin. I looked like the lovechild of a gangster and a sailor. It was EXACTLY the look I was going for.

Also in the box were two cardigans. Ben took the trendy, skimpy black number and I took the thick, granny blue one. We only took items that had been unclaimed for over three months, so as not to get into trouble with any angry tenants. Although, I'm pretty sure the 'finders keepers, losers weepers' defence would have held firm. We also took a baseball cap each. I'm not sure why, but it seemed like a good idea at the time. Ben had an England football cap with a St George's Cross on the front, and I had a retro Manchester United cap. We looked like a couple of chavs. Chavs in cardies.

The final item of lost property that we acquired was a child's pink umbrella. We naively thought that it would shield some of the rain for a while, and we thought it might also be a useful bartering item to swap at some stage of the trip. It proved to be neither.

We were delaying the inevitable.

At some point we were going to have to leave the relative comfort and security of Land's End and start our journey towards John O'Groats. We had scavenged as much as we could from the hotel and it was time to leave. On the way out we bumped into Jemma again. She was armed with two 'official' Land's End t-shirts, which she kindly presented to us. Normal people have to pay for these, but we had told her that payment for anything was prohibited in our world. We pulled these on over our cardigans and we were ready to go. Land's End – been there, done that, and now we had the t-shirts.

Almost fully clothed, we were about to begin our journey towards Scotland. The official start line is in the car park and not by the sign, as you would expect. Crossing it was certainly an anti-climax. Our farewell party consisted of two old ladies, but it turned out that they were just waiting for the toilets to be unlocked. Even so, they uttered a half-hearted 'good luck', raised their eyebrows and smirked at each other.

We were finally on our way.

I was dressed in my suit trousers, which I had to roll up around the waist to keep them from falling down to my ankles. I was also wearing two t-shirts, a blue cardigan, a Manchester United baseball cap (on backwards, because I'm hip), one trainer and one sock. Ben was wearing two t-shirts, a black cardigan, an England cap (on sideways, because he's rad) and no trousers. He was wearing the other sock and trainer. It was still raining, but the wind had died down once we had moved away from the exposed cliffs. It was cold but bearable.

The road climbed gradually away from the coast and the Land's End complex became a distant blemish on the landscape behind us. We had been warned that John O'Groats was just a rubbish version of Land's End, so we were in no hurry to get there.

The ground was painful underfoot. The idea of wearing one shoe each was supposed to minimise the pain for each person, but in reality, it made   things worse, as we constantly had a reminder of what luxury shoes are. We soon established that walking along the thick white line on the edge of the road minimised the discomfort.

Most travelogues such as this have a long preamble about the build up to the journey. This would include extensive details about the preparations and the arrangements involved; sourcing and buying suitable equipment, planning a route and researching the trip in meticulous detail. The training regime would also be discussed to show how a peak level of fitness was attained before undertaking such a physical challenge. You will have noticed that this book contains no such introduction. The truth was, there was no real preparation. As soon as the idea of the trip had taken shape in my mind, I suggested it to Ben who agreed straight away to join me. It then didn't prove too difficult to find three weeks that we both had free, as neither of us had much on in the way of work, or anything else for that matter. We didn't need to source or buy any equipment either, as we weren't taking anything. We didn't need to plan a route as we wanted to allow for spontaneity, and as this was the first time an End to End trip had been attempted in this manner – as far as we were aware – there was nothing productive that we could do in the way of research.

As for our training regime, that was non-existent. Be under no illusion, Ben and I were not experienced cyclists. I did ride my bike several times a week, but this was to cover the 400 metres to the local shop. Ben used his bike even less frequently. We had taken part in the London to Brighton bike ride earlier in the year, which is a distance of 54 miles, and was the furthest that either of us had ever cycled by some way. It took us most of the day and made us both realise that we were not cut out for long-distance cycling. It did however plant the seed in my mind about attempting this journey of more epic proportions.

Originally I had suggested to Ben that we try to acquire our bikes and clothes for free BEFORE heading to Cornwall and then just attempt to cycle to John O'Groats without spending any money.

'Where's the fun in that?' asked Ben. 'If we're going to do it properly then we need to start with nothing at all. No clothes, no money, no shoes and no bikes.'

'What? You want to start from Land's End completely naked? We would get arrested.'

'Maybe just a pair of boxer shorts then, if you're embarrassed about people seeing your tiny penis. But definitely no other clothes, no shoes and certainly no bikes. That would be cheating.'

'Do you really think we'll be able to get clothes and bikes for free?'

'There's only one way to find out.'

We were given a lift down to Cornwall the day preceding by a willing companion and we went through the night in a close by B&B and partook in a 'last dinner' at the nearby bar. Early the following morning we handed our clothes, wallets, shoes and phones to our willing friend, who then waved us goodbye and left us stranded on the cliff tops in our pants.

'Now what?' got some information about a mile up the street from Land's End. I didn't know how to react. We had not actually thoroughly examined entire thing and it out of nowhere occurred to us that we didn't actually have the foggiest idea what to do straightaway. Our point had been to get garments, and that had been more straightforward than anticipated, yet we hadn't thought past that. We kept strolling and expected inspiration.

The previously piece of civilisation we went over was a farmhouse. It was slowed down from the street, yet we could see development through one of the windows. We concluded it merited enquiring about one more pair of shoes. We moved toward the entryway with anxious alert. Ben was still without trousers and it was highly likely that any elderly occupants of the house would have had a seizure at the sight of him cavorting down their driveway in his underwear. We thumped on the entryway and a man replied. He was genuinely old, yet fit enough to withstand the shock of seeing us close to home. He thought we were after cash and was assuaged to hear we just needed shoes. He welcomed us in and we stood clumsily in his front room while he headed out to find an old pair of wellies that he thought he had lying around in a horse shelter. It is extremely challenging to stand to some degree dressed in a more abnormal's home and not feel conspicuous.

He returned a couple of moments later with a couple of wellies close by, and a look of alleviation all over that we hadn't escape with his TV. We said thanks to him and advanced back out into the carport. The wellies were a size 6. We were both a size 10. They were spilling over with straw and spider webs and I gave them a decent shake to eliminate whatever number bugs as could be allowed. I proposed to wear them first and with a touch of exertion and control of my toes I had the option to fit into them. There was no room left for any excess insects

to inhale, not to mention wriggle.

A further half-mile up the street we arrived at a street intersection and we had to settle on our first directional choice. Not really settled, with our fundamental comprehension of British topography, that assuming we kept the ocean to our left side we would be heading toward Scotland. We realized that the street we were on was the A30 and would become more occupied the nearer it got to Penzance. It didn't sound appropriate for seriously dressed walkers, so we turned left and tottered along the calmer street towards St Ives and the sea.

The mist had shut in and we could just see around 20 meters one or the other way. There was almost no indication of something going on under the surface anyplace. I oversaw about a mile in the wellies prior to getting a rankle. I realize it sounds pitiable, however truly, you should take a stab at strolling in wellies that are four sizes excessively little with only one wet sock for insurance. Ben proposed to impart the aggravation to me thus we wore a welly and a coach each. This look is presently a remarkable rage.

The morning had vanished like smoke in the breeze, however we were just three miles from Land's End. We were getting ravenous and chose to look for food at the principal opportunity. It was no longer as cold or wet, and we were practically starting to partake in the experience. Ben appeared totally quiet in his fighter shorts and showed no disgrace. A periodic vehicle passed us and either hooted their horn in a 'ha, take a gander at those oddities' sort of way or just gazed at us with confusion.

The smell of food floated through the air from a unidentifiable source. Out of nowhere, a major white structure arose out of the mist; it was about the size of a little air terminal. Phenomenally, it ended up being a little airport.

We moved toward the structure and saw a little written by hand notice on the door:

'Because of unfavorable climate conditions, all trips to the Scilly Isles have been dropped. *Kindly leave your baggage in the vehicle before entering'*.

We didn't have any gear, or a vehicle, so we entered.

The structure was hurling with individuals, at this point there was a frightful quiet in the room. Older sightseers, inactively standing by to check whether the haze would clear, involved column upon line of seats. We had come to search out the beginning of the smell and we shambled our direction awkwardly through the groups towards what resembled a bistro. This was to be our first solicitation for food and we both turned out to be progressively apprehensive. Assuming we fizzled, we realized it would be a battle from then

on.

There were two older women at the counter requesting their cream teas, so we waited until they had wrapped up. In the event that we planned to bite the dust, we didn't need an audience.

'Hello,' said Ben with an off-kilter grin. 'My companion George and I are headed to John O'Groats. We began toward the beginning of today at Land's End in some fighter shorts and we need to get the whole way without spending a solitary penny.'

'alright?' answered the man behind the counter.

'And we were pondering... ' proceeded with Ben, 'in case you had any food that you were going to toss out that we could maybe have?' There was an uncomfortable delay as he glanced around to check whether he had any ranking staff to check with. The kitchen was empty.

'How does an espresso and a bacon sandwich sound?' he asked.

It was really that straightforward. We had got our first free feast. We were expecting some half-chewed bread at best, or maybe an old lettuce, but we were soon presented with a huge steaming bacon bap and a mug of freshly brewed coffee.

It happened that John – the man behind the counter – was a pilot and had been compelled to assist in the kitchen in view of the flight cancellations.

Ben and I sat peacefully as we ate. John's food had filled us both with a sensation of happiness and there was no compelling reason to talk. He proposed to top up our espressos, as a method of postponing returning outside, we readily accepted.

As we sat, fulfilled, we were drawn nearer by one of the travelers from the lounge area. She had been looking at Ben's legs while we ate. She was around 70 and inquired as to why we were dressed like we were.

'We're cycling to John O'Groats,' answered Ben.

'Gracious, do you need a few grapes?' she asked, and pulled a bundle from her sack. Amazingly, now, others in the lounge area began coming towards us with contributions; chocolate bars, crisps, pancake, apples, organic product juice and more grapes. No one truly comprehended the reason why we were dressed as were we, or where we were going, however it was clearly evident that we were destitute. Their benevolence, which was totally unwarranted, provided us with a reestablished feeling of excitement for our adventure.

'You'll arrive, no issue,' said one of them.

'two or three pleasant folks like you. Simply continue to grin and you'll be fine,' said another.

'Aww, they were crushing? I would like them as my children,' we heard one of the women say as we left the building.

John, the pilot-come-supper woman, pursued us and provided us with a jug of water each.

'You'll require this, fellows,' he puffed.

The entire excursion was unexpectedly genuine. There was currently every possibility we could make it. To Devon, at least.

You are most likely considering how it was feasible to take the photographs in this book assuming we began with only some fighter shorts. Actually, we additionally conveyed a camera, a scratch pad and pen and a wad of postcards printed with the words: 'I'm OFFICIALLY an exceptionally decent individual'. The scratch pad and pen were for me to keep a journal during the excursion. I needed to track our encounters and of individuals that we met, to help make up for my crumbling memory.

Being a photographic artist, I likewise figured it would be a great plan to photo the various individuals who helped us en route, making a montage of Britain's uncelebrated heroes.

The postcards were Ben's thought. He referenced it several days prior to we set off and I at first excused the thought as cheesy and inconsequential. With all due respect, he had initially proposed that the postcards be printed with the expression: 'I'm a FUCKING decent individual.' The prospect of introducing a card like this to an old woman, who had recently given us an apple, appeared somewhat wrong.

'Hi, minimal old woman. Much thanks to you for the apple. Here is a postcard that expresses what a FUCKING decent individual you are.'

In the end, we settled on: 'I'm OFFICIALLY an exceptionally pleasant individual.' It was straightforward, tame and genuine.

I should make plainly neither the camera, nor the postcards, were at any point used to assist us with acquiring favors in any capacity. They were just at any point presented after a decent deed had been done.

The sun had not yet arisen through the mist, and Ben's legs were starting to feel the virus. We thumped on the entryway of the following house that we went over, to attempt to think that he is a few pants. An enormous, round-confronted man addressed the entryway. He was in his thirties and had a face that appeared as though it was produced using crushed potato. He was stocky and north of six feet tall, however his tyrannical casing was balanced by a gigantic grin and delicately spoken voice.

We clarified that we were wanting to get a couple of pants and he welcomed us in while he went to see. He got back with a couple of dark tracksuit bottoms.

'Are these alright?' he asked.

'They look totally great,' said Ben. 'Much thanks. What's your name?'

'Les,' said Les.

Les worked for the coastguard and had purchased his home a couple of years beforehand; it was an old sanctuary, which he had changed over himself. The spot was truly hitting with a low hung roof and sharp lighting giving it a comfortable vibe. The kitchen units were enriched with artworks and drawings done by a little kid. Either that, or Les was very waste at art.

Les additionally offered us a backpack subsequent to seeing our arms weighed down with food, water and an umbrella. We said thanks to him and kept strolling in the haze towards the town of St Just.

The street between Land's End and St Ives is spotted with the remaining parts of tin mines. Mining had occurred in Cornwall since stone-age times, however the revelation of less expensive metal in different pieces of Europe, America and Australia basically obliterated the business. Many mines kept on warding off global rivalry well into the twentieth Century, however on March sixth, 1998, the siphons were at long last turned off for great at South Crofty, simply up the road
– both Cornwall and the UK's last enduring tin mine.

We arrived at the town of St Just with its pleased status as the most westerly town in England. The town is minimal in excess of a major town. At its middle is a charming little market square, which is flanked by a few bars. It had been an intense morning, and we felt like we merited a lager purported into the principal bar to take a stab. Requesting garments and food was a certain something, however requesting free brew was something totally unique. Not at all like food and garments, brew was not really a need, however after a debilitating daytime's strolling and blagging we felt like it was pretty much as fundamental as oxygen.

I picked the most youthful and better looking of the two barmaids and chose to attempt the genuine and direct approach.

'Hello,' I said in a cool and somewhat coquettish way. 'We are venturing to every part of the length of the country without spending a solitary penny, and we were contemplating whether there was any possibility we might actually have a free beer?'

'Errr, alright,' she said with an apprehensive laugh. 'Are two half ales ok?'

I concluded that this was not an opportunity to get some information about attempting one of the neighborhood ales.

'Two half ales would be staggering. Much thanks indeed.'

Seven hours sooner we had been remaining in our fighter shorts in the breeze and downpour. We were presently completely dressed and drinking free brew in a pleasant Cornish town. Life was pretty good.

We begun visiting to a person at the bar called Steve. He was not quite as intoxicated as a portion of different local people, yet his words were as yet slurred. We inquired as to whether he knew anyplace or anybody that could assist us with trip with a bike.

'Assuming you allow me 60 minutes, I'll get somebody to figure you out with a bicycle,' he said.

'Would it be taken?' asked Ben suspiciously.

'Better believe it, presumably, yet you will not get found out,' said Steve.

'Much obliged, yet we were expecting to get a few bicycles legally and really, yet we like the deal,' said Ben.

Steve proposed we attempt one more bar in St Just – the Miners Arms. It was additionally a reason for another beer.

The Miners Arms was genuinely terrible. The dividers were painted dark and there was basically no light, other than the sunshine that jabbed its direction through the shut screens. We bumbled our direction to the bar, knocking from void table to discharge table and stepping on a periodic dozing canine. It was Ben's round.

'Hi,' he said, taking a gander at every one of the four of the folks sitting at the bar, expecting that one of them worked there.

'What would i be able to get you?' requested the most youthful and most unrealistic looking barman from the parcel of them.

'We're cycling 1000 miles to John O'Groats, however we don't have any bicycles,' said Ben. The spot howled uncontrollably. Sniggers could be heard through the murkiness from a table in the furthest corner. 'We were pondering... ' proceeded with Ben courageous, 'assuming you knew anybody that had several bicycles that they were attempting to get freed of.'

The chuckling went up a score. It proceeded briefly or so.

'I'll accept that as a no,' said Ben. 'Any shot at a free lager then,
at that point?' 'Certain,' said the barman. 'You all strong like
you'll require it.'

We plunked down in the haziness and drank our second lager of the day.
We had just strolled four miles, and at that rate, it planned to assume control
more than five months to get to John O'Groats. We had permitted ourselves
three weeks.

By this point, it seemed like my welly had scoured through deep down. I
eliminated it in the desire for showing Ben some horrendous fight twisted,
yet was disillusioned to find a little red splodge on my heel. In any case, we
concluded that appropriate shoes were more vital than bicycles. The
excursion would have been over before it had appropriately started in the
event that we had proceeded in the wellies.

I chose to address the folks at the bar once more. Regardless of giggling at
us previously, they were amicable and approachable.

'Do you know anyplace we could get a couple of old shoes?' I asked, 'We
have one sets of mentors and a couple of wellies that are excessively little.'
The chuckling arrived at new statures and I got back to our table in the
corner.

We were going to leave when part of the gang who had been at the bar
moved toward us. He was in his late twenties, with a missing front tooth and
slicked hair. He had not let out the slightest peep previously and had been the
main individual not to laugh.

'I think what you are doing is moving,' he said unobtrusively, so his
companions at the bar didn't hear. 'I need you to have this.' He then glanced
around to check that his friends weren't looking before removing a small
crystal ear stud from his ear. He then took my arm and placed the crystal
gently in the palm of my hand. 'It will bring you great luck.'

I didn't actually have the foggiest idea what to say. It was whenever I first
had been given gems from anybody, and I didn't envision that I would lose
my adornments virginity to a youngster in a bar in most profound Cornwall.
There was something exceptionally strong with regards to it, which I loved –
in a non-gay way.

'You ought to go with them, Eric,' one of different men yelled. 'Continue,
what's halting you? You haven't found a new line of work or some other
responsibilities. You ought to do it.'

A look of edification disregarded Eric's face and we half anticipated that
he should follow us out of the entryway. He paused.

'Nah,' he said. 'I've actually got 'alf a 16 ounces left.'

We were covertly soothed. However much we loved Eric, we didn't need the outing to transform into a Pied Piper style issue, getting strays at each town. We advised him to get us up, and I attached the stud to my shirt as I had never found time to have my ears pierced.

Outside the bar we met a person grasping a gigantic pair of rigger boots.

'Here you go, fellows,' said the man, who we then, at that point, perceived as being one of different men at the bar. He was around 50, uncovered, with a major grin. 'I got these

for you.'

He given us the colossal boots, that were covered in concrete and each gauged as old as wet towel. They were, nonetheless, undeniably more engaging than the wellies.

'They're from Boomer, a companion of Steve's,' he said. 'He said he had met you in The Wellington an hour prior. He doesn't wear these any longer and says you can have them if you want.'

The Wellington was the suitably named bar we had been to first. 'Splendid, thank you kindly,' I said. 'Kindly pass on our thanks to Boomer and Steve.'

'Surely. Best of luck, folks,' he said.

We had gained our third thing of footwear in under 12 hours. The liberality and energy of individuals that we had met was totally overwhelming.

I removed my welly and mentor and uncurled my toes without precedent for hours. The wellies had been a size 6; the rigger boots were about size 14. I dropped my feet into them easily. Regardless of their size and weight, they felt lavish. They were fixed with hide and my toes were allowed to wander any place they picked. Assuming that I might have just observed one more eight sets of socks from some place, they would have practically fitted me. I consented to do the first change in quite a while and Ben wore the two mentors, which were above and beyond to get us the whole way to John O'Groats

After a two hour bar break we chose to attempt to get a couple of more miles under our figurative belts. We initially had St Ives at the top of the priority list as an objective for the evening, yet this was currently looking totally unreasonable. St Ives was 13 miles away and it would be dim inside a couple hours.

There was no room in the backpack for the wellies, so Ben draped them behind him with the arrangement to pass them onto somebody with little feet and a requirement for wellies. A pixie rancher, perhaps.

Cornwall was staggering. We were unable to see quite a bit of this is a result of the mist, however what we could see was staggering. There was no far off murmur of a motorway that upsets the quiet of numerous different pieces of the British open country. Even the villages had a ghostly silence. The haze hardened the encompassing scene and walled us in a case of cloud. The fields molded erratically and huge bunches of rock spotted them like headstones. The view would have changed very little in a thousand years. Aside from the street we were walking

along, and the hedgerows, there was no sign of modern civilisation at all. It was essentially beautiful.

Just after 6pm we arrived at the town of Pendeen, which, by Cornish norms, was clamoring. The North Star was an appealing looking bar from an external perspective and it didn't baffle within. Britain were playing an European qualifier and everybody in the bar was watching the game eagerly on the TV. We needed to hasten across the floor so as not to obstruct the perspective on those at the bar. I needed to remain in that bar for eternity. There was brew, football and a major log fire. I verged on inquiring as to whether we could remain, yet rather rolled out the routine about bikes.

'Sorry folks, I can't help,' he said.

Disappointed, we stood around at the bar however long we could. We saw Steven Gerrard score prior to withdrawing outside to the cold road.

We were cautioned that once we left Pendeen there was nothing in the method of civilisation until Zennor, which was eight miles away. Interestingly, we had begun to ponder where we may go through the evening. We realized that regardless of whether we wonderfully figured out how to get bicycles, it would be dull when we arrived at Zennor. In spite of the chance of not having the option to find anyplace to remain, Ben and I were still loaded with adrenaline from the test that we had set ourselves, thus it was of little concern.

'What occurs on the off chance that we can't find anyplace to remain?' asked Ben.

'We'll simply track down a bar, remain there until they toss us out and afterward stick around outside until morning,' I replied.

'Goodness,' said Ben. 'Ok.'

Just on the edges of the town we thumped on the entryway of a house with an assortment of odd pieces and pieces flung across the front yard; debris, floats, lobster pots and fishing nets. It was like an elevated tide had regurgitated a wreck in the nursery. We were a few miles inland, so this was very unlikely.

'Come in, come in,' said the wire-haired hippy who addressed the entryway, before asking what our identity was, for sure we wanted.

We had been remaining in her receiving area for a considerable length of time visiting about the climate and her being an analyst and other arbitrary stuff, before she even inquired as to why we were in her house.

'We're searching for several old bicycles to assist us with getting to John O'Groats,'

I said.

'Gracious, I haven't got any bicycles, yet I have a cookout set you can have,' she answered promptly, like she had been pursuing for at some point to dispose of it.

'Fail, great,' I expressed profound gratitude,' 'accepting that she would have been irritated in case we had declined her offer.

The woman's name was Liz and she was a clinician, as I have as of now referenced. I clarified that I was attempting to snap a picture of all of the 'decent individuals' that helped us en route, and I requested to snap a photo of her.

'I don't know whether I can trust you,' she said. 'I work with insane individuals the entire day and it makes me suspicious.'

Now, I'm no therapist, yet perhaps she ought to have thought about that before she let two complete outsiders into her home. Maybe that is the thing that they instruct on the very first moment of Psychology School; welcome quite a few irregular individuals into your home, yet don't, under any conditions, let them snap a picture of you.

She got the cookout set for us, which arrived in a helpful backpack. I had dreams of attempting to convey an enormous wicker hamper the entire way to Scotland, as was mitigated to see it was a sensible size. I had been conveying the backpack that Les had given us, so Ben took the outing set. We expressed gratitude toward Liz and she said thanks to us for lighting up her day. She let us know that we were 'odd and wacky,' which we had never been depicted as, and will likely never again. She additionally proposed, not interestingly, that we were intellectually ill.

We proceeded onwards towards Zennor. Cornwall turned out to be increasingly sloping. The land around us undulated aimlessly like a motocross track. It should be a genuine jerk for ranchers. The haze shut in considerably further and it became risky for us to stroll out and about, so we strolled on the grass skirt however much as could be expected and kept our ears alert for drawing nearer cars.

After one more hour's strolling we arrived at the town of Morvah. Morvah is a little village with a supposed populace of 79. At the point when we went through, they were all secluded from everything. The couple of houses that we could see all had their lights off and there were no vehicles in the carport.

We began to puzzle over whether vehicles and power had been found in Cornwall yet.

The last house that we went over displayed up. There were lights on and a vehicle in the carport. We thumped on the entryway and a lady replied. She was in her mid-forties with a warm, inviting face, bunched up hair and a loose t-shirt.

'I'm truly grieved,' she said before asking what we needed, 'I have quite recently wrapped up draining the cows and I wasn't expecting visitors.'

'We're truly sorry to trouble you,' I said, 'yet we were contemplating whether you had any old bicycles lying around that you were attempting to get freed of.'

'I don't think we have,' she said, totally unflinching by our inquiry. 'We disposed of our own the month before. We may have an old bike in the garden.'

'Truly?' we both reacted, maybe overenthusiastically as it seemed to alarm her. 'A bike would be amazing.'

'alright, what do you want it for?'

'We're cycling to John O'Groats,' said Ben, who then, at that point, depicted our test to her.

'What an experience!' said the woman, whose name was Sue. 'Simply give me a sec, and I'll check whether our neighbors have anything they can give you.'

'Helen, it's Sue,' she said on the telephone. 'I have two young men with me who are making a beeline for John O'Groats and they're after a few bicycles. Do you have anything at your place?' There was a long respite. 'It doesn't need to be a bicycle,' she added, 'anything with wheels.' There was another interruption. 'Indeed, the two of them look woofing,' she said giggling and taking a gander at us both. One more long interruption followed, yet Sue's appearance changed to propose she was having some achievement. 'Brilliant,' she then said, 'any chance Ross could run it over the field with the quad? Thanks, Helen. Converse with you later.'

Our mouths had both dropped open as we remained there hopefully close to home, holding on to hear what Helen had said.

'Ross is our neighbor's child who lives across the field. He will bring over his old bicycle for you,' she said. 'It's tiny and corroded and he couldn't say whether the tires have penetrates, yet it very well may be useful to you.'

We both smiled like lottery winners.

'He'll be over in almost no time,' said Sue. 'I'll simply take a quick trip and check whether I can find that scooter.'

Sue returned a couple of moments later wheeling a bike and a tricycle.

The tricycle was pink with a little bin on the front and was unmistakably planned for a two-year-old.

'I don't think you'll get to John O'Groats on both of these, yet this one will get you to the extent Zennor or St Ives,' she said, lifting up a dark WWF bike. The previous World Wrestling Federation, that is, rather than the World Wildlife Fund. I don't think the last option make scooters.

'Woweeeee,' I said. Indeed, I realize individuals don't say 'Woweeeee' any longer, however I did. It just got out at the time. I'm not glad for it.

Ben was at that point trying out the tricycle and plainly under the heaviness of a grown-up, it would be squashed in practically no time. The other one, in any case, was a monster of a bike. It had a wide skateboard-sized stage, Harley Davidson estimated handlebars, enormous froth haggles decorated with pictures of lubed up grapplers. It would have been the Rolls Royce of bikes 'some time ago'. It likewise had working brakes and a drinking bottle holder.

We could hear the far off thunder of an engine.

'That sounds like Ross,' said Sue as she cleared her path through the yard towards the field.

The clamor became stronger, however we actually couldn't see past the thick cover of fog. Inevitably, a shape rose up out of the fog and we could make out a quad bicycle coming towards us. Ross weaved his way through the field, staying away from cow box and trenches. He pulled up before us and wound down the motor. He was around 13 and was wearing an evaporator suit

'Ross, you are an outright legend, thank you kindly,' said Ben, shaking him solidly by the hand.

'That is alright,' said Ross with the voice of a 60 year-old farmer.

He lifted the bicycle out of the trailer and wheeled it to Ben. It was a smaller than usual BMX, totally rusted over and it screeched as Ross pushed it. There was an unfavorable looking brake link swinging from the handlebars and there was something exceptionally amiss with one of the wheels; it wasn't round. The seat wasn't joined as expected, and the handlebars were at an exceptionally odd point. We couldn't have cared less. At that point, it was the best thing we had at any point found in our lives.

'The back wheel isn't in a bad way on appropriately and it's clasped however I have placed some air in the tires for you. They ought to ideally keep awake,' he said as Ben climbed on.

Despite its conspicuous crapness, it was a magnificent piece of apparatus. The fundamental mechanics of a bike – which we had consistently underestimated – were currently strikingly clear. It truly is a brilliant development. The way that moving your feet around aimlessly could move an awful piece of rust along at a nice speed was very astonishing.

'Goodness, and the brakes don't work,' yelled Ross, similarly as Ben collided with a gigantic metal animal dwellingplace door.

'Brakes are misrepresented in any case,' I said. 'Halting won't get us anywhere.'

We inquired as to whether they had any thoughts of spots that we could spend the night.

'There's nothing among here and Zennor,' said Sue, 'yet I'm certain you'll track down some place to remain there. It even has a young hostel.'

'Yet there's a wedding on this evening,' said Ross, 'so it very well may be totally full. You ought to address a rancher called Harry Mann. He'll allow you to remain some place. Let him know I sent you. He lives in a ranch at the highest point of the slope, right outside of Zennor.'

We said thanks to Sue and Ross for their amazing liberality and gave Ross the wellies that Ben had been conveying. Ross was as near a pixie rancher as we were ever liable to meet.

It was practically dull, and we were as yet four miles from Zennor.

I did the main shift on the bike and Ben accelerated the BMX. The distinction they made was amazing. The field wasn't zooming by like it would on a dashing bicycle, or in a vehicle, however we could feel the advancement that we were making with each transformation of our bicycles' little wheels.

After with regards to a large portion of a mile of consistent uphill we were confronted with our first downhill. Security was not a worry on the bike. The tires were made of froth and it was really lethargic that we needed to push while going downhill. If it came to a wild speed – which it didn't – it had a working back brake to carry it to a slow stop. To make it more elating on the bike, you could stand sideways to cause it to feel like you were snowboarding, though leisurely, and on tarmac.

The BMX, nonetheless, had no such extravagance. Sliding a Cornish slope on that bicycle resembled a skier endeavoring a frigid dark sudden spike in demand for the primary morning of ski school. The best way to keep up with control was to delve each foot into the landing area to attempt to save equilibrium and monitor the speed. We felt a surge of adrenaline after each corner that passed without a terrible mishap. It proceeded with like this the entire way to Zennor; a long, slow, tough trudge, trailed by an exhilarating downhill. We traded bicycles consistently to even things out.

It turned out to be extremely dull that we could don't really see the shapes of the street however we realized we were drawing nearer to Zennor, as we could hear the far off purr

of a messy wedding disco.

We arrived at the town of Zennor at around 9.30pm. I had been to Zennor once already, yet it was so dull on this visit that I didn't remember it. All that I recollected was an anecdote about a mermaid, and a bar with great brew. We thought often nothing about the mermaid, now, so headed towards the pub.

On the way, we enquired at the adolescent lodging, however it was completely reserved with wedding visitors, as Ross had predicted.

The wedding was going full bore in a marquee nearby the bar. There were individuals all over the place, and You Can't Hurry Love by Phil Collins cried out from the tent.

The bar – The Tinners Arms – was slammed. A mix of wedding visitors and townspeople poured out onto the road. There was a little assistance window by the entryway, which opened through to the space behind the bar. Ben jabbed his head through and inquired as to whether he could address the administrator. The administrator, a Brian Blessed copy, seemed a couple of moments later.

'What do you need, folks? I'm extremely occupied here,' he asked while stacking the glass washer.

'We're here to propose to assist you with gathering glasses, clear plates, pour pints, whatever necessities doing,' said Ben, attempting a new approach.

'What's the trick?' asked Brian Blessed.

'We want some place to remain this evening,' yielded Ben. 'Anyplace, simply some floor space or a cabinet. Anything.'

'Sorry chaps, I can't help I'm apprehensive. I'm completely reserved with visitors and I haven't got any space whatsoever. Additionally, I'm completely staffed so you were unable to help anyway.'

We saw a man in a cook coat inclining toward the bar divider and smoking.

'Why you folks need some place to remain?' he said in that strange Godfather type voice that smokers use when they actually have a lung brimming with smoke. He dropped his cigarette interrupt the rock and squashed it with his foot while shifting his head back and extinguishing a haze of smoke as he paid attention to our reply.

'We're cycling to John O'Groats without going through any cash,' said Ben. 'Cool, man. Assume you could do with some food then, at that point. Proceed to stand by over there,' he said, pointing into the murkiness. 'I'll get sacked if my supervisor catches

me.' He strutted off like a Cornish John Wayne towards the providing food tent. We dashed off into the obscurity like a couple of filthy scavengers.

'Here you go, chaps,' he said a couple of moments later, giving us a huge ice-

cream holder brimming with obscure food. 'Better return to work. In case anybody asks, I didn't give you that, right?'

We just barely got an opportunity to absolute a brief 'thank you' as he vanished once again into the evening. We chose to keep the food until after we had tracked down some place to sleep.

We recollected the rancher that Ross had referenced, in this way, as our karma was out at the bar, chosen to check him out. We wheeled our trusty horses back up the slope that we had recently dropped, until the light of the town had blurred behind us. We viewed what we assumed as Harry Mann's home and thumped on the door.

'Howdy, are you Harry Mann?' I asked.

'I'm,' said Harry Mann. He looked exactly how we had envisioned he would look.

'We're searching for some place to remain this evening, and youthful rancher Ross from Morvah said you could possibly take care of us. All we want is some floor space or an outhouse.'

'Indeed, Ross did telephone and caution me that you may call past. You can rest in the outbuilding round the back. There's a lot of roughage to use as bedding, however you'll be imparting to a bull.'

'Cool,' I said.

'Sounds… fun,' said Ben hesitantly.

We finished Harry the dull, around to the rear of the house, through an animal dwellingplace loaded with calves and into a stable.

'Here you go. You can move that roughage around to make yourself a bed and you ought to be really agreeable. Try not to stress over Surprise,' he said, highlighting the enormous bull in the adjoining pen. 'He won't trouble you. He's a prize-champ and is the 6th best bull in the country.'

Surprise was the size of a little train and was fortunately isolated from us by some metal bars. He jabbed his head through and gave an immense grunt to welcome us.

'All in all, what is your take? Is this spot okay for you?' asked Harry.

Ben looked panicked.

'It's awesome,' I said, 'We'll take it.'

'You ought to be sufficiently warm, however I'll take a quick trip and check whether I can find a sweeping or two for good measure. There's a light here, and you can utilize the latrine in our utility room,' he said, and vanished out of the barn.

'This wasn't exactly the thing I was expecting,' Ben articulated, after Harry had left. 'I thought we'd have the option to blag lodgings or B&Bs. I didn't figure we would need to rest in an animal dwellingplace with a bull. That is to say, check out the size of that beast.'

'Relax! Rarely would you get an opportunity to rest on feed close to a prize-winning bull. There's a lot of time for inns, and B&Bs,' I said, attempting to console him.

Harry before long got back with his better half Caroline, who was gripping two dozing bags.

'You can keep this one,' said Caroline, holding up one of the camping beds, 'yet we'll require the other one back toward the beginning of the day. We begin draining at 6am, so you'll likely hear us. Breakfast is at 8am, so come and have something to eat before you head off.'

They addressed us like we were the latest of numerous to go through Zennor and rest in their stable. Not once had either Harry or Caroline addressed what we were doing or why we had no place to remain, yet they had been very inviting, in their own unique way.

Ben had livened up since getting the camping bed, and was at that point moving the bunches of roughage around to make a bed on the floor. We both sank once more into the roughage and let out a concurrent 'ahhhh'. It was potentially the most agreeable I have at any point felt. Following a long, hard day of strolling, cycling, scootering, asking and blagging, the home of roughage was exactly what we needed.

It was 10.30pm and we had not eaten since the air terminal. The time had come to dig into the frozen yogurt holder. Ben ripped the top off the holder and we were given a tremendous heap of cold meal pork, a load of stuffing, a colossal chunk of cheddar, a few bits of snapping and a pile of thick earthy colored bread for certain sachets of spread. We were unable to think about a solitary sight in the whole world that would have looked more alluring.

'The excursion set!' shouted Ben.

'Awesome, we can utilize it to have our supper with.'

It was like our experience was transforming into a type of pretending PC game; gathering things en route to utilize later.

Knock on entryway of
house. Gather excursion
set.
Give wellies to youthful farmer.

Get food from wedding.
Use excursion set to eat
food.

We had nearly finished level one, and assuming we endure the night with Surprise we would have vanquished the malicious finish of-level chief, and moved straight onto level two.

Ben unfastened the outing set so we could have a legitimate glance at it interestingly. It contained, indeed, as you would anticipate from a cookout set, all that you really want for an outing: plates, bowls, cups, blades, forks, spoons and a wine tool. They were all still in their singular coverings and we chose to attempt to grimy as little of it as conceivable with the goal that we could give it to another person. Conveying a whole outing set the entire way to John O'Groats appeared rather strange. Ben opened up one plate and one blade and we started to wrap up to the dining experience. 30 minutes already we had been eager and destitute, and presently we were living like rulers; yet those three insightful men that visited the stable.

Surprise slammed at the bars with his head. Not forcefully, but rather he appeared to be quick to come and go along with us for dinner.

'Essentially we're not eating broil meat,' kidded Ben.

We were simply floating off to rest when a tremendous series of bangs alarmed us. It was the sound of firecrackers starting from the wedding the street. Shock was not an aficionado of firecrackers and darted around his pen like he was at a rodeo. We escaped our camping beds and hurried to attempt to get the firecrackers before they wrapped up. I signify 'get' as in watch. Getting firecrackers is exceptionally perilous – don't attempt this at home, kids. The calves in the nearby animal dwellingplace were on a full rush and they beat around the yard in trouble. We got outside with perfect timing to see the incredibly under-whelming terrific finale, which comprised of three firecrackers detonating at practically a similar time. We could hear the symbolic acclaim and cheers that welcome the finish of each firecracker display.

'Wooo... ahhh... yeeaaah.' Indeed. Back to bed.

On our way back into the horse shelter we saw a little feline measured creature in the obscurity. Ben stooped down to draw a nearer look and found it was an extremely old canine that was sniffing around in the corner. We had been told by Harry to keep the outbuilding entryway shut, so we accepted that the canine ought to be closed outside, rather than in. Ben got the canine and mercifully pushed it out of the entryway, yet the easily overlooked detail hastened straight back in before we got an opportunity to close the entryway. He attempted once more, this time delicately removing it from the entryway. Once more, the bothersome thing bobbed back through the entryway. Ben attempted once more, somewhat more powerfully than previously and again the canine was back in the horse shelter at lightning speed before we knew it. It was now that I heard the chink of metal. I bowed down and found that the poor weak canine was really tied up within the animal dwellingplace, and the explanation that it made want more so immediately was that it was limited by the length of its chain. Ben in a flash acknowledged what he had done and snuggled the helpless canine decently well. I had lost the force of discourse since I was snickering so much.

I had just at any point giggled this much once before in my life. At the point when I was in
the 6th structure, a companion of mine was showing a gathering of us a music video he had made. At the point when his recording had completed it changed to what exactly had recently been on the video tape. It was film of his mum and father shooting each other bare in their room. I have never seen any person or thing move as fast as he did when he jumped across the space for the discharge button. That was, until I saw the speed that this canine returned each time Ben tossed it out.

We shut the horse shelter entryway, with the canine inside where it should have been and we supplicated that it would in any case be alive toward the beginning of the day. The calves had pretty much settled down after the firecrackers and Surprise was perched on the floor and grunting discreetly to himself. We floated off to rest without further incident.

Day 2 – As I was going to St Ives…

Zennor to Camborne – 30 miles

We were shrouded in form when we stirred. Our garments, countenances and hair were canvassed in dark spots, which we chose should be form spores, despite the fact that for some time we were stressed they were fly eggs and planned to incubate into our skin and invade our bodies like a few '50s B-film. I had thought I was being reasonable by eliminating my fighter shorts before I rested, and passing on them to air on a feed parcel. They were currently totally dotted with form, while Ben's, which he had chosen to wear the entire evening, were unblemished, yet somewhat more rancid than mine.

Surprise had been a genuinely peaceful flat mate. He had chosen at around 6am to tell us he was alert by colliding with the bars and thumping over a huge wooden board that had been set against it. This thus overturned onto our BMX and bike that were leant against the divider, and these fell over onto my face.

There were flies amassing surrounding us. I maneuvered my entire body into the camping cot and scrunched it up over my head. Shock was alert, the calves nearby were conscious, the sun was radiating through the window bars, Harry and Caroline could be heard draining the cows and I was overflowing with energy. There was no utilization attempting to return to sleep.

We at last got up and gotten into our inconsistent garments. In transit through to the house we were soothed to see that the canine was as yet alive. In the sunshine it looked much feebler. It whimpered in dread as Ben got it and gave it a cuddle.

Harry and Caroline were both in the kitchen. Caroline was at the AGA with a sizzling dish of bacon, and Harry was at the table perusing the paper. It was a decent estimated farmhouse kitchen with one of the dividers shrouded in postcards and rosettes from their different prize-winning dairy cattle. The rosettes were from the cows, not the postcards, I ought to explain. In spite of the fact that, assuming the steers had composed the postcards it would have explained their prize-winning credentials.

It wasn't until breakfast that we got an opportunity to enlighten Harry and Caroline concerning our test. Up to that point, they had thought we were only a few voyagers searching for some place to remain. Subsequent to hearing our arrangements they opened up totally and we even discovered them grinning two or three times.

Harry had lived on the ranch the entirety of his life. His dad had cared for the homestead before him, and his granddad before that. Caroline had been a medical attendant beforehand, yet presently chipped away at the ranch full-time.

Harry gave me some bailer twine with the goal that I could build a belt for my huge pin-striped suit pants. Caroline demanded giving us two tremendous Cornish pasties and several bananas to take with us for lunch. After a few endeavors, Ben figured out how to crush the camping cot into the cookout set, ruling out whatever else. We got together our things and bid farewell to Harry, Caroline and Surprise. When we got moving it was 10.30am and our plan to be in St Ives by 10am was at that point looking rather unrealistic.

Before we left, Caroline retold us the account of the mermaid of Zennor. The story puts in any amount of work in a long dress – to conceal her off-putting pieces, probably – used to go to administrations at the congregation of St Senara, in Zennor. She was charmed by the performing voice of the chorister, Mathew Trewhella. One day their eyes met and they fell head over heels. He followed her down to the town stream, and afterward to the ocean side at Pendour Cove, and Mathew was gone forever. It is recommended that they vanished underneath the waves together. Certain individuals actually guarantee that assuming you sit at Pendour Cove at dusk in the mid year, you can in any case hear Mathew's voice in the breeze.

This sounds like a heap of old bollocks to me.

What truly happened was that some 'away' slut went through Zennor and enticed Mathew – a suggestible and credulous town dolt – back to her level in Penzance. Mathew then realised that eloping with some girl in the city was a better existence than being a choirboy, and so never returned to the village. Concerning hearing his dulcet tones drifting across the waves on a summers evening – that is simply Phil Collins being played at the wedding disco.

By sunlight, Zennor was an image postcard town. The street from Harry Mann's ranch plunged down to the bar where the wedding had been, and the remainder of the town sat on the slant past. Not at all like different towns that we had passed since Land's End, the fundamental street doesn't go straightforwardly through the Zennor. It had some way or another got its own detour. The area of Zennor likewise has the pleasure of being the last, one after another in order, in the entire of Britain. FACT!

The climate had lit up, however there was as yet a thick torrent of fog noticeable all around preventing the sun from getting through. Our garments were already

tacky with sogginess, so the additional dampness had little effect. Caroline had cautioned us that the landscape among Zennor and St Ives would be pretty much as intense as what we had encountered on the past day.

'Despite the fact that... ' she had said, 'the last two miles are altogether downhill.' It was this

state that continued to rehash in our minds as we pushed our bicycles up the first of numerous absurd hills.

However debilitating and difficult it very well might be, there could be no greater method for seeing the wide open than on a bike and an awful BMX. You travel so slowly that you see absolutely everything; appreciating every inch of downhill freewheeling, and savouring every incline slowly and considerately on foot.

After some time, we detected a going to a setting up camp and troop park, and chose to proceed to look at their lost property. The procession park ended up being a tedious mile-long diversion from the primary street. It was a totally ineffective outing as they had no bicycles and no shoes. The assistant, nonetheless, was perhaps Cornwall's best sight and made the journey completely worthwhile.

On the precarious descending plummet into St Ives, I detected a squash club put off from the street. I figured out how to steer into the drive, however it was past the point where it is possible to caution Ben who shot past on the BMX all the way crazy. The scratching of his boots out and about reverberated up the curious road as he attempted to dial the bicycle back. In a snapshot of lunacy, he connected and took hold of a light post as he passed, and was swung around all around, knocking over-top the check, and completing on the asphalt looking back up the slope towards me. It was a move that any gymnastic specialist would have been glad for. He then wheeled his bike up the hill to where I stood in astonishment.

We had been taking it in goes to wear the rigger boots, yet they were starting to bring on some issues for the two of us. We were presently 'competitors', and mud covered rigger boots are not viewed as appropriate athletic footwear. I had pulled over at the squash club imagining that they may have a lost property that we could rummage through.

The squash club appeared to be a piece of the bar nearby, in light of the fact that the barman ran round when he saw us.

'Would i be able to help you, folks?' he said as he skiped towards us. I mean ricocheted as in a kind of chipper run, rather than genuine bobbing. That would be weird.

'Hi,' I said, 'We were simply puzzling over whether you had an old pair of mentors that had been left behind?'

'Did you lose a couple here?' he asked

'Not by and large,' said Ben, and afterward he clarified the entire circumstance, after which Dave – the amazingly volatile barman – started ricocheting here and there on the spot. This time, I mean bobbing in the exacting sense.

'I love it, I love it,' he said, applauding together like a little youngster. 'I don't think we have any coaches right now, yet you can come and have a look.'

We finished him the passageways to a little brush pantry under the steps. He opened the Alice-in-Wonderland estimated entryway, and eliminated a container containing a couple of arbitrary pieces and pieces. There was one pink sock, a couple of leggings, a baseball cap, a sweat-soaked sweatband, an accessory and a bunch of vehicle keys. Ben held up the sweat-soaked sweatband and the leggings and viewed at me with a look as though to say 'How regarding these? Do you think these may be valuable?' I raised an eyebrow at him, which spread the word about my sentiments. He received the message and set them back in the box.

'Sorry, folks. No karma, I'm apprehensive,' said Dave, sounding nearly as baffled as we were as he set the shoebox back. 'Hold tight a moment, what are these?' He recovered a couple of white Adidas mentors that had been taking cover behind the vacuum more clean. 'I don't know whose these are or where they have come from, however I would simply take them assuming that I were you.'

They were an ideal fit, and, as Ben brought up, they were practically stylish. 'I'm certain no one will miss them,' he said. 'They've presumably been here for quite a long time. Or then again perhaps that is the place where the administrator keeps his coaches.' 'I thought you were the director?' I asked.

'Noooo,' said Dave. 'I simply work at the bar nearby and I'm covering while he's jumped out. I would vanish assuming I were you before he gets back.'

We attempted to leave the rigger boots with him, however he thought it was a poorly conceived notion for us to leave any proof that we had been there. We bounced back onto our bicycle and bike, with appropriate footwear on our feet, the rigger boots on our handlebars, and freewheeled down the last scarcely any hundred meters to the sea.

St Ives was once a flourishing fishing town, yet following a decrease it modified itself as a vacation location and workmanship focus. On account of previous craftsman occupants like Barbara Hepworth and Russian stone worker Naum Gabo (No? Me not one or the other), the town is presently viewed as a significant community for workmanship. Except for Liverpool, it is the main spot outside of London to have a part of The Tate.

St Ives is a little town. We were there on a bright Sunday and the spot was slithering with travelers. It has its reasonable part of tat, however it has still figured out how to keep up with its appeal. For a little coastline town be that as it may, the ocean was truly challenging to track down. We spent some time caught in the labyrinth of minuscule back roads before at last tracking down it. It was the huge wet piece by the harbour.

We halted by a fix of sand by the water. I say 'fix of sand', rather than 'ocean side', as it was a fix of sand, rather than an ocean side. The haze had totally cleared and it was a wonderful day. We leaned against the harbor divider and touch into our Cornish pasties. They were huge. The seagulls dipped and jump besieged us from a higher place, attempting to test our lunch, yet we skilfully guarded our arrangements with dangerous backhands.

Ben set the rigger boots against one of the enormous receptacles along the waterfront. They were in prime situation for a bystander to see, and bombing that, the receptacle man may have been enticed by a difference in footwear.

There was a 'SPEEDBOAT HIRE' sign by the harbor. As yet, we had just requested things we NEEDED for our excursion; garments, food, bicycles… brew. But there we were, basking in the sun, without a care in the world. We had been taken care of, watered and were genuinely all around dressed. It was the ideal opportunity for some fun.

'Hello,' said Ben to the person monitoring the speedboat stand. 'We're cycling to John O'Groats without going through any cash, and en route we're wanting to encounter a portion of the fervors that Britain needs to offer.'

Nice. I preferred Ben's methodology. He was essentially let this person know that by loaning us a speedboat, he would do his touch for old fashioned Blighty.

'Sounds fun,' said the man, somewhat confounded and still uncertain of what Ben wanted.

'Would it be conceivable,' proceeded with Ben, 'for us to lease a speedboat, free of charge, so we can completely encounter St Ives?'

'Errr, alright,' said the man, not actually knowing what else to say.

'I can't track down the gas pedal,' I said to St Ives' form of CJ from Baywatch who had helped us into the boat. Sadly, however, she was a he and he had significantly more chest hair, however with comparative estimated boobs.

'There is no gas pedal,' he said. 'It has a proper speed and you pull this string to stop it.'

'Crap,' murmured Ben, 'this thing may gain out of influence.' in actuality, he need not have stressed. I might have swum quicker than that boat. Its gradualness was agonizing. In any case, we were cruising around the cove in a 'speedboat' we had acquired free of charge. We couldn't complain.

It was in these very waters that an incredible white shark was as far as anyone knows spotted in August 2007. Specialists rushed to bring up that it was bound to be an innocuous porbeagle shark or a lolling shark. At around a similar time, there were comparative sightings of an incredible white shark in Newquay. 52-year-old safety officer Kevin Keeble approached with an image portraying an incredible white with bloodied teeth, straight from a kill. He professed to have snapped the photo in the waters off Newquay and the nearby paper ran the photograph on its first page. The story was before long highlighted in The Sun and different other public media. Kevin Keeble later conceded that the photograph had been gone on during a fishing outing in South Africa and he had just implied it as a joke.

The most astonishing thing we saw on our boat trip was a dead seagull.

All things considered, we accepted it was dead. Either that or it was swimming on its back, with its head submerged, and an opening in its body.

We addressed CJ for some time subsequent to returning the boat, and inquired as to whether he had any ideas of where we may find some bikes.

'There's a ranch a couple of miles out of St Ives where a person ups old bicycles to sell,' he said. 'He is Badcock. Roger Badcock.' Ben sniggered at the name. 'Be cautioned, however, he's a serious odd guy and in the event that he welcomes you in for some tea, I would refuse.'

'Why?' asked Ben, actually smiling at the name Roger Badcock.

'Put it thusly. It's the sort of house where you need to wipe your feet in transit out.'

We had garments and shoes, however there were a couple of different supplies that we figured we would require en route. First up was a frozen yogurt. Indeed, I realize a frozen yogurt is not really a need, however we were at the coastline and everybody was eating them. As the familiar maxim goes: 'When in St Ives, do as the St Ivans do'. With a touch of flattering we got two scrumptious Cornish frozen yogurts from an exceptionally bewildered woman in the frozen yogurt shop.

We set ourselves up a psychological shopping list.
2 x toothbrushes
1 x
toothpaste
Towel
Soap
Plasters for our blisters

It appeared to be a genuinely unobtrusive determination of arrangements. Getting such supplies in a bustling coastline town planned to demonstrate troublesome, so we chose to ask at various shops for each item.

First up was Boots, the 'well known high road scientific expert'. We addressed the supervisor – a youthful, pretty, smiley woman, which is consistently a reward. She appeared to be somewhat interested when we let her know we up to and clarified why we were dressed so incredibly. We requested first from for a few their least expensive toothbrushes, and without a second thought she strolled off and got back with a bunch of Boots esteem toothbrushes and a container of toothpaste.

'I expect you'll require this as wellthpaste, too. Whatever else?' she inquired. We were stunned. We had expected a cool reaction from the perceived high road chains. We envisioned that a severe approach construction would be set up that would forestall individuals like us strolling in off the road and getting things for free.

'That is splendid. Much obliged,' I said. 'Could you spare a little bundle of plasters?'

'Sure,' she said and requested one from different individuals from staff to pass her a parcel of mortars from behind the counter. She most likely would have given us everything on our rundown, yet we chose to leave it at that and attempt somewhere else for the remainder of our things.

There was another neighborhood scientific expert simply up the street and we went in and requested some cleanser. The man behind the counter vanished down into the storm cellar and arose a couple of seconds after the fact holding a jug of rather costly looking shower gel, two huge ocean side towels and two t-shirts.

'Here you go, fellows,' he said. 'Do you have towels as of now? In case not then I'm certain these will be useful.'

'We don't have towels, yet they were on our rundown. Much thanks,' said Ben, surprised. I mean surprised as in 'amazed'. He clearly chats with his mouth open. Assuming he had been a ventriloquist I would have referenced that earlier.

'My pleasure. We get them liberated from organizations when they're attempting to advance another item. You can have the shirts, as well.' The shirts were immense white ones with a sun cream logo on the front and the words 'Surf's up' on the back. We had just been out and about for a day and a half, yet seeing a spotless white shirt that didn't have any hints of form was unbelievably

appealing.

We chosen to proceed to have a dip in the ocean, provide ourselves with somewhat of a wash and afterward change into our 'Sunday best'. It was Sunday all things considered, and it was just correct that we dressed for the event. We wheeled our bicycles and an armload of new effects down to the harbour.

There were at that point a couple of children swimming in the ocean and we sat on the harbor divider to attempt and repack our sacks. Two little youngsters, matured around seven and nine, were taking it in goes to ride their bike down the long boat incline and into the water. It was a pink Barbie bike and they before long saw our unrivaled WWF bike inclining toward the divider, and they looked at it with envy. They understood that their bike was absolutely lame, and that our own was the daddy.

'What about we show these smaller than normal Evil Knievels some things about scootering,' proposed Ben.

'I'm not even certain that 'scootering' is a word, yet better believe it, I figure we could encourage them how to do it appropriately,' I said.

Ben took the bike and I took the BMX and we prepared ourselves at the highest point of the slope. The young men remained back and looked on in wonderment. Ben and I took a gander at the young men, gestured at one another, and afterward set off down the ramp.

We collided with the water in astounding design. The water was totally freezing, however we imagined it wasn't. We swam around for a couple of moments and gave a valiant effort to clean ourselves however much as could reasonably be expected. Ben swam out somewhat further and I began to follow him.

'Don't come any nearer,' he said. 'I'm doing a piss.'

We fished our bicycles out of the ocean, and afterward got dry with our matching towels, hung our matching fighter shorts out in the sun to dry and put on our fresh spotless matching shirts. We made a beautiful couple.

Realistically, we ought to have cut one of the massive towels in half there and afterward and taken a large portion of each, however they were overall quite rich that we chose to attempt to keep them both.

The two young men, who probably been siblings, moved toward us and began pointing whimsically at our bicycle and scooter.

'You need to get our own?' I asked.

They gestured enthusiastically and began pointing wildly at the ocean. 'You need to ride our bicycles into the ocean?' asked Ben.

They gestured much more enthusiastically. 'I believe they're hard of hearing,' said Ben.

They began marking to one another and it became clear that they were hard of hearing, yet in addition quiet. They got our bicycle and bike and went through the following ten minutes riding down the incline into the ocean. At a certain point, one of the young men wheeled the BMX over to me and began stepping his feet, pointing at the bicycle's chain and afterward waving his finger at me. The chain had tumbled off and it was obviously my shortcoming. I reattached the chain and they continued. They might have been somewhat impolite, yet Ben and I felt a feeling of prosperity that we had been liberal to two distraught youngsters. This ended up being an enormous mistake.

'Where have our bicycles gone?' I asked Ben inevitably.

'They're around some place. One of the young men is still there.' 'Yet the other kid isn't there nor are our bikes.'

'I'll proceed to address him,' said Ben, who got up and strolled over to the more youthful of the two boys.

'Where did you put our bicycle and bike?' he asked, utilizing signals to guarantee that he would understand.

The kid shrugged his shoulders and began to stroll off.

'Then, at that point, where is your brother?'

The kid shrugged again and kept strolling. His sibling before long showed up and gave similar articulations when we asked him what had befallen our bike and BMX.

'We're not leaving them, Ben,' I said, getting up off the harbor divider to go along with him. 'How about we follow them until they show us where the bicycles are.'

The more seasoned sibling started to make motions to show that they were returning home and afterward they began to run.

We pursued them.

I saw that the more youthful of the two siblings needed to gather his shoes from the divider in transit past, and I arrived before him and got them. Presently, this might appear to be brutal to take a helpless minimal hard of hearing quiet kid's shoes, yet you need to trust me, those young men were evil.

I held his shoes noticeable all around and he leaped to attempt to recover them.

'You'll get them back when we get our bicycles back,' I said like an elementary school teacher.

We followed the young men for a couple of moments along the waterfront and we soon

saw the BMX set against a divider on a close by street.

'I figured you didn't have a clue where the bicycles were, you poops?' Ben yelled angrily.

The young men smirked.

'Let us know where the other one is,' I demanded.

The more established kid began pointing toward Land's End, back down the coast.

'alright, then, at that point, show us where,' I said.

He shook his head and began pointing the alternate way, as though to say they resided in the other direction.

'Well we're going any place you go,' I

said. He stepped his feet again.

They lead us out of the harbor and round into the following narrows. Sufficiently sure, after around five minutes he brought up the bike, which was set up behind a dustbin. The more established kid held up his hands as though to say: 'I have no clue about how that got there.'

It was totally surprising. We had almost been looted by two young children. There we were, on a 'excellence visit through' Great Britain, and the two generally guiltless and weak individuals we had met enjoyed taken full benefit of our liberality and attempted to take our BMX and bike. They expected to confront the consequences.

We revealed them to the police and after an extended and costly legal dispute they were requested to serve eight years in an adolescent remedial facility.

'Now clear off, both of you,' is the thing that I really said, prior to giving the more youthful sibling his shoes back. They gave us both a snide grin then, at that point, turned and strolled off to find their next victims.

'You truly showed them,' Ben said with a chuckle.

It was weird how joined to the bicycle and bike we had become in under a day. They were conceivably the most refuse type of transport that always existed, yet to us they were beyond value. They were something beyond bicycles, they were our technique for getting from A to B speedier than by walking, and without them we would have been back where we began. I imply that figuratively, obviously. We weren't assuming some part playing game that would have implied returning to Land's End in case our bicycles were stolen.

Another gathering of more seasoned young men had been sticking around the harbor and had seen our quest for the young men. One of them moved toward us and asked what

we were up to.

'I realize where there's a bicycle you can have,' he said enthusiastically. 'There's one up by Co-operation. It's been there for quite a long time and we simply use it for playing on. I'll proceed to get it for you.'

Before we even got an opportunity to ask whose it was, or where it had come from, he had turned and ran up one of the limited roads into town, actually wearing his trickling wetsuit. He had reestablished our confidence in humankind. One moment 'the young people of today' were denying us of our cherished bicycles, and the following they were running shoeless across town to help us out.

He returned around five minutes after the fact wheeling what looked from a distance to be a good looking off-road bicycle. After looking into it further, it was a mind boggling heap of shit.

'It'll require a touch of work,' he said, 'however you're free to take it in the event that you need it. I don't think it has a place with anyone.'

There were no pedals, no chain, no brake links or brake cushions. The back wheel was seriously clasped, neither one of the tires had an inward cylinder and the seat was absent. However, it had a working ringer. We felt genuinely horrendous turning down a bicycle, yet the measure of work that this one needed to make it useable implied that we would have made an enormous stride backwards.

'That is extremely sort of you,' I said, 'however it appears as though it needs a lot of work. We can't go through any cash and it would require some investment and exertion for somebody to repair this for us.'

'Definitely, thanks mate,' said Ben. 'We truly like the deal, however I think we'll stay with what we have, for the present, and hold in the mood for something better. Evidently there's a barely out chap of St Ives who has a great deal of bicycles at his farm.'

'Definitely, his name's Roger Badcock,' said the kid. Ben sniggered again at the notice of his name. 'Also no stresses over the bicycle. I don't believe it's worth you folks keeping it. I just idea I'd show it to you. Best of luck with the remainder of your trip.'

We assembled our stuff and tied our fighter shorts to our backpacks so they could complete the process of drying. Indeed, we were both going commando. In a couple of thick woolen suit pants, it felt amazingly liberating.

The street out of St Ives climbed steeply away from the ocean. We strolled for about a mile as there was essentially no point attempting to ride the bike up slopes. It was more slow, and undeniably more debilitating than walking.

The street then, at that point, arrived at a level prior to slipping bit by bit into the

town of Lelant. We observed Roger Badcock's home reasonably effectively in the wake of sorting out an assortment of bearings from various people.

His home was a kind of long-lasting manufactured house, assuming such a Catch 22 is conceivable. It was on the edge of a fix of no man's land and the entryway was secured with a cross section fly screen. The entire spot was straight out of a 1970s awfulness film.

We thumped on the entryway. There was no answer.

I had held out incredible expectation for Mr Badcock, and notwithstanding Ben recommending we attempt a couple of spots in the developed city that was St Ives, I was resolute that Roger was our man.

We gone to leave and looked down in disgrace. It was at that point 5pm and it was improbable we would find bicycles elsewhere that day.

'I surmise we'll simply need to head into the following town and search for… ' I began, prior to being hindered with a voice behind us.

'Would i be able to help you?'

Roger Badcock was remaining in his entryway. He was north of six feet tall and his mass filled every last trace of the door jamb. He was wearing a green polo shirt that was canvassed in different messes. His hair retreated nearly to the rear of his scalp; he had an immense shock of dark hair splashing out from behind every which way and a great handlebar moustache.

'Hello, we're truly sorry to upset you,' I said. 'Are you Mr Badcock?'

Ben sniggered to himself.

'Yes,' said Mr Badcock. 'That is me.'

'We've been told by a few group that you could possibly take care of us,' said Ben. 'We're cycling to John O'Groats without going through any cash and we were contemplating whether there was any possibility that we could trade these bicycles for something a touch more appropriate for significant distance cycling.'

There was a respite while he attempted to clean his spread glasses on his shirt which possibly made them worse.

'Well I couldn't say whether I have anything reasonable right now,' he said, 'yet we can see.' Roger ventured down from his home with a mammoth battle. He strutted across the carport and opened the way to the contiguous barn.

The structure was stuffed loaded with bicycle parts. There were whole bikes, half bikes, bike wheels, chains, inner tubes, saddles of all shapes and sizes; they hung from the ceiling, they were piled against the wall and they were strewn

across the floor. We followed Roger into the stable and Ben went to me, gripped his clench hand and mouthed the words: 'Goodness. My. God.' We were in bicycle heaven.

'Why you have such countless bicycles?' I asked.

'It's simply a leisure activity of mine truly. I can't work due to disease, so I fix bicycles. I don't actually bring in any cash from them however it keeps me busy.'

'So what kind of bicycle are you after?' he gasped, obviously exhausted by the 20-meter stroll from his house.

'Whatever you can save,' said Ben. 'We're searching for anything that is superior to the bike and BMX that we have.'

He watched the outbuilding like a General, seizing a periodic bicycle and weighing up to him whether he could leave behind it, and regardless of whether it was reasonable for our needs.

On his second lap of the animal dwellingplace he stopped at a little, startling pink young ladies' mountain bike.

'You can have this,' he said, 'however it's presumably not the sort of thing you're... '

'It's ideal,' I said, before he had completed his sentence.

Despite its appearance, it appeared to be a good bicycle. Every one of the different pieces seemed to be set up and it seemed to have a few pinion wheels. It was marginally on the little size, yet it was a tremendous overhaul from both of our other bikes.

'That is presumably everything I can offer you,' said Roger. 'The wide range of various ones are either incomplete or I would rather not part with them.'

'You've been amazingly liberal to give us this one,' I said.

I admired see that Ben was over on the furthest side of the animal dwellingplace, probably stroking a tiny hustling bike.

'Ben!' I brought over, 'Roger will mercifully give us this pink off-road bicycle. Isn't that great?'

'No doubt, that is underhanded. Much appreciated so a lot,' said Ben not taking his eyes off the racer.

'I surmise we would be advised to take off now, and attempt and track down some place to remain,' I said.

'That's right, I surmise we ought to,' said Ben, who had now ridden the racer and was inclining forward claiming to be on a downhill.

Roger strolled over to the bicycle and began tinkering with the brake links. It was a 1970s junior Sirocco Falcon. It had 5 pinion wheels and the handlebars were concealed with multi-shaded tape. It was fundamentally a dashing bicycle for a youngster, however it had a specific retro charm.

'Goodness, continue,' he said. 'You can take that

one, as well.' 'Are you genuine?' said Ben.

'Well, you got me feeling great, and I've had both of these bicycles lounging around for some time now,' he said.

'Well I trust you can put our own to some utilization, so we can basically go some method for reimbursing the blessing,' I said.

Roger laughed to himself.

'I could possibly give the bike to somebody,' he said, 'and I'll likely have the option to get some valuable screws and orientation off the other one, however there's nothing else to it. Best of luck to you both. I'll place some air in the tires for yourself and they ought to be great to go.'

We had gone around 14 miles on the bike and BMX. This may not seem like a great deal, yet I had never felt more depleted in my life. The energy it takes to push a bike with froth wheels up a Cornish slope, or pedal a small

BMX over a significant distance, is immeasurable.

Our thigh muscles were consuming, our knees were wounded from getting the handlebars on the BMX, our heels were totally rankled from wearing the rigger boots and our backs were hurting from being in such unnatural positions. Looking back, it would have been undeniably less agonizing and presumably faster assuming we had strolled from Land's End.

After only a couple of moments on our new bicycles we felt like we had been brought back to life. We chose to substitute the bicycles routinely, as they were both altogether different yet each enjoyed their benefits. The pink young ladies' trail blazing bicycle – or 'Pinky' as we innovatively called it – had a comfortable seat, 12 cog wheels and fair brakes. It was somewhat little, however, and the fat tires implied it was very lethargic. The racer – or 'The Falcon', as it became known – just had five pinion wheels, a seat made of the hardest material known to man and handlebars that were about a foot lower than the seat. It had pleasant smooth street tires, however, and appeared to be quicker than Pinky.

I did the principal shift on Pinky and Ben began The Falcon. We chose to endeavor another 10 miles or so to attempt to compensate for the time we had spent in St Ives playing in boats and pursuing hard of hearing kids.

For the initial time since setting off, we abruptly felt like we were gaining ground towards John O'Groats. The street had opened up before us and we could feel ourselves destroying the 1000-mile course that lay ahead.

We presently couldn't seem to set up a course for the excursion. Seeing as we needed to get everything free of charge, we couldn't bring a course book or guide. We knew at some stage we would need to discover how to get to John O'Groats, however meanwhile, we realized that in case we generally followed the A30, we would head in the right direction.

We had made it our intend to stay away from A-streets notwithstanding much as could be expected. They may be speedier and more straightforward, however they are unpleasant to cycle along and you don't get to see the country similarly that you do by means of the dirt roads. We made an exemption on this event, however, as we needed to have covered a good distance. We joined the A30 soon after the town of Lelant, and expected to get to Camborne before dim. It was 7.30pm on a Sunday, and we had the whole A30 to ourselves. Not that you really want the two paths of a double carriageway when you are on a bike.

We arrived at the town of Camborne eventually. It was still light and there was a lot of movement in the town place. By action, I mean there were gatherings of individuals sticking around outside shops and dallying on traffic intersections. Camborne was once the focal point of the Cornish mining industry and one of the most extravagant mining regions on the planet. It has as of late been the objective of an enormous recovery venture to inhale new life into the town.

We chose to attempt to track down some place to remain first, and got two dismissals with hardly a pause in between from a lodging and afterward a pub.

'I guess we would do well to begin searching for a horse shelter,' said Ben dejectedly. 'We've just been going after for ten minutes,' I said. 'We knew this wasn't

going to be simple. I'm certain we can track down some place to rest. In addition, I don't think they will generally have stables around centres.'

'That is valid. I get it doesn't make any difference an excessive amount of where we end up. Essentially I have a camping cot now.'

'You have a hiking bed?' I asked furiously. 'I thought it was both of ours.'

'Well we can't actually both use it and I have been conveying it the entire day.' 'Fine, whatever. You have it, Mr Selfish.'

A man drinking a jar of Special Brew began snickering at our pink bike. He influenced and spilled as he

talked. 'Super nice boike,' he

spluttered.

'Much appreciated,' I said. 'Do you know anyplace we could remain this evening for free?'

'There's a bar up there called the Veeeeervan Aaaarms,' he said, pointing in three unique headings. 'They have modest rooo… ooo… ooms.'

'Tragically we can't go through ANY cash whatsoever. We're on a test to get to John O'Groats without spending anything.'

'Goodness,' he said. 'That sounds idiotic. All things considered, you could ask at the Veeeeervan Aaaarms at any rate. Let them know Big… ig… ig… Mick sent you.'

The Vyvyan Arms was a major corner expanding on an intersection at the top finish of town, and we wheeled our recently procured bicycles around to the vehicle leave at the back. This was whenever we first would need to leave them unattended, and we unexpectedly understood that security was a slight concern. The BMX and bike that we'd had before did not merit taking, yet they had been taken. Presently we had bicycles that were worth stealing.

Pinky had a bicycle lock folded over under the seat, however we didn't have the foggiest idea about the blend. Ben speculated 4856. I speculated 1234. Neither worked.

We attempted again.

Ben speculated 1111 and I speculated 2199. Once more, neither worked. This proceeded for at some point, until we undersas welld it was purposeless. With a touch of exertion, we figured out how to unravel a portion of the bicycle lock from around Pinky and afterward circle it over the Falcon's seat, too. To the relaxed bystander it created the impression that the bicycles were locked together.

The inhabitant DJ was simply setting up his unit when we entered the Vyvyan Arms, and there was a table of men crouched in the furthest corner. The woman behind the bar was in her forties, very short and had the greatest bosoms we had at any point seen. We didn't actually see them, yet we found out about their size by the way that she was by all accounts laying them on the bar to stop herself falling over.

'Howdy, are you the proprietor?' Ben asked.

'Indeed, I guess I am,' she said, as though she had just barely acknowledged it.

'We were contemplating whether there is any work we can do here in return for some place to sleep.'

'We're great at cleaning, cleaning up, finishing, and we needn't bother with a bed. All we really want is a rooftop,' I added.

'Errrr... errrr… hold tight,' she said. 'I'll need to check with my husband.'

Scotty, the landowner, was a scary looking person. He was fabricated like a prop forward. He had long fair hair that was tied back in a braid and he

had tattoos down the length of the two arms. To go against his threatening biker picture, he wore a shirt with a tremendous image of Taz, the Tazmanian Devil animation character, enhanced across the front.

'I hear you're searching for some place to remain this evening free of charge,' he said.

'We're genuinely calm this evening and I question we'll have additional visitors showing up, so I'm certain we can figure you out with a room.'

'Would you say you are certain? There should be some work we can do consequently?' I asked.

'I don't think so,' said Scotty. 'As I said, we're extremely tranquil so there's very little necessities doing. I'll proceed to make sure that your room is prepared. What would i be able to get you both to savor the meantime?'

'Let me get those, Scotty,' said one of local people who had been listening in. 'Seems like both of you really want it.'

'Right you are, Colin,' said Scotty. 'The following round's on me, however.' Colin, as the majority of different men, had been in the Vyvyan Arms for the greater part of the day. They demanded that we go along with them, and we recounted to them the tale of why we were in Camborne.

Scotty and Billy – his significant other – showed us to the room, where we were given a selection of beds. The room had two single beds and a tremendous four-banner bed. Ben and I were not exactly prepared to share a twofold bed right now, so we selected the singles

We both sank back onto the beds and lay there peacefully for a couple of merry minutes, letting the sensations of help and solace go through us. We actually had our brews down the stairs to get done, so we washed our countenances in the sink and got back to the bar.

After our lager, Scotty offered us some food, however we concluded that we would have rather not misuse his cordiality thus strolled into town to attempt to find some food elsewhere.

'I extravagant a Chinese,'
said Ben. 'Sounds great to
me,' I said.

We before long arrived at Tse House, a Chinese café on the high road. We could see through the window that the spot hushed up. For a typical individual, this is generally viewed as an awful sign, however for us it was great. We had developed more sure with regards to requesting things, however we actually liked to have as little a crowd of people as possible.

We entered through the beaded shade and moved toward the youngster behind the counter who then, at that point, advised us to address the manager.

Becky Tse, the supervisor, was quickly stacking glasses behind the bar. We apologized for disturbing her and clarified what we were doing, and inquired as to whether we could accomplish any work in return for some food. She gestured all through, however didn't look remotely interested.

'alright. Eat in or important point?' she asked when we had finished.

'Yet we don't have any cash,' I rehashed on the off chance that she had not understood

us.

'It's alright. Eat in or action item?' she said.

'Goodness… thank you… eat in then please,' I said.

'Two chicken chow meins?' she asked, and highlighted a table over in the far corner.

'Whatever is least demanding and least expensive for you,' said Ben.

'TWO CHICKEN CHOW MEINS,' she yelled through the drapery into the kitchen. 'Five minutes,' she said to us, 'I bring it over to table.'

'Much thanks,' said Ben, 'Is there any tidying or cleaning up we can do in return?'

She grinned for the first time.

'No,' she said. 'Five minutes. I bring it over to table.'

And so she did. Two enormous plates of steaming Chicken Chow Mein were before long sitting before us and we appreciatively gobbled up each and every noodle.

We got once again to the Vyvyan Arms where the disco was going full bore. I imply that the lights had been darkened, and the DJ had begun his set. The dance floor was unfilled, however, and the solitary table of regulars were as yet the main individuals in the pub.

We put in a couple of hours visiting to local people, playing pool and being purchased drinks. At around 11pm, we hit the sack, stuffed loaded with Chinese, somewhat tanked and totally knackered.

Day 3 – The lawnmower man

Camborne to Nanstallon – 48 miles

We ate our direction through a colossal heap of toast that Billy had made for us, drank a tea kettle loaded with tea, and ate a few dishes of grain each. The neighborhood paper had an article about a few terrible street mishaps, and it made me ponder how conceivably perilous our outing could be. We had dodgy bicycles, no head protectors, and little experience of cycling. I referenced this to Ben and we both consented to attempt to shake off the lighthearted mentality we'd had for the initial two days. We likewise consented to attempt to find helmets.

We said our farewells to Scotty, Billy and the occupant DJ who was as yet in the bar, wearing the very garments that he had been wearing the prior night. Ben gave them a frisbee that we had found by the roadside close to Lelant. It was all we had in the method of a gift, yet they appeared truly touched.

'We'll leave it here behind the bar to help us to remember your visit. It's been so exquisite to have met you both,' said Billy. She then gave us a couple of green t- shirts that they had been given from a brewery. They turned into our new Sunday Best, which we chose to put something aside for the nights, and not to wear while cycling.

We followed the old street to Redruth, which ran straightforwardly corresponding to the A30, and we then, at that point, cut back towards the coast.

We were on a lofty plummet into the town of Porthtowan when I saw a crane over to the right.

'See that crane!' I yelled to Ben who was before me. I have no clue about why I chose to bring up the crane to Ben, as it was not in a tiny smidgen amazing, and I didn't know that Ben had a specific interest with cranes.

'What?' called Ben, who couldn't hear as expected in view of the speed we were going. He banged on Pinky's brakes and she slipped to a stop. The Falcon, nonetheless, presently couldn't seem to be tried on a downhill.

I applied the brakes. They squeaked. Nothing occurred. There was no an ideal opportunity to stay away from Ben and I collided with the rear of him getting my leg on his back tire machine gear-piece. I was then tossed advances and arrived with my balls on the crossbar.

My leg was draining somewhat, however it was not much, and after a slight rearrangement, I concluded my balls would recuperate, too.

'There was a major crane simply back there,' I said
to Ben. 'Goodness, right. A debt of gratitude is in
order for that. Are you alright?'

'Definitely, I'm fine much appreciated. I think we want to get The

Falcon's brakes looked at.'

'No crap, Sherlock.'

Porthtowan is a wonderful town that is home to one of Britain's most well known riding sea shores. It clearly has some 'debilitated breaks' and 'phat tubes', whatever that implies. Once more, the town was once a significant mining spot, however it presently depends vigorously on the travel industry. In the event that you were pondering, the name Porthtowan is gotten from the Cornish words 'porth' and 'tewynn' signifying 'Inlet of Sand Dunes'. You will rest tight now.

Just on the edges of the town we passed Porthtowan Garage. Presently, I'm no bicycle master, yet we assumed if we acquired a spanner and fixed a couple of nuts to a great extent The Falcon would be cured.

'Wheel it in and I'll investigate it,' said John the technician when we requested to get a spanner.

'The brakes are gone,' he said. 'I'll put forth a valiant effort to fix them up, however they're essentially finished.'

He fixed a few nuts, stretched a few links and abbreviated some others. He then dribbled oil from one of those old-fashioned oilcans with the ridiculously long nozzle, over various bits of The Falcon's anatomy. I could nearly hear it murmuring. The Falcon, that is, not the mechanic.

The street out of Porthtowan was idiotically steep. Interestingly since getting our 'genuine bicycles' we got off and strolled. We didn't have a liable outlook on it. At the point when it gets to the stage that you are cycling uphill at the very speed that you would stroll, there is just no real reason for busting yourself.

Once we had come to the highest point of the slope, the landscape evened out and the cycling became more straightforward. The sun was out so we removed our shirts. We actually had restricted apparel and we concluded that the less we perspired onto our garments, the better.

I was still commando now, as I had endeavored to wash the pungent ocean water from my fighter shorts in the sink at the Vyvyan Arms and have them dry by the morning. I had prevailed in the washing part, yet fizzled miserably in getting them dry. I'd hung them out of the window around evening time, gullibly anticipating that they should dry by the light of the moon. I then attached them to my backpack so they could dry during the day.

Going topless with my suit pants left my lower half rather uncovered. The bailer twine had not actually helped, and to stop the pants tumbling down totally, I needed to turn the belt north of a few times. This made them hang incredibly low, uncovering a perspective on pubic hair. Presently I'm certain that this is a psychological picture that you didn't need shaped, yet I feel that it is my obligation to paint as precise an image as possible.

The street among Porthtowan and St Agnes was saved money with high supports, so in spite of cycling along the coast, we just had infrequent looks at the sea.

We had wanted to eat in St Agnes, yet we arrived at the town by early in the day so halted for a brief reprieve all things being equal. The tracksuit bottoms that Ben had been given by Les-the-coastguard were superfluously massive, and they continually surged out behind him like a breeze sock. He chose to make a shifty move and went to get some scissors from the scientist on the high road. He arose before long in some huge loose shorts and a tracksuit base leg on each arm just because he thought it was amusing. It was a bit, so I had a go at wearing them, too.

I was very envious of Ben's shorts, but didn't feel that I could do the same to the suit trousers. What if I had another wedding to go to on route, or a job interview? I would need to look my best, so I decided to roll the legs up to make them feel like shorts. Albeit, thick heavy woollen ones.

Ben had 'lost' his water bottle some place since Camborne. We were all the while utilizing the containers that John from the air terminal had given us, and we were topping them off at each opportunity.

'I'll proceed to get a jug of water from the shop,' he said as he stepped off.

'Wouldn't you be able to simply track down an old restrain and fill it from some place?' I called
after him.

'Nah, I'll get another one from the shop up here.'

He returned void handed.

'What a total and utter moron,' he said.

'What happened?'

'I went in there, right, and clarified what we were doing and requested a jug of water and he said, 'Bring cash like most of us.   You're
anticipating that people should pay for your 'oliday.' What a tosser.'

'Yet wouldn't you say you were being a thrower by going off and hoping to be given another jug of water?'

'It's just a container of water, for the wellbeing of Christ,' he said.

'I know. That is the point. Water is something that we can go anyplace, and you could find an old container without any problem. You were being presumptuous requesting something only for it.'

Ben twisted his lip and thought about that maybe I was right.

I imparted my water to Ben and we bested it up from an external tap in the bar vehicle leave. We requested that somebody point us an easterly way, and they advised us to head towards the towns of Perranporth and afterward Goonhavern.

Ben and I initially met in the mid year of 1998, when we cooperated at Althorp – the home of Earl Spencer and the resting spot of Diana, Princess of Wales. We filled in as superintendents when the domain made its ways for general society for July and August soon after Diana's demise. We went through our days grinning at guests, addressing questions and playing with walkie-talkies. I appeared to be the main individual on the 14,000-section of land bequest that liked Ben's odd funny bone and we hit it off instantly.

There was a piano in the staff room which Ben spent each lunch break playing. The more established individuals from staff loved him, while the remainder of the staff – including the chiefs – all thought that he is somewhat bizarre. I worked an aggregate of four summers at Althorp. Ben was not asked back after the first year.

Perranporth was a bustling little coastline town. Its clamoring high road was slithering with mentor parties who were stripping the shops uncovered of their souvenirs.

It was noon and there was an unmistakeable smell of Cornish pasties noticeable all around. We before long tracked down the source; Berrymans Bakery with a line loosening up the entryway. They were obviously famous pasties, and we concluded it merited the shame and conceivable embarrassing dismissal, to join the line and request a freebie.

The little youngster who served us was very smiley and didn't actually get what we were doing, however she checked with her director and afterward gave us two enormous pasties. We drove our bicycles further up the way to where we observed admittance to the ocean side and we sat and ate our scrumptious pasties in the sand dunes.

There was one more tough area out of Perranporth, where we followed signs to Goonhavern until we became diverted by a sign for The World In Miniature. We couldn't resist.

The world in Miniature was, all things considered, the world, yet in smaller than expected. The vast majority of the world's most conspicuous tourist spots were there to see, in decreased sizes. They had the Leaning Tower of Pisa, the Statue of Liberty and the Egyptian pyramids, to give some examples. We had an agreeable world visit in around 20 minutes. It was nearly just about as great as the genuine thing.

The administrator of the spot, Donna, was especially liberal and she heaped us high with more pasties, wiener rolls, pick 'n' blend and caffeinated drinks (which gave Ben another drinking bottle). We asked her for bearings east, following the tourist detour, and she rolled out a rundown of towns for us to pay special mind to. These included: Fiddlers Green, Kestle Mill, St Columb Major, Withiel and Nanstallon. It seemed like we were characters in a Charles Dickens novel. In reality, it didn't feel like that at all.

We acquired a spanner from the laborer who was caught up with fixing the smaller than normal Buckingham Palace, and we raised Pinky's seat. Neither one of the bicycles was agreeable to ride, yet the seat on Pinky had been particularly low and was especially excruciating on the knees. Raising the seat made an immense difference.

The Falcon's chain stuck as Ben attempted to overwhelm me at speed on one of the numerous downhills. It was wedged between the primary stuff pinion and the casing yet he had the option to freewheel for one more a large portion of a mile before we needed to pull over.

Conveniently, at the lower part of the slope was The Lappa Valley Steam Railway. We appeared to be doing an accidental visit through Cornwall's most famous vacationer attractions.

The Lappa Valley Steam Railway was little, as it appeared were most traveler things in Cornwall. We attempted to no end to free the caught chain, however no measure of yanking would deliver it. We chose the best way to deliver it is relax the back wheel.

I lined up at the ticket office and they guided me towards the train driver who was simply rising up out of the train. He had a major white facial hair growth and every last trace of his face was shrouded in oil and ash. He resembled a dark Captain Birdseye. He joyfully loaned me a movable spanner and I got back to Ben who was at that point getting into his pick 'n' blend. We had concurred that we

would save it until we were truly frantic. It appeared to be that we were truly frantic as I too got my pack and begun scooping modest bunches of desserts into my mouth.

It was the main sugar we'd had since the air terminal and our bodies positively were shrinking in its nonattendance. I had begun to get the shakes a couple of hours prior, and I could feel the moment impact of the sugar. I have never attempted heroin, and never plan to, yet I can't envision that it's any better than the surge we got from that pick 'n' mix.

We lay on the grass, totally sugar-stoned. Donna from World in Miniature more likely than not given us somewhere around a kilogram of pick 'n' blend each, and in around 30 seconds we had eaten half of it. Subsequent to fixing the haggle the spanner, we proceeded onwards with the sugar actually dashing through our veins.

We spent the remainder of the day cycling along paths that were really calm that grass filled in them. It was wonderful and quiet, yet very difficult. Notwithstanding trading bicycles routinely, partnerships were starting to be shaped. Ben unmistakably preferred Pinky, and I favored The Falcon – notwithstanding Ben guaranteeing it was actually difficult to ride it up slopes. Cycling uphill on The Falcon was a workmanship that Ben won't ever dominate. Indeed, he didn't adapt much better on Pinky, and she was evidently a 'mountain' bike.

'These bleeding slopes!' Ben yelled, getting off to push once more. 'For what reason wouldn't we be able to adhere to the A-roads?'

'The A-streets have slopes as well, you know.'

'Better believe it, dislike this. This is ludicrous. We've not seen any level ground in two days.'

'Yet it's overall quite tranquil. Clearly you'd like to cycle along these country paths than the bustling A30?'

'No chance. Essentially we'd get some place on the huge road.'

'That is assuming we didn't get hit by a truck. Also, there's really no need to focus on how rapidly we do this excursion, it's tied in with seeing pieces of the country, too.'

'I think I've seen enough already!'

We quit talking for a couple of moments and I thought he had quieted down, until I heard a yell of 'FUCKING PIECE OF SHIT' behind me. I went to see Ben tossing Pinky into the fence. She fell back out again and arrived at his feet, where he gave her a kick.

This appeared to clear his framework, as he appeared to be marginally more joyful afterwards.

The slopes smoothed fairly, and we felt like we were gaining ground again.

Half an hour after the fact, we were lost. We had been covering the distance yet we had no clue assuming we were heading the correct way. It was some time since we had seen any of the towns that Donna had referenced, so we halted at a ranch to inquire as to whether they had a map.

'Sorry, I was KILLIN' chickens,' yelled the woman, after we had been meandering capriciously around her farmstead for quite a while. She was in her mid thirties, with blanched light hair. Her hands were shrouded in blood that she was cleaning on her pants. 'What would i be able to get you? Is it chickens you're after?' she said, highlighting a sign on the entryway. *New Meat – For Sale.*

'Really, we're somewhat lost. Do you perhaps have a guide we could have a brief glance at, please?'

'I think somebody left one 'ere once. I don't have no requirement for a guide,' she said and moved into a train, which appeared to be her house.

'There you are,' she said, giving us a street chart book dated 1988. 'I can't peruse so great, so you'll need to sort out it for yourselves.'

'Whereabouts on the guide we are presently?' I asked.

'I think somewhere near here,' she said, highlighting a touch of the guide miles from anywhere.

'Nanstallon! That is one of the spots that Donna referenced,' I said.

'No doubt. Seems as though we're putting in any amount of work then, at that point, Ben.'

'So in case we continue to head toward this path for around eight miles, we ought to get to Nanstallon. It looks very huge on the guide, so we should track down some place to remain there.'

Ben sighed.

Soon subsequently, we were at a junction and lost again.

We turned right and the grass in the street started to get to knee stature, and clearly no measure of traffic had been down there in Thusme time. We attempted one of different turns all things considered. It drove into a field. So, by a course of disposal, we calculated the third and last choice must be the right way.

The chain stuck on The Falcon, once more. This time it was on a long tough. Once more, we couldn't free the chain manually, so I pushed the bicycle to the highest point of the slope, and afterward freewheeled down the other side.

We halted at an adorable little bungalow at the lower part of the slope. We were in certain woods, and we half anticipated that Little Red Riding Hood should open the entryway. Tragically, the woman who addressed looked more like the Big Bad Wolf.

Not just did she furnish us with a spanner, however she gave us a Kit Kat every, which we gulped down as the surge from the pick 'n' blend had begun to wear off. We inquired as to whether we were heading toward Nanstallon. 'Sure you are,' she said. 'You can either go up this slope, which is truly long and steep and I wouldn't suggest it. Or on the other hand, you can turn left there and afterward take the long way round, however in case you put in any amount of work a truly long and steep slope which I wouldn't recommend.'

'So we can go regardless, yet you wouldn't suggest it is possible that?' I inquired. 'Not on a bicycle, noooo.'

'But rather we are on bikes.'

'Well I wouldn't suggest it.'

As it ended up, we had been up far more extreme slopes currently that day, and we came to the top without breaking sweat. It was great for the long plummet into the town of Nanstallon, which ended up being a colossal frustration. Not that there was anything amiss with the town, but since we had expected it to be brimming with cafés and inns offering free convenience. The idiotic spot didn't have a pub.

We remained close to the congregation pondering where to attempt first. It was 8pm, so we actually had bounty time to track down some place to rest, yet it was adequately late to imply that individuals would not have any desire to be disturbed.

A man wearing an ER shirt had been taking care of the lawn at the congregation. I mean ER the TV series – he wasn't a specialist. Subsequent to stacking the trimmer into the rear of his vehicle, he unwound his window and inquired as to whether we wanted any assistance. 'There's a rancher not too far off there who may have an outbuilding you can stay in bed,' he said in the wake of hearing the abbreviated adaptation of our story.

Ben chuffed. He wasn't in the mind-set for another barn.

'Albeit, last time he let individuals stay they torched one of his outbuildings, so he may be somewhat dubious. Best of luck,' said the lawnmower man as he hurried away. He proceeded up the path, and we remained there discussing what to do. 'There should be a camping area some place close here,' said Ben after a while. 'Certainly they'd have an old tent lying around that we could borrow?'

'Excuse me,' I said to a simply man escaped his vehicle with his dog. agonizing over what she could prepare us for supper. We demanded that we didn't require taking care of and that we actually had some pick 'n' blend, however she was having none of it. None of our demand, I mean, not our pick 'n' blend. Despite the fact that she was having absolutely no part of that either.

'Right. I'll figure out a type of pasta dish,' she shouted, hopping up from her seat. 'David will show you to your room. Have a shower and afterward supper will be prepared in with regards to a large portion of an hour.'

David showed us to the loft room, which we got to through a mysterious entryway, somewhat like Narnia, just not. It was a major white room with a twofold bed in it.

'I'll leave you both to it. The washroom is at the lower part of the steps,' said David as he left.

'So who's having the bed, and who's having the floor?' I asked Ben.
'Well I'm resting in the bed, and assuming you have gives then you can have
the floor, any other way we can share.'
'Fine, we'll share. Yet, take a stab at nothing funny.'

Annie had made a beast dish of spaghetti and pureed tomatoes. This was no Dolmio (other pasta sauces are accessible), however new pureed tomatoes produced using natural tomatoes filled in their own nursery, seasoned with onions and garlic filled in their own nursery, decorated with basil filled in their own nursery, served on plates terminated in their own furnace and with cutlery made in their own manufacture. I lied about the plates and the cutlery, however they were exceptionally glad to show how independent they were. Not that I fault them. I developed some cress once I actually consider it perhaps my most noteworthy accomplishment in life.

The food was scrumptious. It was the kind of supper that cyclists ought to eat. I can't help thinking about the number of Tour de Frances Lance Armstrong would have won on a tight eating routine of Cornish pasties and pick 'n' mix.

We ate seconds. And afterward thirds. And afterward tremendous cuts of nut cake, probably produced using a determination of natural products filled in their own garden.

'Do you have any socks?' asked Annie randomly.

'Indeed, all things considered, we have a couple between us,' said Ben. David, who had been sitting unobtrusively at the opposite finish of the table, spat his wine across the table.

'A couple between you?' he snickered. 'My god!'

'We can't have that,' said Annie. 'I'll go nearby and get a few socks from our neighbour.'

'What might be said about MY socks?' asked David.

'Your feet are excessively little, dear. Bill nearby is a size 11.'

David didn't get an opportunity to guard his lacking feet as Annie had effectively left through the front entryway. I didn't inspect David's feet especially intently, yet he didn't seem as though the sort of individual that would have had particularly little feet. I'm certain we would have serenely fitted into any socks that he had, yet Annie had been resolved that we really wanted greater ones.

She got back with six sets of the greatest socks I had at any point found in my life. In case they'd been held tight the chimney at Christmas, even the most liberal Father Christmas would have battled to fill them.

'Annie dear, they're going to Scotland, not Iceland,' said David.
'Indeed, but rather it can get freezing up there around evening time. They'll see the value in them.' 'We do for sure, thank you kindly. What's more kindly thank your neighbour,
as well,' said Ben with a grin.
'Gracious, I didn't let him know I was taking them. He's north of 90, and was quick asleep.'

After supper, Ben engaged David and Annie with an amazing piano presentation and afterward we made a beeline for bed.

'What the heck are we going to do with this large number of gigantic socks?' asked Ben when we returned to our room.

'I can't really understand. I surmise we'll need to wear a couple each and attempt and stuff the rest in our sacks some way or another.' We took it in goes to pick a couple and I wound up with the best of the bundle; a couple of knee length ski socks enhanced with pictures of sheep wearing Christmas hats.

Annie had sympathetically proposed to wash our fighter shorts, and the pair of socks that we had been sharing for three days. She was concerned we would get a type of parasitic contamination, and she was likely correct. This implied that I needed to rest in my suit pants and Ben dozed in his shorts. I appreciated Ben's conversation, however our relationship was as yet far from exposed bed sharing.

Day 4 – A new hero

Nanstallon to Okehampton – 52 miles

We woke before David and Annie, so had a shower each, and afterward went through 15 minutes reworking our sacks with the goal that the socks would fit. Once more, our hosts demanded that we eat so we happily acknowledged. Annie gave us our spotless and dry fighter shorts and socks and acquainted us with their chicken Diamond Lil. Local eggs, too.

We checked out a guide over breakfast, and for the principal we had an abrupt acknowledgment of exactly how huge Great Britain was. We had been out and about for three days yet we had covered just a minuscule part of the island. We actually had almost 900 miles among us and the highest point of Scotland and it was unbelievably overwhelming. Even with our new bikes we had only managed 48 miles, and if there was any hope in us reaching John O'Groats within three weeks, we were going to have to significantly pick up the pace.

Outside, David was doing something to our bikes.
'I saw that the handlebars on this pink one looked truly awkward,' he said.
'Definitely, they are a little,'
said Ben. 'Well I think I have
fixed them.'
We strolled over to him and saw that Pinky's handlebars had developed into enormous wipes. He had taken a part of froth pipe protection from the lines in his carport, and cut them into handlebar-sized pieces, which he had then taped onto the bicycle. The Falcon likewise had a major shower wipe taped to its seat, determined to make it more comfortable.
'Much obliged, David. They look... blunder...
incredible,' said Ben. 'No doubt, they look stacks
better,' I said suspiciously.

We gave our gratitude to Annie and David and left Nanstallon. David had recommended following a course known as the Camel Trail for a couple of miles. The Camel Trail was a stretch of old railroad that had been changed over into a way for strolling and cycling. It had two sections; one extending from Padstow to Bodmin, the other segment extending east towards Camelford, which was the bearing we were heading.
We joined the way soon after leaving Nanstallon. It was a joy to cycle along, considering it was the main piece of level ground that we had cycled along since the vehicle leave at Land's End. Joined by an ensemble of birds, we wound our direction through woods and along the bank of the stream Camel.

'Excuse me, is this the way to Camelford?' I asked an old walker, who was strolling the other way to us, with a woman who had all the earmarks of being his daughter.
'Yes. It's only a couple of miles further down the path,' he said. 'Is that where you are heading?'
'Until further notice, indeed, however we're en route to John O'Groats,'
said Ben.
'Gracious truly? I strolled from John O'Groats to Land's End a couple of years prior. I'm really referenced in the gallery at Land's End, similar to the

most seasoned individual to walk the course. I'm simply along the divider from Ian Botham.'

'And the narrative of the one who attempted to push a pea with his nose the whole way,' I added.

'Indeed, believe it or not. The inept dolt,' he said.

Reg Savill was the main individual we had addressed since setting off that morning, and it worked out that he was a Land's End to John O'Groats record holder. What were the chances?

He was 74 when he finished the outing and he had strolled the whole distance all alone. Genuinely from the beginning in his outing, he got an opportunity meeting with a man named Gil Campbell who was out driving in his campervan. He had seen Reg strolling at the edge of the street looking lazy, and offered him a lift to the following town. Reg declined the deal, however inquired as to whether the man could drop his backpack at the following B&B along the course. Not exclusively did the man oblige, yet he additionally did likewise each day, the entire way to Land's End. They had been dear companions ever since.

'He really was a lifeline,' said Reg. 'I sincerely accept assuming it hadn't been for him I couldn't have ever finished it.'

'That is inconceivable,' I said. 'We've met our very own couple adaptations of Gil currently on our trip.'

'And you'll meet bounty more. There are bunches of them about.'

'In this way, it seems as though you are as yet keeping yourself fit then, at that point, Reg?' asked Ben 'Well, indeed, I used to be a Navy commando, so I was genuinely fit. Until last year, I was doing my military preparing system each day; 100 press-ups, 100 sit-ups and 40 jawline ups. I had a hernia activity last year, so presently I can just oversee 20 jawline ups.'

Ben and I were both in stunningness. We had tracked down another saint. We needed to hear whatever number of Reg's accounts as could be expected under the circumstances, thus went through 45 minutes remaining in the Camel Trail, being blessed to receive stories from his journey.

'I wound up on a motorway one day, accidentally. I was strolling along and I took what I thought was the right street, however it ended up being a slip street that drove onto the motorway. The street was genuinely peaceful so I chose to continue to stroll, as it was past the point where it is possible to turn around. The police got me after a couple of miles and drove me back to where I'd went along with it. I had to take a different route then, and ended up walking 38 miles in one day. I wouldn't suggest that.' 'Jesus, that is nearly to the extent we cycled yesterday. What's more you strolled it!' I said. 'What's more a specific features of the excursion for you?'

'The good countries in Scotland are fabulous. Assuming that you believe it's really round here, simply delay until you get to Scotland.'

'How far are you strolling today?'

'Around 12 miles. My significant other and I attempt to do around 12 miles per day,' he said, highlighting the young woman adjacent to him. His significant other? Pleasant one, Reg. You da man!

We left Reg with blended feelings. We had been really enlivened by his accomplishments, inspiration, and obviously his young spouse. If I can be half as fit as him when I'm in my late seventies then I'll be very happy. But on the other hand, it made us both feel that our challenge was somewhat inferior. We were genuinely fit youngsters and we had bicycles. He was almost multiple times our age, and had strolled every last trace of his 868 miles on foot.

Camelford was a little market town on the edge of Bardmin. I say was as I am composing this book all things considered. It very well may be a poop opening now, for all I know.

It was, in any case, home to some extremely odd individuals. We plunked down on a seat in a square off the central avenue. It hushed up, aside from an alcoholic over in the furthest corner, who was drinking from a jug in a paper pack and yelling indistinguishable indecencies to passers-by.

It was nearly noontime and we were ravenous again.

We were drawn nearer by an odd looking woman. She was around seven feet tall, mid sixties, with a mass of brilliant light hair. I thought she was a cross dresser from the beginning, and Ben thought she was a witch. She later became known, among us, as Tranny Witch.

She had spotted me utilizing my camera and had meandered
over. 'What are you taking pictures of?' she asked.

'We're cycling to John O'Groats and we're simply taking some photographs along the way.'

'How fascinating,' said Tranny Witch.

Her mouth began to froth in one corner, and the more she talked, the more it frothed. Before the finish of the discussion she appeared as though she had a marshmallow adhered to her face.

She ended up being an extremely fascinating (ish) woman and recounted to us an account of a journey of sorts that she had embraced a couple of years beforehand, when she and a gathering of others had strolled to London. They had likewise depended on individuals to assist with taking care of them and give them cover en route. She said the gathering they got from everybody was shocking. Luckily, she didn't set off in some jeans. That is something I would rather not even imagine.

'Recall that you're not in England presently, you're in Cornwall,' she said as she was leaving. 'Meur ras. Dyw genes.'

'I'm grieved, what was that?' asked
Ben. 'That implies thank you and
goodbye.'

There was a butcher's inverse and we meandered over to attempt to top off our water bottles.

'Ahhh, no issue,' said the woman behind the counter.

She asked us what we were doing thus we told her the story.

'You'll be needing some lunch then, at that point, as well. What about some chicken thighs?'

'That is extremely kind,' I said, 'however we don't have any means to cook them.' 'Goodness, I see, all good. What about a few pork hacks then?'

'Errr, once more, I think we'd battle to track down some place to prepare them for lunch. Much obliged anyway.'

'Well, so I surmise bacon wouldn't be any utilization either then, at that point? What about some ham?' she asked, not having any desire to be defeated.

'Some ham would be splendid, much obliged. I'm certain we could get some bread from somewhere.'

'There are a few treats for you there, as well,' she said, giving us a transporter sack containing ham, treats and our water bottles.

I found that in 1988 Camelford's water supply was inadvertently defiled when 20 tons of aluminum sulfate was filled some unacceptable tank at the neighborhood water works. The drawn out consequences for the inhabitants are as yet under question. Everything I can say in the wake of meeting local people is that it

clarifies a terrible lot.

There was minimal possibility that we would have effectively explored ourselves to John O'Groats without the guide of a guide or course book. Asking irregular outsiders 'what direction is Scotland?' was demonstrating vain. We understood that we really wanted a more coordinated way to deal with navigation.

'THE LIBRARY!' I yelled.

'Shouldn't something be said

about the library?

'We could get a guide or a course book from the library. It takes care of every one of our concerns. It will make getting to Scotland quite much simpler, and we don't need to spend any money.'

'Virtuoso,' said Ben.

The library didn't credit out maps, nor did it have an immense choice of Land's End to John O'Groats course books yet it had one – Bike Britain, by Paul Salter. This was to turn into our book of scriptures over the accompanying three weeks.

Borrowing the book demonstrated far simpler than we anticipated. Regardless of having no recognizable proof, we had the option to enchant the bookkeeper with our grins. We vowed to return the book to our nearby library after we had gotten done and for it to be moved back to them.

The book was awesome. It point by point a course from Land's End to John O'Groats following generally minor streets. It was fanned out more than a 21-day plan. The main issue was that Camelford was on Day 2 of the book. We were partially through our fourth day, and had the slight impediment of youngsters' bicycles. We expected to get cracking.

It would have been a long evening, so we chose to attempt to do a couple of more miles before lunch. The town of Launceston was a couple of miles up the street so we set off determined to stop there for a break.

The course followed the bustling A39 out of Camelford, and afterward remove from the fundamental street and cut its direction through the wide open towards Launceston.

Just prior to arriving at Launceston, the street dropped pointedly into the town. We before long found that in spite of all his Benevolence, David had really changed over Pinky into a passing snare. The froth on the handlebars was really thick that it made it difficult to press the brakes enough for them to work successfully. Ben, who was riding Pinky at that point, needed to steer around a transport that had pulled over, steer back to keep away from a head-on impact with approaching traffic, zigzag all around a line of vehicles that had upheld at a

thin convergence, before in the end arriving at an unexpected stop against a wall.

'What the heck was David playing at?' shouted Ben. 'Was he attempting to fucking kill me?'

We both

laughed.

'Definitely, moronic David. What a fucking thrower!' I said. 'He took us in for the evening, gave us supper, a blistering shower, a comfortable bed, delightful breakfast, and afterward he proceeded to mess our bicycles up. What a knob!'

Launceston appeared to be a town of two sections. One section – the poop part – is at the lower part of the slope, with only several shops and some featureless roads. The other part – the less poop part – sits on the highest point of the slope overwhelmed by the noteworthy Launceston Castle.

There was no charge to visit the space of grass right inside the external dividers of the palace, so we sat on the bank and ate ham and old bread that Ben gained from a close by cook. We had the remaining parts of our pick 'n' blend for pudding. The view from the palace was staggering, and the 'poo part' of Launceston – that I had evaded only minutes prior – gazed especially delightful from upward high.

Ben discussed his annoyance from the other day, when he had tossed Pinky in the hedge.

'What you saw was uniquely around 10% of the fury that was within me,' he said.

'Truly? I thought you were simply kidding near.'

'Noooo, that was all real.'

'Were you annoyed with me?'

'No, I was getting irritated with myself. I disdain holding individuals up.'

'You weren't holding me up. I like it when you get off and stroll, as then, at that point, I can get off, too.'

'Well in any case, I'm feeling better today.'

The Cornish Stannary Parliament dispatched Operation Chough in 1999, which brought about the evacuation or ruining of English Heritage signs from large numbers of Cornwall's vacation spots. One of which was Launceston Castle. The explanation being, as Tranny Witch had brought up, was that they weren't in England, they were in Cornwall. A legal dispute resulted, and charges against the Cornish Stannary Parliament were in the end dropped after they returned every one of the signs and paid remuneration to English Heritage.

Cornish or English, it was as yet a delightful spot. The actual palace just costs a couple of pounds to visit and appeared to be definitely worth a trip.

'Will we check whether Launceston has a Police Station? They may have some legitimate bicycles lying around that they can give us?' asked Ben.

'What do you mean? We've got proper bikes, haven't we?'

'Yeah, I mean bikes to get us to John O'Groats.'

'I believed that is what these were?'

'What? No doubt, right. Extremely amusing. These are simply

impermanent things until we get something better.'

I was befuddled. I had believed that we planned to take Pinky and The Falcon the entire way to John O'Groats, yet Ben had various thoughts. They weren't the best bicycles on the planet, as a matter of fact, however they were doing the work. Individuals had most likely done the outing on more terrible bicycles in the past.

'alright,' I surrendered, 'how about we attempt the police headquarters.'

Launceston Police Station was situated on the outskirts of town, fortunately in the direction we were heading. A smiling bald man manned the desk.

'We do get stolen bikes in occasionally, but if they're not reclaimed then they get sent to Torquay,' he said.

'How far is Torquay from here?' asked Ben.

'Oooh, I would say it's about 70 miles or so.'

Ben looked at me. 'That's not too far,' he said. 'It's probably worth a try.'

'Are you serious?' I asked, in shock. 'You want to cycle 70 miles out of our way, to somewhere that may or may not have bikes that are better than the ones we already have?'

'No?'

'No!'

Ben looked dejected.

'Is there a tip in Launceston?' he asked the policeman.

'Yes, follow this road down for half a mile. Right at the roundabout then it's on the right.'

'It must be here somewhere,' said Ben after we had taken every possible exit from the roundabout and still not found it.

'Do you really think the tip is likely to have bikes better than the ones we already have?'

'They might. It's worth a try.'

'Are you hoping that Lance Armstrong might have been holidaying in Cornwall and needed to get rid of a couple of his racing bikes? It's 3pm already and we want to do another 30 miles today.'

'You do. I don't,' snapped Ben.

We eventually found the tip. They had an exercise bike, half a Raleigh Chopper and a fold-in-half shopper bikes with no wheels.

'It doesn't look like they have anything,' accepted
Ben. 'That's surprising.'
'What did you
say?' 'Nothing.'

'What's your problem with upgrading our bikes?'

'My problem is that we've got bikes, and we've just spent the last TWO HOURS trying to get bikes, and we've covered about a mile.'

'But if we can get better bikes, then we'll be able to cycle more miles each day and we'll get there quicker.'

'Why do we need to get there quicker? It's not a race.'

'No, but these bikes aren't even comfortable to ride. You seem to like to suffer. They are not even adult bikes, they were made for children. I don't understand you!'

And so it went on.

I could see Ben's point. If we had got better bikes, we would have made better progress, and the cycling would have felt less painful. The truth was, I was secretly falling in love with The Falcon. Yes, it was far too small for me. Yes, its handlebars were hacking my palms to pieces. Yes, it had the hardest saddle ever invented, and because of the position of the handlebars I was swiftly becoming a hunchback. Riding a stegosaurus to Scotland would have been more comfortable. But there was something about The Falcon that was winning me over. It was partly the added challenge of completing the trip on an inadequate bike; I imagined that it would perhaps make me feel more of a man.

I was also intensely aware that our trip was all about stripping things back to basics. People have been cycling the length of the country for years, on far crapper bikes, and just because we were living in the 21st century did not mean I needed a 21st century bike.

The first recorded 'End to End' cyclists were two Leeds policemen,   who completed the trip on penny-farthings in 1882. It took them 14 days. If the trip could be done in two weeks on a penny-farthing, then I could sure as hell do it in three weeks on a child's racing bike.

Reaching the Devon county sign was a pivotal moment, and it caught us completely by surprise. We just turned a corner and there it was. *'Devon', it said, as you would expect it should.*

We had cycled across an entire county. We had been warned that Cornwall was the worst bit, and so felt a real sense of achievement having successfully conquered it. We took an obligatory picture of the two of us at the signpost, for which I had to run back through a nettle patch to get in place before the self-timer fired.

From then on, it promised to be easy. The contours of the land would level out, and we would be in John O'Groats in no time.

Or so we hoped.

Devon had other ideas, however, and presented us with a huge big sodding hill straight after welcoming us. It stretched on for about six miles until just before the town of Okehampton, where it allowed us a brief downhill to gain its forgiveness.

It wasn't the best start. We had only been in Devon for a couple of hours and already thought it was shitter than Cornwall.

Okehampton looked like Devon's answer to the Wild West. Its main high street – which is called Fore Street, as many in Devon and Cornwall are for some reason – was unusually wide. Imposing flat fronted buildings banked each side of the road, and we half expected a gunslinger to swagger out from a dusty saloon. Only this was Devon, and there were no dusty saloons, or gunslingers for that matter. Instead, a blue-rinsed granny hobbled out of Specsavers.

The town is right on the northern edge of Dartmoor, and is considered one of the gateways to the national park. The main A30 used to pass straight through the town centre, which explains why Fore Street is so wide. A bypass was built in 1988 and the town now enjoys a little more peace and quiet from the traffic.

We arrived in Okehampton at about 7.30pm and decided to ask at The White Hart Hotel – a huge hotel on the edge of town – about the possibility of doing some work in exchange for somewhere to sleep.

The manager's name was Glyn – a small bird-like lady.

'So what you're saying is that you'll do some jobs for me around the hotel, and in exchange I'll give you some dinner and somewhere to sleep,' she said with a strong Yorkshire accent.

'Well, yes, but you don't have to feed us.' 'But you don't have any money or food.' 'No, that's true.'

'So if you have something to eat, and a bed for the night, I can write you a list of jobs and you'll do them. Is that right?'

'Yes, that's right.'

'I have to say this is a first, but, ok, take a seat and I'll write a list of things.'

This was more like it. Good honest work in exchange for board and lodging. She returned with a handwritten list.

Remove ALL leaves from car-park Clean out bin room
Wash outside of hotel

The White Hart is probably the biggest hotel in Devon – possibly the world. And we had to wash it.

Glyn gave us a tour of our duties and described exactly what she wanted doing.

'You see these leaves on this path? I want EVERY LEAF picked up. EVERY LEAF... You see all these leaves all over the car park? I want EVERY ONE of those picked up. EVERY ONE. This bin room needs sweeping, and clearing up, and the bins need wiping down... Take a large bucket with some soapy water – NOT TOO MUCH SOAP – and wipe down the black bit all the way down to the floor... Leave THAT bit, the council own that, so they can do it... Wipe down all the door frames and window frames, and that should just about do it.'

It was dark by the time we started.

As we scraped up huge piles of soggy leaves with our bare hands, it was obvious that they were all coated in urine. It was clear that people stopped to relieve themselves on their way back to their car after a night on the beers. Don't drink and drive, kids. In fact, if you're a kid, don't drink at all. Or drive for that matter.

The bin room was rank, too. It looked like foxes had been at the bins, as the contents were strewn across the floor. We scooped up eggshells and rotten vegetables with a shovel and put it all into black bin bags. As I knelt to reach under a big wheelie bin I managed to get rotten egg all over my suit trousers. The smell lingered with me for several days.

Whilst cleaning we met Arek, a Polish chef who had been in England nearly a year. He began working in the kitchen in the main restaurant, and then helped set up a pizzeria at the back of the hotel.

'My name iz Arek. I come from The Poland. My English izza not so good. I learn English for tree manths.'

'Your English is very good,' I said. 'It's almost better than mine and it's definitely better than Ben's. So, do you like living in England?'

'Yessa. I come to England and see English people they only eat steak and kidney pudding, chips and graaavy. I think I want show English people something new, something different, so I cook them pizza. So we bring piiizzas, 11 manth ago, to England. Is gone down very well.'

Pizza? How groundbreaking. Ben and I had to ask Arek what it was as we had never heard of pizza before. Apparently it's some sort of radical food that consists of a dough base, baked with tomatoes, cheese and various other toppings. They're going to become very popular in the UK, thanks to Arek. You heard it here first.

We told Arek why we were washing the hotel, which amused him greatly.

We explained that Glyn was giving us a bed for the night and some food.

'I cook you piiiiizza!' he shouted.

'I'm not sure that's what Glyn had planned for us,' said Ben.

'Is ok. I speak her. I cook you piiiiizza. You come find me after and I cook you piiiiizza. Then we go uppa to my house abovva hotel and we drink beers from The Poland, ok?'

'Ok.'

Washing the hotel didn't take as long as we had thought. We slopped hot soapy water over the walls (with NOT TOO MUCH SOAP) and although we couldn't see what we were doing, it felt as though we were cleaning it.

It was 10.30pm by the time we had finished our chores. We had cycled 52 miles on children's bikes, had to scrounge our lunch and then spent 2 ½ hours cleaning a hotel. We were in need of our piiiizza.

Not only did Arek manage to wangle us a pizza each, but he also poured

Reg Sewill – Land's End to John O'Groats record-holder

Bedrooms in Camelford

Devon, obviously

Andi, Okehampton

Late night beers with Andi and Oakash

Gen, White Hart Hotel, Okehampton

Andi making pizza

Day 5 – Mrs Rogers

Okehampton to Walton – 81 miles

I felt like I had been in a car accident. We had stupidly requested an alarm call at 6.45am with the intention of having an early start. My body felt like it belonged to someone 50 years older.

Again, I had foolishly tried to wash my boxer shorts late at night and have them dry by the morning. Again I had failed.

Glyn, the manager, was at the reception when we went downstairs.

'Good morning. Dave will sort you out with some breakfast in the dining room, and then I'll do an inspection to see if you did your jobs properly. Then I'll decide whether you can have your bikes back.'

She didn't look like she was joking.

Dave was in his sixties and clearly wanted to be anywhere else, other than serving breakfast in a hotel in Okehampton.

'Morning, Dave. Sleep well?' asked Ben.

'Too well. That's why I was late this morning. So what will it be? Two full Englishes?'

'Sounds perfect. Thanks.'

During breakfast, the ketchup bottle exploded when I opened it. It covered my t-shirt, face, suit trousers, the table, the surrounding tables, the old couple on the next table, the ceiling and the window. Ben, who had somehow escaped unmarked, howled with laughter.

'Everything alright?' asked Dave when he came to offer us more tea.

'Errrr… I kinda covered the room in ketchup,' I said. Dave took one look at me and then began laughing and pointing.

'Ha ha, look it's all over your face and clothes.'

'Yes. I know.'

'How strange. I wonder how that happened?' he said, with the smirk of someone who knew exactly how it happened. He handed me a napkin, picked up the ketchup bottle and walked off.

It didn't take a genius to work out that he and the other kitchen staff probably had something to do with it. A couple of teaspoons of baking soda would have probably done the trick. I could hardly blame them; they had cooked and served breakfast to a couple of dirty, non-paying guests. I probably would have done the same thing.

After breakfast Glyn led us round the hotel checking we had completed the jobs to her standard. In the daylight it was clear that we had missed most of the leaves.

'It must have been really windy last night, because this car park was spotless when we finished last night,' I said.

This seemed to do the trick, and she seemed happy enough with our efforts. There were also several patches of the outside of the hotel that looked like we had failed to clean. We made sure that we were deep in conversation with Glyn whilst she checked these, and we managed to distract her sufficiently to get her seal of approval. We passed with flying colours and she allowed us our bikes back.

Arek was still asleep when we left.

We were both feeling like death. A combination of the Polish beer, the lack of sleep and the fact that we were cycling to Scotland on tiny bikes had started to take its toll. For the first few miles of that morning, neither of us enjoyed the ride. The road climbed yet again after leaving Okehampton. Devon was just one big fat hill after another, and we still had 2 ½ weeks and nearly 900 miles to go. It was demoralizing.

We were following what was once the main road between Cornwall and Somerset, before the A30 was built parallel to it. It was satisfying to hear the distant buzz of traffic on the very busy A30 that many End to Enders follow from Land's End all the way to Somerset. The road we followed, however, was completely deserted, and it didn't take long for us to get back into the spirit of the trip.

We gradually warmed to Devon. Its hills became less severe, and the countryside it offered us was breathtaking. Our route led us through the tiny villages of Belstone Corner and Coleford, which were little more than collections of houses. Dogs barked at us as we passed through these places, as though we were the first visitors in many years.

Quiet country roads are obviously a pleasure to cycle along, but they also have their drawbacks. As there are so few vehicles about, many of the vehicles that do use the roads assume that they are the only ones to be doing so. I turned a corner to be met with an oil tanker that was travelling in the middle of the road at a ridiculous speed. It would have vaporised me had it

made contact. Fortunately, I managed to dive into the relative comfort of the hedge. I turned to see if Ben had survived, as he had been trailing slightly behind. There was no sign of him. I heard the screeching of the tanker's brakes and so feared the worst, but Ben soon emerged round the corner, looking like he had also taken refuge in the hedge.

Ben was becoming increasingly frustrated with me and The Falcon. Its chain had got into the habit of falling off at regular intervals for no apparent reason, and these occurrences were becoming more frequent. As if that wasn't irritating enough, its front wheel then fell off midway through the morning. It quite literally detached itself from the bike as I was cycling.

Fortunately, I was moving relatively slowly at the time, trying to avoid a pothole, but when I pulled at the handlebars to attempt to hop over it, the front wheel stayed in contact with the ground and continued rolling. The bike's front forks then hit the ground and scraped along the road surface as I tried to regain my footing.

'I don't believe it,' said Ben. 'Is there anything else that can go wrong with the bloody bike?'

'Calm down. It's only a wheel. I'll get it sorted.'

'ONLY a wheel? Because it's not like wheels are important on bikes or anything.'

I flipped the bike upside down and reattached the wheel, tightening the bolts as best I could with my hands. It needed to be fastened with a spanner, though, or it was going to become a regular event. We were in the middle of the countryside and miles from anywhere.

'I'll just take it easy until we pass a house or garage or something, and we'll borrow a spanner there,' I said.

'But you might be dead before we get there.'

'At least you won't have to keep stopping for me then.'

'That's true.'

Just as I was climbing back on my bike, I saw Ben running off down the road, waving his arms at a passing campervan.

'Excuse me! Excuse me! Can you stop for a second?' he shouted. The van pulled over, and I immediately saw what Ben had spotted. The campervan – a badly converted transit van – had three BMX bikes on the back, and another two on the roof.

'Hello. I'm really sorry to bother you,' said Ben, 'but I saw your bikes and thought you might have a spanner that we could borrow. The wheel has just fallen off one of ours.'

Max was a very cool, dreadlocked man in his early thirties. He happened to be a professional BMX stunt performer, who was on his way to do a show in Cornwall. The back of his van was like a bike repair shop. He had tools and parts of all descriptions, and he set to work immediately. After securing the front wheel, he tightened a few other bolts, and gave both bikes a spray of oil.

'There we go. As good as new,' he laughed.

'Thanks so much. I don't suppose you want to swap this bike for one of yours?' Ben joked.

'Unfortunately not. Mine are all specially designed stunt bikes.'

'So is mine,' I said. 'I can do this great trick where I detach the front wheel whilst I'm cycling along.'

'Ha! I'll have to try and put that one in my repertoire. Good luck with the rest of your trip, guys.'

We arrived in the village of Thorverton shortly before midday, having covered about 20 miles that morning. After our long breakfast, the ketchup incident, and Glyn's inspection, our planned early start had become 10am. We had made good progress, though – considering the issues with The Falcon – so decided to try for an early lunch, and then embark on a mammoth afternoon of cycling.

Thorverton is a relatively small village with an attractive little garden in the middle. Unlike usual village greens, this one was an actual garden. It had a stream running through it, flowerbeds, trimmed shrubs and a bench. We sat on the bench for a few minutes and assessed the two pubs that we could see and decided on The Thorverton Arms. We pretended to lock our bikes in the beer garden at the back and entered the pub.

A sporty looking lady was manning the bar. She was in her forties and gave the impression from the way she was rearranging the bottles that she was the landlady.

'What can I get you?' she said with a smile.

'Hello. Do you have any work that needs doing in exchange for some food?' asked Ben.

'What do you mean?'

'We're on a mission to get to John O'Groats without spending any money and thought we might be able to help you out with some jobs, in exchange for something to eat.'

A large bearded man appeared behind the bar. He looked sporty too, in his own special way.

'There's some washing up you can do, if you want. One of the lads called in sick today so they could do with a hand back there,' he said, as though it was the most natural thing in the world for two people to walk in off the street and do the washing up. 'Then when that's done, I'll sort you out with some lunch.'

'Brilliant,' I said. 'Which way is the kitchen?'

The sink was piled several feet high with dirty pans and dishes, but between the two of us we figured we would have it all washed in no time.

'Then when you've finished all the stuff in the sink there are a few things behind you that need doing,' he said.

We turned around and every inch of the kitchen's serving station was stacked with plates, cutlery, pots, baking trays, knives and mixing bowls. On the other side of the carnage, we could just about make out two guys working away at the stoves.

'Hi, guys. I'm George and this is Ben. We're here to help you with the washing up in exchange for some lunch.'

'Cheers, dudes,' said the younger of the boys. 'We've been completely swamped and haven't had a chance to do any all day. We've been washing stuff up as we need it.'

'That technique has worked for me for years,' said Ben.

Their names were Ryan and Matthew. They looked around 17 and 19 individually. They were both hopeful youthful cooks who voyaged thirty minutes every day to the bar, in light of the standing it was acquiring. It won the Newcomer of the Year Award 2006, however regardless of whether this was a public honor, or a rivalry at the Thorverton Village Fete, I don't know.

They were investing an enormous measure of energy and fixation into their cooking, yet were as yet quick to talk and look into our outing. They were making what appeared to be opulent cheddar on-toast.

'Sounds like something insidious to do, man. The entire length of the country?

Jeez. All things considered, basically

you're almost there.' 'Really, we

began at Land's End.'

'Gracious, crap. That is intense,' giggled Matthew.

We were given a short guidance on the most proficient method to utilize the sanitizer. It was essentially a machine that steamed off any excess microorganisms subsequent to washing. Ben concluded it would presumably bend over as a dishwasher as well thus heaped it high with pots and container. The thing came to a standstill following a couple of moments, and we needed to request that Ryan assist with unblocking the channel that had become stopped up with rice and peas.

Each time we began to make advances into the heap of cleaning up, Matthew and Ryan were available to renew the heap. They were some way or another spending container and plates faster than we could wash them.

We were eager when we showed up in Thorverton, and after north of an hour in the kitchen, we were voracious. We began to pick at the extras on plates that were being gotten back from the lounge area; cold chips, salad leaves, half-eaten slices of bread. Ryan and Matthew looked on in disgust.

The noon surge in the end finished. It was 2pm on a Tuesday in September in no place. Where on earth had this multitude of individuals come from, and shouldn't they have been at work?

We sat on one of the outdoor tables outside the front of the bar and Garth presented to us a major glass of Coke each (other colas are accessible). He likewise carried with him two shirts. One was a green polo-shirt with the logo of a neighborhood distillery on it, and the different was a dark polo shirt with Thorverton Arms composed on the back, and TITS composed on the front.

'It represents Thorverton Impotent Tossers Society,' he said. 'That is the name of the bar's darts team.'

I'd had first dibs of the last shirts we were given, thus Ben had best option this time. He picked the TITS one, obviously, and I was left with the somewhat second rate green one.

The food was definitely worth every single dirty plate that we had cleaned and there was sufficient to take care of the entire of Thorverton. We each had an enormous sizzling lasagne, a monster bowl of chips, a garlic loaf and a side plate of mixed greens. Food tastes such a great deal better when you've acquired it, and we had absolutely procured it. Be that as it may, the extent that it being a reasonable supper to have halfway through a drawn out day's cycling goes, I wouldn't suggest it.

We ate without question, everything. Indeed, even Ben, who generally has the craving of a daddy long-legs, destroyed the part. We were full that we could scarcely talk, not to mention cycle.

A major, furry dark feline strolled towards us from across the street, right inverse where we were sitting. Simultaneously a mentor was tearing downwards through the town and there was the thunder of something important coming the alternate way. The feline was totally courageous and stopped in the street to clean its paws. The mentor shrieked to a stop, thus did the gigantic join reaper that arose out of the other bearing. The two vehicles stood by calmly until the feline had cleared the street, prior to proceeding with their individual excursions. The cat then hopped up on to the picnic table where we were eating, discovered there were no leftovers, licked the plates then jumped down and went through the front door of the pub. At the point when we took our plates through to the kitchen, it was sleeping on one of the bar stools.

'He's one of our regulars,' said Garth. 'He comes in many days about this time.'

Spurred on by our titanic lunch, we chose to focus on a record-breaking day on the bicycles. We expected to do another 40 miles yet it was 3pm when we set off, and our lasagne sat vigorously in our stomachs.

After leaving Thorverton the street crossed the River Exe by a weir and afterward climbed continuously for a couple of miles. We went through the town of Bradninch and the tree-lined roads of Cullompton without even stopping.

We were tearing up the miles. We were beating Devon's ass.

We arrived at the town of Wellington by around 5pm, having covered 43 miles, which incorporated a 10am beginning and a 2 ½ hour lunch. Taunton was a couple of miles up the street so we proceeded onwards. All I was aware of Taunton was the M5 administration station Taunton Deane – one of my top choices on the M5. I realized that assuming Taunton was half pretty much as great as that assistance station, I'd be a cheerful man.

We followed the bustling A38 among Wellington and Taunton. It was the primary stretch of A-street we had been on since Camborne, and it rolled out an astonishing improvement. It was busy time and the traffic was spilling in the two ways, yet we could feel the advancement that we were making. The bearings we followed took us on the A361 sidestep around Taunton focus without us even realising.

Taunton Deane administration station is still all I am familiar with Taunton.

The sun was sitting low in the sky and we chose to attempt to track down convenience at the following conceivable chance. The A361, notwithstanding, had different thoughts. The street before long fixed into an endless passage

across the Somerset moors. The heavy traffic had scattered and we were left alone in a scary calm.

Ben had not represented with regards to an hour and this was an obvious sign that he was in a foul mood.

'You alright back there,

Ben?' No response.

'Ben?'

'No doubt, I'm alright. Simply getting somewhat annoyed with

this cycling.' 'Better believe it, me as well. I'm certain we'll pass

some place soon.'

'That is assuming we are as yet alive and not tossed into the field by some sodding hatchet killer. This spot terrifies me.'

'I know. I thought it was simply me.'

The light was blurring, there was no indication of any close by houses, and the boggy bogs on either side seemed as though the ideal unloading ground for a few eviscerated cyclists.

'It's minutes like this I wish you had your Disco Bike to ease up the mind-set,' I said.

Ben and I had cycled together only once previously, however it was an encounter that caused me to understand that he would be the best individual to go along with me on the outing. Prior in the year we had partaken in the British Heart Foundation's well known London to Brighton Bike Ride. Ben, for reasons unknown, chosen to change over his trail blazing bicycle into a 'Disco Bike' for the afternoon. He shrewdly mounted his iPod (other mp3 players are accessible) onto the handlebars just as an enormous pair of speakers. To power this setup, he then strapped a car battery to the back of the bike, which was then wired, via a transducer, to the iPod. Subsequent to testing his sound framework the other day, he wasn't content with the sound quality, so obtained a football-sized bass sub-woofer, which he likewise mounted to the rear of the bike.

The subsequent 'Disco Bike' was totally astounding. From the solace of his bicycle seat, Ben had the option to impact whatever music he wanted, across the encompassing open country. A significant number of the other 20,000 cyclists were in wonder of his development, and we were encircled for the whole 50 mile trip by multitudes of Ben's groupies.

What Ben hadn't considered was the monstrous load of his sound framework. His bike was a similar load as a motorbike. Cornering turned out to be extremely challenging, and on a few events, he verged on having a significant accident.

'I would do anything for my Disco Bike at this moment,' he said.

We endure the fields and afterward crossed the Greylake Bridge at the King's Sedgemoor Drain, which, in the event that you were pondering, is a fourteenth century ditch that is utilized to deplete the encompassing moorland.

We talked momentarily with two Scottish men who were fishing by the bridge.
They had driven as far as possible from the north of Scotland to fish in a trench in no place. At last, we'd met two individuals more idiotic than us.

'Yes, you could attempt the small bar just there. That is the place where we're stayin'.
They could possibly help on the off chance that you ken whit ah mean,' said one of the men.

The bar was shockingly occupied with considering we had not passed a house in hours and there appeared to be no different structures past it.

'Splendid, it's test night, as well. Possibly assuming they have some place for us to rest, we can come and do the test later,' I said, rather optimistically.

It worked out that the bar just had two rooms and that pair of trench fishing Scottish nitwits were involving the two of them. As enticed as we were to package the pair of them into the King's Sedgemoor Drain and take their rooms, we chose to pass on them to their fishing and proceed onwards to track down some place to stay.

It was dim and we were totally dim. We headed over to the roadside each time a vehicle elapsed, which implied that progress was ludicrously lethargic. We in the long run arrived at the town of Walton at around 9pm.

Just on the edge of the town was the sign for a camping area and we followed the path up for a large portion of a mile until we arrived at Bramble Hill Camping Park. It was a beautiful, tranquil looking campground adjoining a farmhouse. Without a doubt a spot with such a storybook name couldn't deny two frantic young fellows. 'Hi, would i be able to help you?'

asked a very articulate woman. She seemed in her entryway with a look of fear all over like 70-odd long periods of life were going to reach a sudden conclusion on account of two peculiarly dressed, sweat-soaked youthful scallywags. She had a major, styled, brilliant white bouffant, a dark dress and a white cover on. She seemed as though she had left Jane Eyre.

'I trust so,' said Ben. 'Do you, by any possibility, have an old tent that we could utilize or anyplace for us to rest this evening, free of charge. We are going with practically no money.'

'I'm grieved, I am apprehensive I don't. We are only a little site, and individuals bring

their own tents. We don't have any extras for individuals to utilize. What are you doing out in the center of no place this late anyway?'

'We're on a test to cycle to John O'Groats without going through any cash. The entirety of our food, convenience, garments and bicycles have been given to us. We were wanting to track down some place to remain, however we've not passed anyplace until now.'

'No, I am terribly grieved, there is very little around here. I would envision that there are a few camping areas in Glastonbury, however you have left it somewhat late to arrive this evening. I'm sorry I can't be more help.'

'alright, thank you in any case. I'm certain we'll track down some place,' I said as we went to leave the entryway. We bowed our heads in dissatisfaction and pulled the most despicable, sorry, penniless countenances imaginable.

As an investigation of human consideration, this bicycle ride must be attempted by complete nobodies like us. Any type of superstar carries with it acknowledgment, which makes a huge difference. I watched Ewan McGregor's narrative – Long Way Round – with incredible adoration. Ewan McGregor – of Star Wars, *Trainspotting and The Da Vinci Code distinction – exceeds all expectations round the world on his bike*, with his companion Charley Boorman. It was an amazingly noteworthy accomplishment, and I'm not contrasting our own excursion with his brave experience in any capacity, however the truth of the matter is that he is Ewan McGregor. Even people in Kazakhstan and Mongolia recognised him; I often don't get recognised by my own family. What I am attempting to say is that when requesting favors from irregular outsiders, you are at an unmistakable benefit in case you are Obi-Wan Kenobi.

We probably won't have had the ability to lead any Jedi mind stunts, yet these pitiable countenances of our own were our mystery weapon.

'Well... one moment,' she said reluctantly. 'Is it simply some safe house you are after?'

'Indeed, anything,' I said.

'Well I could possibly assist you with excursion all things considered. Follow me.'

She drove us through to a dusty old toilet, which had dividers on only two sides.

'You can set your bicycles in a tough spot there,' she said, and we then, at that point, anticipated that she should let us know we could rest on the floor close to them. It was a wonderful evening and we would have been glad to rest there.

But she wasn't done yet.

'And you can snooze here,' she said, opening the way to an independent annexe. 'There's a room higher up and you can utilize the camping area latrine block, which is directly across the yard.'

It was extraordinary. We had been seconds from strolling back out into the night with no place to go, and afterward unexpectedly we had been offered our own little level. Ground floor was a kitchen, and higher up was an enormous room with a twofold bed and a sleeping pad on the floor.

'I can't offer you any food, I'm apprehensive, however there's a bar about a large portion of a mile not too far off where you could possibly get something.'

'Many thanks, you're a lifeline,' I said. 'What's your name?' 'Mrs Rogers.'

Mrs Rogers bid farewell, and we guaranteed we would clean the campground latrines for her in the morning.

'Look at this. We have our own level!' said Ben prior to plunging onto the twofold bed. 'Bagsie having the bed.'

'I guess you're having the camping cot, as well?' 'Too right I am. I conveyed it all day.'

'You are such a dick. Appears as though I'm resting on the floor then, at that point. Would i be able to acquire your towel, please?'

'Yes. How about we proceed to attempt to grab a bite,' said Ben. 'The bar will quit serving food soon.'

'Definitely. We should go straight there now. Britain are playing another European qualifier this evening. We'll ideally get the finish of the game.'

'Better believe it, goodness, that will be fun,' said Ben snidely, as he cares very little about football whatsoever.

'Old fashioned Mrs Rogers,' I said as I followed Ben across the room towards the stairs.

'No doubt, I'm going to roger her in the first part of the day,' said Ben, for no evident reason.

And then, at that point, he froze.

He turned and gazed toward me as though he had seen a phantom. I've never seen anybody look more froze in my life.

Mrs Rogers was remaining at the lower part of the stairs.

Ben was mostly down the steps and kept on gazing back up at me with a look as though to say: 'Help me, George. Say something to get me out of this awful situation.'

I didn't say anything. Mrs Rogers at long last spoke.

'I simply needed to show you where the light switch is for the first floor kitchen. It is only here at the lower part of the steps. Could you ensure you turn it off when you go out and before you go to sleep.'

'Yes. Obviously. Blunder. Roger that. Much thanks to you, Mrs Rogers,' said Ben, still unmoving on the steps. She turned and left the latrine, and shut the entryway behind her.

'Gracious. My. God. What have I done?' said Ben, measuring his face in his hands.

'What the heck did you say that for? What had you to say you were going to roger Mrs Rogers?'

'Gracious god, I don't have a clue. I figure I should have Tourettes or something like that. Assuming I hear a name like that I need to poke a moronic fun at it. Do you think she heard me?'

'She must've done. She was remaining around ten feet from you. You imbecile!' 'I know. Bollocks. Goodness fucking bollocksy, bollocksy, bollocks.'

'I don't have the foggiest idea why she said nothing. Or then again even hurl us back out into the street.'

'Possibly she didn't hear me. Or then again perhaps she wasn't sure what it implied? She's most likely in her home presently flicking through a word reference. For what reason am I such a twat?'

'I've no thought, however you are. It was exceptionally interesting, though.'

'There's nothing entertaining with regards to it by any means. That caring old woman has given us a spot to remain this evening and afterward I said I was going to roger her. Poop, that was the most humiliating snapshot of my life. How could she come in without us hearing her? She resembled a phantom. She must've dissolved through the divider or something to that effect. We should escape here.'

We followed the completely dark country path back down to the fundamental street, and afterward saw the bar a little not too far off. We barely talked the whole way. Ben was all the while wincing regarding what he'd said, and I was being egotistical that it hadn't been me.

The Pike and Musket was genuinely occupied for a Wednesday. It was brimming with youngsters playing pool and yelling exorbitantly uproariously at one another over the commotion of the jukebox. A few of them were wearing England shirts however there was no TV and in this manner no football.

'Any thought what the score is?' I requested one from fellows, who had quite recently sent the white ball flying across the room.

'Nah, mate. They're showing it at the bar at the opposite finish of the village.'

The young lady behind the bar looked extremely youthful. She snickered at us before we had even addressed her. She was unmistakably in wonderment of the fine examples of manliness that had quite recently entered the bar. Either that, or loose moved up suit pants, sweat-soaked shirts and cut off tracksuit bottoms are not the most recent pattern in Walton, Somerset.

Had I referenced we had arrived at Somerset by this point? Maybe not. Indeed, we had vanquished Devon and had arrived at our third province in as numerous days.

'Hi,' said Ben to the as yet smiling barmaid. 'We've cycled north of 80 miles today on youngsters' bicycles, and we don't have any the means to purchase food. Do you have any extras at all that you could spare?'

'Why you have no cash? Is it some kind of challenge?'

'Yes. We're cycling to the highest point of Scotland without going through any cash. We began in pants. Every one of these garments have been rummaged, as well. That is the reason we're dressed like this.'

'I was asking why you both looked so asinine. I think they've quite recently shut the kitchen yet I'll proceed to address the gourmet expert and check whether he has anything. Sit down around there and I'll see what I can do.'

There were several others wrapping up their suppers yet other than that, the café a piece of the bar was vacant. If by some stroke of good luck we'd been there the prior night; Tuesday night is 'Curry and a 16 ounces night' at The Pike and Musket, if at any time you are passing.

She strolled over to us a couple of moments later.

'The gourmet specialist will concoct you something. I'll bring it out to you in a little. Do you all need a lager meanwhile?' asked the barmaid, who plainly liked us. Checking out the room, we were most certainly awesome of an awful bunch.

'To Mrs Rogers,' I said, toasting my half quart to Ben.

'Don't. I would rather not ponder that. I actually can't really accept that it occurred. I will not have the option to check out her in the morning.'

'She may be anticipating it. Who can say for sure, she's likely preparing herself at this very moment. Putting a meager minimal number to the side to wear in the morning.'

'You're debilitated, do you know that?'

'You're the person who said you were going to roger her in the first part of the day.' 'Okay! Enough! We should never discuss it again.'

'Ham, egg, chips and peas,' said Siobhan the barmaid, as she put two gigantic plates of food before us. 'The gourmet specialist heard what you were doing and thought it sounded extremely entertaining so needed to ruin you.'

It was our greatest day's eating of the whole outing; a cook for breakfast, lasagne, chips and salad for lunch, and ham, egg and chips for supper. We would not have eaten so all around had we had our wallets with us.

Only an hour ahead of time, Ben and I had been eager, destitute, drained and factious with one another. Furthermore there we were partaking in an enormous bar dinner and a brew, prior to going to our own little level for the night.

Life couldn't have better.

'Quite recently got a text from my mate at the other bar,' said one of the youthful chaps in an England shirt. 'Britain won 1-0. Peter Crouch scored.'

Life settled the score better.

We cleared our plates and completed our brew. It was almost 11pm when we scrabbled our direction back up the dull path to Bramble Hill Camping Ground.

Ben climbed straight into his hiking bed and lay on the bed.

'Night, mate,' he said.

My suit pants were moist from a day's cycling, so I chose not to rest in them regardless of it being a significant cold evening. I put on the colossal ski socks rather that Annie had given us in Nanstallon and set down on the bedding with two towels over me.

'Night, Mr Selfish,' I said.

Somewhere, near somewhere else

Ryan and Matthew, Thorverton Arms

Garth and Melissa, Thorverton Arms

Max – the BMX world man

Mrs Rogers, Watton

Mrs Rogers, flat

Day 6 – Michael Eavis in a pair of hot pants

Walton to Bath – 27 miles

'Morning, George,' said Ben.

'Morning,' I said grumpily.

'Did you rest soundly? I didn't awaken once.'

'No. I dozed actually severely. It was fucking freezing. I needed to get into my suit pants in the evening, alongside the entirety of my shirts and my sweatshirt and I was still cold.'

'Goodness. Sorry. It's a disgrace you don't have your own camping cot. In any case, it resembles it's a great day today.'

'A decent day for rogering Mrs Rogers?' I asked.

'Kindly shut up. You said you could never make reference to that again.'

There was a line of around five young ladies holding up external the shower block, notwithstanding there being a void cubicle.

'Is the shower not working in that one?' I asked.

'Yez, it eez, however a major creature eez in there,' said one of the young ladies in broken English.

'What kind of large creature? Is it expected to be in there?'

'No! Eeeza creature with wings. It extremely startling. It go whoosh, whoosh,' she said, making jump besieging signals with her hand.

I was charmed. A huge, alarming, winged creature had assumed control over a shower desk area in Somerset. I needed to examine. I made the way for the desk area and looked warily inside. Whatever the monster was, it was stowing away. Either that or it was an expert of disguise.

I turned on the light and a moth began to move around the light. 'Is that the creature you are talking about?'

'Yez, close entryway. Ezza evil.'

'It's simply a moth. Would you care if I feel free to utilize the shower?' 'You frantic. Be that as it may, alright,' she said.

I had a shower, and afterward Ben did, and thereafter the young ladies were all the while lining. I then, at that point, gotten the moth, utilizing my BARE HANDS and the young ladies acclaimed me like a hero.

Mrs Rogers was in fine spirits when we went to answer to her for latrine cleaning obligations. She didn't appear to hold any disdain over Ben's remark the prior night, and in spite of our offers, she would not permit us to do any

cleaning to reimburse the favour.

We had high expectations for the afternoon. We left Bramble Hill by 9am, which was a promising beginning by all accounts. It was a brilliant, crisp morning and we both felt the most energetic we had done since leaving Land's End.

'I figure in case we attempt and find something rapidly to eat in Glastonbury, we could be in Bath on schedule for lunch and afterward who realizes how far we may scrape by this evening,' said Ben uncharacteristically.

'Sounds great to me. I think we've turned the corner and fired heading up the country.'

'That is all in all too profound and significant for this season of the morning.'

'No, I mean it in a real sense. Since we left Land's End we've quite recently been traveling east yet I think we've presumably turned north at this point. Do you get me?'

'Actually no, not really.'

We arrived at Glastonbury town focus quickly. Ben and I had both been to Glastonbury celebration twice before however neither of us had visited the town appropriately. It was brimming with interesting little hippy shops, with hand-painted signs outside. Gatherings of individuals sat in the little square selling different pieces of stuff or having a quiet dissent about who knows what. The entire town had a truly loosened up energy to it.

We set out toward the Glastonbury Backpackers, which sits on the principle square. However much we were getting a charge out of absorbing the hippy climate, we were ridiculous hungry.

It was 9.30am and noisy music was playing in the bar region. There were two or three individuals lounging around at tables, and an appealing Dutch-sounding young lady was looking at herself. That is to say, leaving the lodging, rather than gazing at herself in the mirror. The young lady behind gathering guided us towards the chief in the wake of hearing our request.

'How would i be able to help both of you?' he asked.

'We're venturing to every part of the whole length of Great Britain and we're not permitted to go through any cash. We needed to check whether you had any work that requirements doing in return for some breakfast.'

'Sounds like a reasonable arrangement,' he said without delaying. 'Are you doing an End to End trip?'

'Better believe it, this is Day 6, and we've permitted ourselves three weeks.' 'You're traveling north, I presume?'

'Tragically, yes.'

'You've actually got far to go then, at that point. We get loads of End to

Enders going through here. Some of them do it in under seven days, however they're crazy. However at that point both of you should both be crazy, too.'

'You're not the principal individual to propose that,' I said.

'Every one of the floors in here need wiping, as does the floor around the pool table and in the latrines. Assuming you do that, I'll get the young ladies to figure you out with some breakfast.'

The bar region was genuinely long, yet it just took us 30 minutes to clean the floor. I say 'us', yet there was just one mop and Ben provided himself with the job of 'boss', which included mumbling 'you missed a little,' every couple of seconds.

We sat on bar stools along the morning meal bar that watched out onto the square. Claire – the young lady from gathering – brought north of two enormous cappuccinos, two fry-ups and several newspapers.

We'd just been going for six days, however we both felt all the way withdrawn from what was happening on the planet. I'm a news addict. I can't go for an hour without really taking a look at the BBC site. I normally have the radio on, or the TV, and routinely read the paper, as well. Since setting off from Cornwall, we had barely seen a TV, had no radio updates, and I don't think The Internets has arrived at the South West yet.

I had figured I would experience serious withdrawal, however I was adapting fine and dandy. Truth be told, I hadn't missed any of it. Unexpectedly, I cared very little about the thing was going on the planet. The first page of both The Mirror and The Guardian declared something that David Cameron had said or done, yet I didn't peruse it to discover what. Even the match report of England's win the night before received little more than a cursory glance. I had become isolates from this present reality and felt no direness to rejoin it.

Whilst we had breakfast, we read through the 'What to take' area in our course book – the brilliant Bike Britain by Paul Salter – which records all of the hardware that is required while endeavoring a Land's End to John O'Groats bicycle ride.

The rundown, which reaches out to a few pages, varied only somewhat to our own pitiful possessions. Here is the rundown of all that you should take, close by our real belongings in italics.

<u>Bike</u>
Bike with racks – lacking bicycles, no racks Panniers
and handlebar pack – backpack and pockets Water
containers and enclosures – water bottle, yes.
Confines, no Cycle PC – as if

Small blazing LCD back light – Tony the Tiger reflector

<u>Clothing</u>
<u>Raincoat –</u>
<u>no</u>
Rain pants (with versatile sleeves or clasp for right leg) – uncovered legs
Mid-weight downy top – cardigans
Polypropolylene clothing (aches and tops) – Union Jack fighter shorts
(cotton, not polypropolylene, whatever that is)
Hat – baseball caps
Gloves – no
2 T-shirts or cycle tops – 4 shirts each
1 Pair of lightweight shorts – moved up woolen suit pants for me, cut off
tracksuit bottoms for Ben
1 or 2 sets of cotton socks – 3 sets of ski socks each
1 or 2 sets of lightweight aches – woolen suit pants for me, no pants for
Ben
1 or 2 sets of cycling shorts – moved up woolen suit pants for me, cut off
tracksuit bottoms for Ben
Cycle gloves – what were different gloves for then, at that point? Evening
wear? No
1 Pair of shoes – old trainers
Sunglasses – no
Reflector scarf – this isn't a marvel show. *No*
Bicycle protective cap – no

<u>Tools</u>
<u>Pump –</u>
<u>no</u>
Puncture fix pack – no
Tire switches – spoons in excursion set
Spare internal cylinder – no
Tire fix or extra tire – spare tire? It is safe to say that you are significant?
Where might we keep it? Just the ones around our waists
Spare spokes – I have never broken a spoke in my life, nor do I know any
individual who has. *The main explanation a spoke would break is a result of
the*
weight of all of this shit
Spokes for the back bunch side – no. *What or where is the back bunch
side?*
Spoke wrench – no spokes to wrench

Cluster eliminating device – eh?

Chain breaker and extra chain joins – for what reason would we need to break the chain?

Spare brake and stuff links – no

Spare stray pieces (counting rack fasteners) – KP nuts, does that count?

Appropriate Allen keys – who's Allen and for what reason would we have his keys?

No

Wrenches, forceps, screw driver – No, no and no

Zip ties – what for?

Grease and lube – what is this, some kind of unusual shit?

Duct tape – I knew it! No

Small cloth – that is the thing that pants are for

Miscellaneous

Bike lock – indeed, kind of. *However, not one that we could really unlock*

Pocket blade with can opener – indeed, in the cookout set

Small First-Aid and sewing unit – plasters

Plastic packs to enclose gear by wet climate – what gear? No

Camera and film – It's the 21st century. *Get with the program. Everything's computerized, man. Yes.*

Toiletries and meds (counting sun screen and bug repellent) – *toothpaste, toothbrush and cleanser. What more do you need?*

Maps – course book, yes

Compass – no. *Asking individuals for bearings is far easier*

Personal archives – no. *Like what?*

Water Purification tablets or channel – this is Great Britain, not Ethiopia

Camping

Tent – no

Sleeping sack – indeed, 1 between 2

Sleeping mat – no

Small towel – 2 tremendous ocean side towels

Small light – no

Plate and spoon – 6 plates, 6 spoons, 6 dishes, 6 blades and 6 forks

Optional Extras

Waterproof overgloves and shoe covers – Overgloves? Just as the evening gloves and cycle gloves? My god, no

Matches and flame – in the event of a birthday celebration? No

Stove – no

Fuel – no stove

Pot – no oven and no fuel

Rear view reflect – it's a bicycle, not a car

Bottom section evacuation apparatus and parts – I don't have a clue what a base section is, so for what reason would I need to eliminate it?

Light plastic sheet with tent to cover bicycle while setting up camp – awww, bless.

No

Handheld GPS – No, that is cheating

'Any thought what time it is?' I asked Ben after we'd been sitting and staring

out into the square for what felt like hours.

'Errr... ,' he said going to take a gander at a clock behind gathering, which I had not put forth the attempt to search for. 'It's 11.30am. That can't be right.'

'Gracious, cool, that implies it's almost noon. We've completed two miles up to this point today. Some way or another I don't figure we'll make it past Bath today. Also even Bath may be a piece ambitious.'

'Anyway. This day is somewhat of a discount. Do you fancy proceeding to look at Glastonbury Tor? I've seen it in spending heaps of times yet never been.'

'Definitely, sounds cool. I believe we're expected for a break.'

Glastonbury Tor was a knave to climb.

It's a conservative, however conspicuous slope neglecting the town, with a lovely stone pinnacle enhancing the top. It was especially intense in light of the fact that we needed to convey our inept bicycles as far as possible up. Assuming we had left them at the base, there would have been a possibility that somebody would have taken them. Our hopelessness would have been jumbled by the reality we would have had the option to watch everything occur from the top, however been not able to do anything about it. It did not merit the risk.

The highest point of the Tor was abandoned with the exception of a peculiar looking man conveying a huge wooden staff. He had long white hair and a facial hair growth and he resembled a person from The Lord of the Rings.

'Great morning, courteous fellows. Or then again should I say evening,' he said, checking the time. 'Is this your first time up here?' He was either being friendly,

or had attempted a genuinely horrendous talk up line.

'Good evening. Indeed, it's our first time. What an incredible view,' I said, turning round and taking in the view interestingly. It was spectacular.

'It sure is. It's anything but a terrible
work environment.' 'Accomplish you
work up here then?'

'Well, yes. I'm a kind of informal local area
expert.' 'Aha, was that local escort or Tor
guide?' I kidded. 'Indeed, local area expert, as I
just said.'

He didn't get it.

'Cool. It should be an incredible spot to go through your day? What's your
name?' 'Rod.'

Ben sniggered.

'For what reason is that entertaining? That is my
name. Bar,' said Rod. 'In any case, you're holding a
rod.'

'Indeed, I am. So?'

We didn't push it any further.

'I can give you a visit and let you know a portion of the historical
backdrop of the spot, in case you need,' he said.

'That is exceptionally kind, yet we don't have any cash at all to offer you
I'm apprehensive,' I said.

'Goodness, that is alright. Simply jump into my next one then, at that point.
You don't have to pay.
I'm certain there'll be some more individuals here soon.'

Sufficiently sure, a gathering of around ten others showed up before long
and Rod offered them one of his visits. We snuck behind the scenes
expecting some valuable data, yet it before long turned out to be evident that
we would have gotten familiar with the Tor by mystery, than from Rod.

'You see around there somewhere far off… ' he said, 'simply behind that
huge telephone pole,' he stopped while we as a whole searched for a major
utility pole. 'Apologies, not telephone pole, I implied slope. You see that
slope around there? Well that slope and the one close to it are known as the
Bra Hills. Since they resemble a major pair of tits.'

The remainder of Rod's Tor visit was totally vast and we picked up
nothing of the spot's set of experiences aside from that it had some
association with Jesus or perhaps King Arthur. However, it didn't make any
difference. It's a wonderful spot and it doesn't cost a penny to visit,
regardless of whether you are a scrounger like us, or a fair citizen.

Seeing as we were in Glastonbury, we figured we should bring in to see
Michael Eavis, the legend behind the Glastonbury celebrations. It would have

been inconsiderate not to. Everyone we asked, even Rod, knew where Michael Eavis resided, and it wasn't some time before we observed his homestead close to the town of Pilton.

We finished the long carport the farmland and up to the house and advanced toward the Site Office.

'Hi. Would i be able to help you?' requested the woman on the opposite side from the little office window.

'Hi. This will sound somewhat bizarre,' I said, 'yet we're cycling to John O'Groats and as we were passing we thought we'd bring in and check whether we could make proper acquaintance with Michael Eavis.'

'Gracious. He's not here right now. He's out on the ranch some place,' said the woman. 'Also you simply need to make proper acquaintance? Does he know you?'

'No.'

'And he's not anticipating

you?' 'Errrr, nope.'

'Would i be able to inquire as to why you need to see him?'

'Just to make proper acquaintance truly,' I said, understanding that I was sounding very odd. 'Is it worth us sticking around so that a piece might be able to check whether he appears?'

'Not actually. That is to say, I'm not going to stop you, yet he probably won't be back for ages.'

'I figure we should stick around so that a piece could check whether we see him. We have come this way,' said Ben as we sat on the grass outside and drank our water that the woman in the workplace had compassionately beaten up.

'We haven't cycled this method for seeing Michael Eavis. We're en route to Scotland, recollect? However, I figure as we're here now we should hold tight for a bit.'

'He'll be cool when he discovers what we're doing. He should get heaps of insane Glastonbury monstrosities who just come to see him cos he's, y'know, Michael Eavis. He wouldn't fret talking to several typical guys like us,' said Ben.

'Hold tight. That is actually what we are. We're simply insane Glastonbury monstrosities who need to see him cos he's, y'know, Michael Eavis. We are only a few dismal freaky stalkers, aren't we?'

'When you put it that way, better believe it, we are. It's past the point where it is possible to avoid now though.

Isn't that him getting with regards to the red Land Rover over there?'

And there he was. He was wearing, what I can just portray as, denim hot pants. They were the littlest, most secure shorts that I have at any point seen. To supplement these, he was wearing a white vest (the sort regularly worn by rappers and undershirts) which was skin tight and gotten into his shorts. As though this fashion proclamation was not striking enough, he polished off the outfit with a couple of wellies. We had rescued garments from a lost property, the coastguard, elderly folks individuals, cyclists and ranchers, at this point we actually missed the mark concerning Michael Eavis' varied blend. But somehow he pulled it off.

We strolled over to him.

'Hello there, Michael. I am Ben and this is my companion George.'

'Hi, chaps. Ideal to meet you both,' he answered while strolling towards the workplace, apparently attempting to move away from us as fast as he could.

'We're cycling to John O'Groats without going through any cash and we thought we'd bring in, as we were passing,' proceeded with Ben unfazed.

'alright, best of luck with the excursion,' he answered as he arrived at the ranch door.

We believed that was it. We'd cycled all that way. We'd covered that multitude of miles. We'd rested in an animal dwellingplace, and suffered hunger, thirst, a throbbing painfulness. We'd creepily shown up on the doorstep of our saint, similar to a couple of frenzied weirdoes, and all we planned to receive consequently was a short 'Best of luck'. I made one final dumped endeavor to connect with him in discussion before he went into the house and was away for good.

'Thus, would you be able to uncover any insider facts regarding who will feature the celebration next year?'

'ha, pleasant attempt,' he said, stopping at the entryway. 'Did you say you were going to John O'Groats? Accompany me, I have something to show you.'

Now, typically when a man says a line like this to you (particularly a man wearing a vest, wellies and hotpants) you should shout and flee as fast as could really be expected. For this situation, seeing as it was Michael Eavis, we chose to go with our impulses and follow him.

He drove us back past the workplace and around into the yard. Inclining toward one of the dividers was a gigantic metal ring, around eight feet in diameter.

'a few fellows went through here around 25 years prior,' he said. 'They set off from Land's End, similar to both of you, and had this gigantic wheel that they intended to push the entire way to John O'Groats. I don't have a clue why, however they figured it would be fun, I presume. At any rate, they went to the celebration here and had such an extraordinary time that they concluded they couldn't be tried to go to John O'Groats and they never made it any further.'

'That is stunning. Also this is the wheel that they were pushing?' asked Ben.

'That's right, it's been here from that point forward. It was a beautiful looking wheel in those days. A sort of cart wheel, I presume. This center piece was wooden yet it's decayed away throughout the long term and all that is left is this metal edge. They called me up a couple of years back and inquired as to whether I actually had it. I let them know the wood had gone, yet they could come and get the rest in the event that they needed. I never heard from them again.'

We were dearest companions with Michael Eavis by this point. Or then again, should I say Mikey Boy, as he loved us to call him. After just a tad longer he let us know we could call him The Mickster, and afterward some time later we got to call him Eavo. When we left, we had shed names generally together, and had set up our own uncommon handshake, that main Ben, Eavo and I comprehended. We were inseparable.

After some long goodbye embraces and a mournful farewell we got back on our bicycles and left his ranch. In doing this we had outperformed the two failures with the huge wheel.

It was 3pm and we had cycled an aggregate of five miles in six hours. 1.2 mph was not especially amazing advancement. We had missed lunch thus proceeded to get to Bath before the day's end. The A39 avoided around the city of Wells, which they say is a charming business sector town. I'll need to trust 'them, as we didn't get to see it. The film Hot Fuzz was shot for the most part in Wells. FACT.

After Wells, there were a few long difficult areas that turned our legs to mush. We were feeling the impacts of a cook being our main wellspring of energy for the day.

From high up on the slope when we initially saw it, Bath resembled some other city. Starting from the earliest stage, in any case, it was especially beautiful.

Pinky and The Falcon arrived at record speeds as we shrieked into the town community at around 5.30pm, drained and frantic for lunch. I was greedy, yet Ben had different things on his mind.

'There's a cop!' yelled Ben. 'I'll proceed to inquire as to whether they have any bicycles at the station.'

'Yet… uh… pause… can't we…'

It was past the point of no return. Ben had dropped his bicycle and was pursuing a cop up the road. Following a couple of moments of energized gesturing and motioning he returned.

'That police officer says we could attempt the station down here. It's simply down

this street, turn both ways, then, at that point, right and afterward it's on the left. He says you can't miss it. Come on, we should go there now and have a look.'

'For new bicycles?' I asked.

'No, to hand ourselves in. Obviously for new bicycles, you bellend.'

'Wouldn't we be able to attempt to get food first? The police headquarters will in any case be there later, however I probably won't be in the event that we don't eat soon.'

'Okay, yet we'll check it out later, definitely?' 'Better believe it, yeah.'

We wheeled our bicycles up the central avenue keeping watch for some place to get food. We passed a bread kitchen that had shut for the afternoon, yet there was a heap of decline sacks stacked up outside. Ben and I had discussed dustbin-plunging a couple of days already, and this was our first potential opportunity.

Dustbin-jumping, or 'freeganism' as it is currently stylishly known, has acquired another rent of life lately. Freegans embrace an enemy of consumerist way of life and an elective method of living. They go after the disposed of misuse of stores, eateries, shops and bistros and attempt to insignificantly affect the economy. Because of a mix of rigid cleanliness laws and an expanded longing by the customer for food to be of the best quality, the stuff that is tossed out is frequently impeccably edible.

Ben and I both had a cycle of hostile to industrialism in us and a sharp craving to 'beat the framework'. We began scrounging through the container packs, individually. They all appeared to be brimming with void cake wrappers.

We burrowed deeper.

'Crap, a needle,' screeched Ben, holding his finger with a look of frenzy across his face.

'Fuck. Goodness poop, you… ' I began, prior to seeing his huge smile.

'You idiot.
That's not funny.'

We continued searching for a couple of moments until Ben tracked down a goliath tub of egg mayonnaise. The pot actually had its name on, yet showers of egg were overflowing from the sides.

'Hello, George, look at this. What is your take? It's best before tomorrow.'

'Definitely, cool, it looks… fail… incredible, yeah.'

'You can have it in case you need. I'm not a major fanatic of egg mayonnaise.' 'No, you have it. Locater guardians, washouts weepers, and all that.'

'No. Think of it as a gift from me to you.'

'That is exceptionally sort of you, however I couldn't realistically accept.' 'Well I'll simply leave it here where we tracked down it, assuming you're not going to eat it.' 'Great arrangement,' I said. We were the world's most exceedingly terrible freegans.

'To be reasonable, however,' I said, 'I'm almost certain genuine freegans don't eat egg by the same token. I think the word freegan likely comes from 'free' and 'vegan'.'

'Valid statement. Will we attempt those packs then, at that point?' asked Ben, highlighting one more heap outside the secondary passage of a restaurant.

We were part of the way through the primary sack when a huge, sweat-soaked culinary specialist ventured outside his eatery for a cigarette break.

'Oi! Get the damnation out of my receptacles, you hikes. Continue, clear off,' he yelled. We hastened off like a few sick rodents. It's a hard life being a freegan.

'Will we simply take a stab at asking in Caffè Nero for some food all things considered?' asked Ben. 'Indeed, that sounds substantially more civilised.'

We asked the woman behind the counter what the organization strategy was on extras, and she let us know that any extras were packed away up and afterward put outside the accompanying morning.

'The number of sandwiches do you need to toss out every day?' asked Ben. 'Not very many,' she said, 'Perhaps three or four packs. We're very great at requesting our stock so there's very little waste.'

'So assuming that we returned the morning and went through your receptacles before the container men arrived, we could have some free packs of sandwiches?' I asked.

'Indeed, I assume so. Or then again I could simply give them to you now. I'm shutting shortly anyway.'

This It's just plain obviousmed like a vastly improved thought. She scoured the chiller bureau searching for sandwiches that had arrived at their best before date, and got back with three packs of sandwiches and an extravagant looking plate of mixed greens. See, we were freegans all things considered. Yet well mannered and modern freegans. I don't intend to suggest that freegans are rude and unsophisticated, I recently implied that... gracious, never mind.

We sat on a seat outside Caffè Nero and ate our sandwiches.

'God, I'm starving. We've just cycled around 20 miles today. Why we're so ravenous?' I asked.

'It's all that psychological energy we've been spending,' said Ben. 'What do you mean?'

'Did you realize that our cerebrums go through 33% of our energy?' 'Truly? That would clarify why you don't eat much.'

'Extremely interesting, you idiot.'

'So... ' I considered, 'does that imply that you could go to the library for exercise?'

'Well, no, it won't give you enormous muscles.'

'No, yet you could consume calories just by understanding books and learning stuff?' 'Yes. I assume so.'

'We could begin another eating regimen frenzy. Disregard Atkins or Dukan, the Ben and George Diet sounds way better.'

We sat for some time discussing this until we recollected that we didn't have anyplace to stay.

We got visiting to three understudies (two female and one male) back on the central avenue. It took us some time to clarify what our test was, as they had no clue about where either Land's End or John O'Groats were. Pah, the young people of today! We let them know we were searching for somebody who might allow us to rest on their floor.

'We can help!' shouted the blonde.

'No doubt, you can rest on our floor,' added the brunette.

'Truly? That is extraordinary. Much appreciated. Where do you live?' asked Ben. 'Bristol.'

'Oh.'

'Yet you could get the train there with us, and afterward you would be somewhat nearer to Scotland when you set off tomorrow,' added the guy.

'It's exceptionally enticing. However, that would be cheating, though it pains me to say so. We must cycle as far as possible and we wouldn't have the option to pay for the train charge. Much obliged especially for the proposition though.'

It's not frequently that two flawless young ladies stop you in the road and afterward beseech you to proceed to remain at their home. Yet, such was our commitment to the test that we waved them farewell and set off to track down some place to stay.

'We should go to the bar,' said Ben, after we had been meandering the roads for another hour.

'You read my psyche,' I said.

We stopped our bicycles right inside the entryway of a bar so we could watch out for them. It didn't take long for us to enlist that it was a gay bar. I know it's not socially sensitive to generalize gays and lesbians, however the customer base resembled, indeed, cliché gays and lesbians.

The barman, a youthful blushing cheeked kid, paid attention to our story while he held his head with his hands.

'Are you alright?' I asked, after we had clarified our test and that we were expecting a free beer.

'Better believe it, no doubt, apologies. I'm simply feeling like poo from the previous evening. Piece of a wild one, if you catch my drift,' he said with a smile as he hesitantly glanced over to a gathering of folks in the corner who all raised their glasses at him. 'I just got up around ten minutes prior and I feel like outright poop. No doubt, I can sort you both out with a lager, though.'

'How long have you been going?' yelled part of the gang in the corner who had clearly caught us recounting our story to the barman.

'Six days,' I said.

'And the number of miles have you done?' 'Around 200.'

'And you figure you will finish it in three weeks?' he snickered. 'No doubt. We'll do it.'

'No you won't, mate. You're screwed. You've just completed 200 miles and you have 15 days left. Math says you're fucked.'

'We'll make it. We're somewhat delayed yet we'll get up to speed,' said Ben. 'It's unrealistic, mate. Arithmetic says you are fucked.'

One of the ladies joined in.

'What the heck would you say you are doing savoring a bar, when you ought to cycle? He's right y'know. You're fucking fucked.'

The entire gathering emitted into attacks of laughter.

Of the multitude of innumerable individuals that we met during our 1000-mile venture, these were the main individuals who at any point questioned we would finish the outing. They kept on deriding us in a whimsical manner, and we gave as great as we got. Their remarks reverberated through our psyches for the remainder of the outing and we felt not really set in stone to refute them. I sent Adam – the most vocal of the bundle, and the conspicuous instigator – an email after the outing to delight in our wonder. I didn't get a response.

The table of cynics got us half quart after 16 ounces. It seemed like we were being prepped, had it not been for the way that not a single one of them offered us a bed for the evening. There we were, two alluring, guileless, destitute, tanked men in a gay bar we actually couldn't track down a bed for the evening. We staggered out of that bar at around 10.30pm and into another.

This one was brimming with underage Goths blending in affectionate gatherings. We expected to work rapidly in light of the fact that end time was drawing closer we actually had no place to remain. Five pints of lager had given us additional certainty so we adopted it in goes to strategy the different cliques.

'Okay, folks. We're not mental or anything, so don't be apprehensive. I don't assume any of you have a story that we can rest on this evening?' asked Ben.

Blank stares.

'We're cycling to Scotland with practically no cash and we want some place to remain this evening,' I added.

There was still no feeling of acknowledgment at all from any of the countenances. They all watched totally stoned out of their cerebrums, and attempting to understand whatever that we said was extremely burdening. We had the very same reaction from every one of the various gatherings. The barman gave us a large portion of a 16 ounces of ale among us, and we withdrew to a table to settle on our next strategy.

'Did you say you were searching for some place to remain?' asked an imposing voice over our shoulder.

'No doubt. We have no place to remain this evening. Have you got any thoughts?' I asked.

The voice came from a young fellow wearing armed force battles and a dark Guinness shirt. He had floppy light hair and a goatee facial hair growth that was so goat-like that I was astonished when words emerged from his mouth, rather than a bleat.

'You could possibly remain at my place. I'll need to give my housemates a speedy call, however I figure they'll be cool with it.'

'That would be splendid. Much thanks to you. What's your name?'

'Max. Apologies, I've lost my voice,' he murmured, highlighting his throat. 'I'll simply proceed to call them and I'll be back in a minute.'

Max returned a couple of moments later.

'Better believe it, they were cool with that,' he murmured, 'yet they requested that I check that you're genuine and not some kind of sharp con individuals. I realize it sounds moronic, yet have you got any ID or anything?'

'No. We haven't got anything by any means, though it pains me to say so. We set off from Land's End with only some fighter shorts and all that we have we have blagged from individuals en route,' I said, attempting to console him.

'Errr, cool, that sounds fiendish, man. You truly began in boxer

shorts? Regard. No doubt, man, you both appear to be authentic, however my housemates needed me to check. There are some dodgy individuals about.'

'We totally comprehend. Please accept my apologies we haven't got any ID or anything. However, I can guarantee you that we are 100% certifiable. We wouldn't ask arbitrary individuals except if we were truly frantic,' said Ben.

'That is cool. You can remain at mine. I haven't got anything worth nicking anyway, so if you are con men then you'll be pretty gutted. I'll simply proceed to complete my brew and I'll give you a yell when I'm leaving.'

By this point, Max's voice had totally vanished, so the possibility of him giving us a yell was improbable. We had left it late, yet by 11.15pm we had in the end tracked down ourselves some place to sleep.

We strolled with Max back to his home, which was a short ways from Bath town focus. He talked – all things considered, murmured – to us about the course that he was learning at college, his fantasy to coordinate music recordings and the way that he had just lived in England for a very long time. His father had worked for the military and Max had spent his youth at different bases all over the planet. In the two years he had lived in Bath, he had effectively fostered a solid South West accent.

Max was having relationship issues. Sarah, a young lady we had met momentarily in the bar, had been in surges of tears. She and Max should be a thing, however at that point had got exceptionally bothered in light of the fact that she had seen a young lady that she preferred snogging another young lady. It was an extremely confounded circumstance that Max neglected to clarify appropriately, yet he had essentially understood that his sweetheart favored young ladies to him. Ben and I, being 'men of the world', offered him the best guidance we could, and he appeared to be truly contacted to have gotten direction from us more seasoned, more experienced folks. In spite of the fact that, I need to admit that my involvement in lesbian circles of drama is tragically non-existent.

Max's two housemates – Sonnie and Mark – were as yet up when we got back. They were playing some PC game on a monstrous widescreen TV with massive speakers either side.

'Bleeding heck, Max. I figured you had nothing worth taking,' I said

'Ha, definitely, well I didn't think you'd get much of anywhere with the TV on your bicycles. Talking about bicycles, would you like to wheel them through the kitchen and stick them in the garden?'

Like any remaining understudies, Max, Sonnie and Mark were totally unequipped for cleaning up. Each and every utensil in the kitchen was grimy and had either

been heaped in the sink or on the cupboards. It was actually as old as kitchen had looked when I was at University, however according to a full grown man, very much prepared by a neatness fixated spouse, the entire spot was profoundly distressing.

Ben and I made them each of the some tea as we began work on the kitchen. We dealt with the savagery, piece by piece. We cleaned up everything, we purged the canisters – which had ejected all around the floor – and put out the reusing. All things considered, we expected it was the reusing. Either that, or Max was storing for a huge papier-mâché session.

Back in the parlor, the understudies were sitting in front of the TV. It was the initial occasion when we began the outing that we sat and sat in front of the TV. The recognizable sparkle of the TV was captivating and we felt a feeling of fervor like we had been let out of isolation. Two minutes of channel jumping later, we understood we had not been missing anything. Even the students were defeated, and switched the TV off with a frustrated sigh.

'I'll show you where you can rest,' murmured Max.

Max's room was on the ground floor, neighboring the lounge. Its floor was heaped profound with garments, CDs, books and unopened gas bills.

'You can rest on the floor. Simply push a portion of that crap aside. I have an extra hiking bed somewhere.'

We scratched at the floor with our hands until we had cleared adequate space for two bodies. For reasons unknown Max decided to rest in a hiking bed, as well. There was no sheet on his sleeping pad, nor pillowcase on his pillow.

'Why you're in a camping cot?' I asked.

'I've simply never got round to purchasing any sheet material. Also I very like resting in this. It causes me to feel like I'm on holiday.'

'You're on a long-lasting occasion, mate. You're an

understudy.' 'Better believe it,' he hacked, 'that is valid.

Night, guys.'

I scarcely dozed at all.

The hiking bed Max had allowed me to acquire was a 5-season one. In the event that I had dozed out in the snow in Antarctica in it, I would in any case have been excessively hot. In a little, twofold coated, halfway warmed room in Bath, it resembled resting in an oven. I unfastened it almost the whole way down and let half of my leg lie in the relatively cool air. Had I not been wearing my tight Union Jack fighter shorts, and been in a more abnormal's room, I would have quite recently lay uncovered, yet I felt it best for the prosperity of Max that I concealed as much as possible.

I needed to dare to the latrine in the early hours of the evening, and Max almost crapped himself when he woke him up to see a half-stripped man wearing oddity clothing sneaking across his room. Following a couple of moments he enlisted what My identity was, and he gave a little wave prior to covering his head with his resting bag.

Day 7 – The Severn Bore

Bath to Newent – 50 miles

Max had early talks to get to, so we were out of the house by 8am. It was one more bright day and we wanted to make up certain miles following the simple time we'd had the earlier day. Max's voice was as yet missing however he waved us farewell and murmured that he believed he had made several new companions, and that he trusted one day he could accomplish something like we were doing.

That was essential for the adventure of our test. Assuming I had been Max and had met us, I would have been extraordinarily desirous, and it was this kind of response that we got from incalculable individuals en route. We were the fortunate ones and we had no one to be jealous of.

Bath town focus was a whirlwind of individuals en route to work. We called into a bread shop where a young lady named Suzie gave us two newly heated hotdog rolls, in return for two grins. We remained outside on the asphalt and gobbled up them in a flash, regardless of them being the temperature of liquid lava.

An exceptionally tall man moved toward us. He had an immense, white, ragged facial hair, and was shrewdly wearing suit pants, cleaned shoes, a shirt, sweatshirt and a panama cap. He was truly unsteady on his feet and smelled of liquor regardless of it being before 9am.

'Hold these, will you?' he slurred, giving me the calfskin sack he was conveying and putting his panama on my head.

'You're not going to disrobe are you?' asked Ben.

'Don't be silly,' he spluttered, laying his hand on my shoulder to consistent himself. He pulled a penny whistle from the pack and began to play. Regardless of not having the option to string a sentence together, his fingers skimmed over the whistle like an entertainer. With the whistle in his mouth he became animated. He jigged on the spot like Michael Flatley, having been not able to try and stand upstanding just minutes prior. It was very extraordinary.

'I'm... an... Attt... Atttten... Attenborough, you know, as in... one of The Attenborough family,' he said, when he'd got done with playing. 'Peter Attenborough, however individuals call me Peter... Peter... The... Potter. I'm a busker... furthermore a potter. I make pots.'

'It's great to meet you, Peter the Potter,' I said. 'Assuming we had any cash, we'd give you a few, however I'm apprehensive we have nothing.'

'Nooooo, that was a gift. A melodic gift... for you. I could perceive you really wanted it. Best of luck... on your movements, any place you are going.' And with that he strutted off down the road into the morning clamor.

I looked into Peter half a month after the fact, to attempt to find a smidgen more with regards to him. In spite of our concise gathering, he'd hugely affected the two of us and he appeared to be an amazing person. I was disheartened to discover that he had passed on seven days after we had met him. He had tumbled down certain means while visiting a companion in their cellar flat.

He was, as he had said, a relative of Richard and David Attenborough, and had been one of Bath's best-cherished buskers. His burial service occurred at Bath Abbey and was gone to by north of 1000 people.

Ben advised me that I had guaranteed him that we could call into the police headquarters to check whether they had any bicycles. Notwithstanding my earnest attempts to persuade him in any case, we advanced towards the primary police headquarters in the town centre.

'Hi,' said Ben to the representative behind the glass in the banquet room, 'Do you end up having any lost or taken bicycles that you are attempting to get freed of?'

I prowled behind the scenes, wincing at Ben's audacity.

'Indeed, we do have bicycles, yet any that are unclaimed are delivered off to Africa. Assuming you can hang on brief I will get the Lost-Property Officer to come and address you.'

I remained there surprised. Since I had been discredited, but since there was such thing as a Lost-Property Officer. It was a task that had all the charm of being a police officer, however without the problem and risk of genuine crooks; simply an assortment of others' assets to watch out for. In case I was a cop, I would need to be a Lost Property Officer. However, i don't know there is a lot of degree for advancement. Lost Property Inspector? Lost Property Commander? Head of Lost Property?

The Lost Property Officer's name was Kevin. He was a wonderful, grinning man, who might not have watched awkward in an animation. He clarified that, indeed, they had bicycles, yet that they were totally transported off by a cause to Africa in case they were unclaimed.

'Sadly we can't simply part with bicycles to the overall population as the foundation will miss out,' he added.

'obviously, we totally comprehend,' said Ben, and I went to leave accepting that Ben would follow. He had different thoughts however.

'Yet what might be said about if we somehow happened to give you our bicycles all things being equal, and that way individuals in Africa would in any case get their bicycles, and everybody would be happy.'

Kevin looked confused.

'Assuming you as of now have bicycles, why do you need various bicycles?' he asked.

'Great inquiry,' I said.

'We're cycling to John O'Groats and we just have a pink young lady's off-road bicycle and a youngster's racer. We were wanting to overhaul them to something more substantial.'

'Well, I guess that could work. I can't see it being an issue. Do you have your bicycles here? Wheel them in and we'll take a quick trip and see what we can find.'

We had been intrigued by the breadth of Roger Badcock's bike cave, however this was on something else altogether. Roger's horse shelter had been filled for the most part with bike parts, and those bikes that were unblemished were genuinely fundamental looking; as both Pinky and The Falcon were confirmations to.

Bath Police Station, in any case, had a column of around 30 brilliant, glossy bikes arranged all set to Africa. Some of them looked nearly pristine, as I accept many taken bicycles are.

'Your bicycles look sufficiently nice,' said Kevin. 'We may need to fix up guarantee they satisfy the security guidelines before we transport them, however assuming that you see something you like the vibe of here then I'll do you a swap.'

'Would you say you are not kidding? Any of these bicycles?' spouted Ben like an energized school boy.

'Indeed, that is fine,' said Kevin.

Ben watched here and there the length of the sanctuary where the bicycles were arranged, really looking at every one thus. Sooner or later he stopped close to a monstrous silver professional bicycle. It was without a doubt the greatest bicycle that had at any point been constructed, overshadowing all the other things in the row.

'What is your take on this one, George?' asked Ben.

'I think it looks, all things considered, it looks extremely huge. Are you certain you can come to the pedals?'

'ha, exceptionally interesting,' he said, despite the fact that I had not been kidding. 'No doubt, I love this one, Kevin, assuming that is ok.'

'No issue, let me simply take these foundation names off. What might be said about you?
Which one do you need?' he asked me.

'Really, I believe I will keep the one I have,' I answered, nearly apologetically.

'What? Gracious come on, George,' said Ben, astounded. 'This is our opportunity to at last get fair bicycles that will get us the entire way to John O'Groats. This is the thing that we've been looking for.'

'No, it's why YOU have been looking. I'm content with The Falcon.'

'Don't be idiotic. Is this some kind of infantile mope since you didn't want to go to the police headquarters? Since, supposing that so then, at that point, that is really disgraceful.' Kevin turned away to try not to engage in our argument.

'Actually no, not in the slightest degree. I've generally been content with The Falcon and I've for a long time needed to accept it to the furthest extent that I can, and I don't feel that I have yet.'

'However its dumb chain tumbles off each couple of hundred meters!' he woofed. 'Ideally it'll get itself straightened out and it hasn't dialed us back too much.

Besides, it doesn't feel right sending a little dashing bicycle to Africa. It wouldn't have a potential for success on the streets out there. Basically Pinky is an off-road bicycle and would be fit to the spot. The Falcon would be annihilated right away. Additionally, I question that it has any possibility of breezing through the security assessments, taking into account that the chain tumbles off, the brakes don't work and the back wheel is wobbly.'

'Okay, fine,' surrendered Ben. 'Yet, you would be advised to not begin whinging that my bicycle is far superior to yours from now on.'

'Relax, I won't.'

We expressed gratitude toward Kevin, and said our farewells to Pinky – which was neither passionate nor nostalgic for Ben – and headed on our way.

'I can't arrive at the pedals appropriately when I'm perched on the seat,' gasped Ben around 30 seconds subsequent to leaving the police headquarters. 'I need to rise up to have the option to pedal.'

I made an effort not to sound self-satisfied but rather I couldn't resist.

'And you told me not to whinge. What did I ask you back in the station about the pedals? That bicycle looks silly. It is the size of a horse.'

'No doubt, all things considered, it could give a thumping to your awful little bicycle no issue,' said Ben, making an effort not to snicker. 'Alright, so it's enormous, and hard to pedal, yet it's a legitimate bicycle. I will initiate it The Horse.'

Cycling behind Ben was exceptionally interesting. The seat was extremely high that when he rose up to pedal it was situated in his back.

There was a Halfords (other vehicle and bicycle shops are accessible) that we passed in transit out of Bath, so we brought in to check whether they could assist us with trip with some fundamental bicycle repairs.

'What kind of things do you want doing?' asked Jason, the business collaborator and bicycle mechanic.

'You know, only a couple of minor things like the brakes not working, and the chain tumbling off. That kind of thing.'

After a couple of moments fixing screws, and nudging machine gear-pieces he gave his diagnosis.

'The chain is essentially buggered. I've put some oil on it, yet the back derailleur has had it. It needs replacing.'

'Is there anything that you can do?' I asked, seeming like somebody who had recently been informed that their cherished pet would have been put to sleep.

'I'm apprehensive not. Derailleurs for bicycles this old are truly difficult to get hold of nowadays. It may endure somewhat longer before it goes completely.'

'alright, much obliged, shouldn't something be said about the brakes?'

'Well, they're essentially buggered, as well. The cushions are extremely worn out that for you to have the option to utilize them to stop they should be fixed so they limit the wheels from going round.'

I could hear Ben moaning behind me, yet not really set in stone not to be defeated.

'Is it conceivable to fix them enough so I can dial back?' 'That's right, can do, yet you will not have the option to stop quickly.'

'alright, that is fine.'

After Jason had gotten done with The Falcon, Ben inquired as to whether he could bring down The Horse's seat. It worked out that it was at that point at its most reduced setting, which interested me greatly.

'Do you all have protective caps?' asked Jason as we were taking off of the shop.

'No, however we wish we did,' said Ben.

'Stand by there a moment. I want to likely figure you out with a head protector.' When he had said 'a cap,' we accepted he had signified 'a cap each,'

yet it turned out he implied only the one cap. In any case, we chose to take it in goes to wear it, hence making us fundamentally more secure half of the time.

We took off of Bath through Pulteney Bridge. Pulteney Bridge is one of just four scaffolds on the planet to be lined by shops on the two sides. Indeed, it seems such a lot of like a typical road that we experienced the humiliation of asking somebody which heading the extension was, just to be given the answer, 'you're on the scaffold, m'duck.'

Having successfully crossed the Avon, we then continued with renewed enthusiasm in what we thought was the direction of Scotland. after 45 minutes we had to backtrack our means to the Pulteney Bridge and attempt once more. In the energy of getting another bicycle and a cap we had traveled west towards Bristol as opposed to proceeding north.

We then took a wrong turn and ended up having to take a lengthy detour around Colerne Airport and then through the sinister sounding villages of Slaughterford and Thickwood before joining the busy A420 for a few miles to correct our mistake.

We showed up in the town of Nettleton with exclusive standards of a long comfortable bar lunch, yet were significantly frustrated to find that the town didn't have a pub.

It did, nonetheless, have a very much supplied Post Office.

Di, the woman who ran the Post Office, appeared to be excessively energized by the appearance of two unusually dressed 'tourists' to her shop. At the point when we clarified our main goal she settled the score more energized and appeared to observe the entire thing exceptionally entertaining. We proposed to assist in the shop in return for some food yet she just laughed.

'Does it seem as though I want assistance in here?' she laughed. 'Both of you simply take any sandwiches or cakes that you want.'

'We would rather not remove your stock like that. Do you have anything that you were tossing out?' asked Ben.

'There's two or three prawn sandwiches out the back that terminated yesterday. I had one for lunch I'm as yet alive,' she said.

'That would be awesome. Thank you.'

'Basically take a cake and a chocolate bar every,' she said. 'Gracious, go on then, at that point. In the event that you insist.'

We found a seat at the outdoor table outside and ate our gone-off prawn sandwiches, Eccles cakes and Snickers (other nut, nougat and caramel chocolate bars are accessible). We were partaking in the harmony and calm of the Wiltshire field when I felt an abrupt surge of frenzy through my body.

'Gracious SHIT! It's my mum's birthday tomorrow. I haven't got her a present.
I haven't sent her a card.'

'She'll comprehend, won't she?' said Ben. 'You can make her something when we've completed the excursion. She knows you're not permitted to spend any money.'

'No doubt, yet that is somewhat weak of me, right? That is to say, we've figured out how to get convenience consistently, food, most suppers, bicycles, garments and a lot of brew. I ought to have a card, at least.'

'Well, we're at a Post Office. What better spot? How about you proceed to ask Di?'

I returned inside and nonchalantly disclosed my situation to Di without really asking her for a birthday card.

'I can give you a card and a stamp,' she said before I had even completed the process of talking. 'Proceed to help yourself from the rack over there.'

Di was one of those uncommon diamonds of humankind that you at times run over. I could envision that she was the pride of the town and had a deep understanding of everybody. Not in a gossipy manner, but rather basically due to her glow and liberality. I explored Nettleton while composing this book, to attempt to set up what district it was in (it turns out it's in Wiltshire. Truth be told, I didn't understand we had gone through Wiltshire. I don't think I even knew where Wiltshire was). My hunt uncovered another intriguing truth. I found that Di was granted the honor of Best Village Shop/Post Office in Britain 2007. This was a really peculiar fortuitous event, considering it was the main Post Office that we visited on the whole excursion, and furthermore that Di's liberality and grant winning potential was so obvious. I quote one of the adjudicators, who summarizes it far superior than I could:

'This is a massively troublesome classification to judge on the grounds that our town businesspeople and sub-postmasters structure the hearts of each provincial local area, however Di Bell is an exceptionally uncommon woman who motivates genuine commitment from her clients. She received dozens of nominations from people of all ages, all praising her warm nature and the fact that she is a lifeline who always goes above and beyond the call of duty. With the danger of conclusion approaching over many Post Offices in the locale it is the ideal chance to stress that our branches are about the spirit of nation life, not just with regards to stamps and vehicle charge. A considerable lot of Di's clients said that the town would change for the more regrettable without her, which is the reason I am pleased to respect her in this opposition and raise the profile of our beset Post Offices. Long may Di continue!'

'Why have you marked the card 'DW', you fruitcake?' asked
Ben. 'Gracious, no excuse, it's a boring tale,' I said coyly.
'Well we have a lot of time. Truth be told, around 800 miles worth of
time.' 'It's simply something my mum calls me, that is all,' I said,
nonchalantly hoping
that would fulfill his interest. It didn't.
'I accumulated that much, however what does it
rely on?' There was a long pause.
'Dordie Wardie.'

Ben howled uncontrollably and almost gagged on the Eccles cake that he was eating.

'What the hell? Ha. Dordie Wardie? My god, what's going on with all that?' he spluttered.

'When I was nearly nothing, I used to call myself Dord in light of the fact that I was unable to say George appropriately. My folks continued calling me Dord, and afterward for reasons unknown throughout the long term it steadily got reached out to Dordie Wardie. That is the thing that my mum, Dad and sister call me now.'

'ha, that is strange. Dordie Wardie! Your family are wicked strange.' 'Your mum should have a name that she calls you? What does she call you? Benny Boodles? Benny Wenny? Benji Bunny?' I

examined. 'Ben,' he said.

'Oh.'

My mum got the card the next day, and Dordie Wardie got some genuine brownie points.

We had been perched on the seat by the Post Office for more than an hour prior to we understood it was 2pm and we had just cycled ten miles. We proceeded through the curious towns of Sopworth and Leighterton, prior to coming to the bustling A46 which we followed to Stroud. We halted momentarily at a bar on the edges of Stroud on the grounds that Ben was peckish for some peanuts.

'Do you truly need to proceed to get peanuts? Wouldn't you be able to simply delay until some other time when we can attempt to eat appropriately?' I asked.

'No, I truly need something now and I think peanuts are the appropriate response.' 'They won't give you any. This is a bar. Do you truly think they'll just

give you peanuts in case you stroll in and ask?'

'obviously. For what reason wouldn't they? We've not had any issues up to this point.' 'Definitely, however that is on the grounds that we haven't actually been requesting explicit things,

and we've been asking due to legitimate need rather than in light of the fact that we extravagant a tidbit,' I said, attempting to legitimize my expanding dissatisfaction. 'Recall that time you requested another jug of water?'

'That was on the grounds that that chap was an arsehole. Fine, well you won't need any of my peanuts when I get them, I assume?'

'No, I most certainly won't.'

I held up external the bar with the bicycles, as I was too humiliated to even consider going in with him. Some portion of me trusted that he would come out with essentially nothing having endured embarrassment before a bar loaded with local people. The other piece of me trusted he would arise conveying peanuts, as I also was eager. I guaranteed myself that I would decay them in any case, just to point out that I didn't require them.

He seemed a couple of moments later with four sacks of peanuts; two parcels of salted and two bundles of dry roasted.

'See, simple. The person didn't address it. He just gave me these,' said Ben with a self-satisfied smile. 'Do you need two or three bags?'

'Certainly,' I said timidly. 'Thank you.'

Following a long trudge up Scottsquar Hill we were then compensated with a long downhill into the Severn Valley. We halted for a lay on the M5 flyover. We had gotten over the M5 multiple times already – either side of Taunton – however hadn't yet halted to watch the traffic. I comprehend that this may not appear to be a pleasurable leisure activity, however there was a dreamlike thing about watching others' lives proceed at high velocity. We had effectively become acclimated with carrying on with life at an extraordinarily lethargic rate, and we had failed to remember what it resembled to have the option to get in a vehicle and be at your objective a couple of moments later. It was peculiarly fulfilling to move back on our bicycles and proceed onwards at our own relaxed pace.

It was practically dull when we arrived at the town of Newent. There appeared to be a choice of bars and B&Bs in the town community, so we both were hopeful with regards to the possibility of observing some to be good accommodation.

'I'm grieved, young men, yet I'm totally full, what with the Onion Fayre and all,' said the proprietor at The George Hotel.

'Onion Fayre? What's the Onion Fayre?' asked Ben, viewing at me like I would know.

'Why, it's the Newent Onion Fayre tomorrow!' she said. 'Why, it's the greatest day in the town's schedule. I believed that is the reason you were visiting.'

'No, we're simply going through. We didn't be aware of the Onion Fayre,' I said. 'It sounds fun. We're glad to rest in a latrine or carport in case you have one?'

'I'm truly grieved. Every last bit of room is brimming with provisions and onions for later. There'll be around 20,000 individuals visiting the town tomorrow and

50,000 onions.'

'20 THOUSAND PEOPLE? 50,000 ONIONS?' I repeated

back to her, accepting she had got her figures wrong. 'I had no clue about that onions were so popular.'

'Neither did I before I moved here five years prior. It's the just one of its sort on the planet and it's been going – in some structure – for 800 years.'

'Blimey, it seems as though a serious party,' said Ben, making an honest effort not to sound wry. 'Would you be able to suggest some other spots around that could possibly help us?'

'I'm apprehensive you'll get similar reaction at the wide range of various spots around. Wherever books up months ahead of time during the current end of the week. Apologies, young men, best of luck.'

Once outside, Ben and I checked out one another with a combination of energy and discouragement. We felt advantaged to have shown up in the town on the most significant evening of the year, yet we were likewise confronted with the problem of not having anyplace to remain. Assuming we proceeded onwards we would pass up what the fayre brought to the table, in any case, in the event that we waited, we may go through the night on the street.

'We'll get something arranged here, I think. We haven't flopped such a long ways on the excursion,' said Ben.

'I believe that is the principal piece of certified confidence I have heard from you.'

'I know. It's the possibility of the Newent Onion Fayre. I can scarcely hold back my excitement.'

We wheeled our bicycles down the central avenue as we attempted to build up a game plan. At the point when we arrived at the principle square there were individuals dumping a goliath trailer heap of onions and stacking them under an old Tudor-looking building.

'So this is the place where everything occurs,' said Ben. 'I surmise so. That is a LOT of onions'

'We could check whether they need any assist setting with increasing all the stuff and afterward perhaps one of the laborers will actually want to offer us some place to remain,' recommended Ben.

'Sounds great. It's certainly worth an attempt.'

There were clear gazes from the onion stackers as Ben pitched his suggestion. They kept hurling sacks of onions to each other in a line from the trailer to the stack. There was still no reaction after Ben had completed the process of talking. I tapped Ben's arm to propose that we let them have at it, when one of the men toward as far as it goes spoke.

'So you set off from Land's End and you're cycling to Scotland without going through any cash?' he asked as he kept on pulling

onions. 'Better believe it, fundamentally,' said Ben.

'Sounds exceptionally venturesome,' he said, grinning interestingly. 'You can rest at mine assuming you need. I could do with a hand setting up in the morning.'

It truly was actually that straightforward. We had been milliseconds from leaving and abandoning Newent and its onions, and out of nowhere we had been offered some place to stay.

We spent the following hour assisting the folks with emptying the remainder of the trailer of onions. The one who offered us a room was named Rob – a neighborhood rancher and the principle provider of onions to the celebration. Loot was in his mid forties, thin, gorgeous and un-endured – contrasted with some other farmers.

After we had wrapped up stacking the onions he proposed to get us a lager at the bar across the square. The greater part of different men looked like nearby farmhands, yet one of them was unmistakably unique. He was in his mid twenties and he had a ceaseless full-confronted smile like a jokester. His dress sense looked, all things considered, how might I put this graciously? Eastern-European. He was wearing a couple of those loose hued designed pants that were in style for about seven days in 1988. He then complimented this with a shiny red bomber jacket and a yellow baseball cap. None of different men had said a word to him each and every evening. He had been one of the connections in the onion line, yet was extremely ineffectual that different men would in general sidestep him and give the sack straightforwardly to the individual on the other side.

I grinned at him when he visually connected and he accepting this as a challenge to come over and address us.

'Helllo-a. My name-an iz Rooballs,' he

said. 'Rooooballs? Hello I'm George.'

'Roooooooballs,' he rehashed, changing the accentuation

somewhat. 'Hello there Rooooballs, I'm Ben.'

'I from Slovakia,' he said, shaking us both by the hand. 'You England?'

'Indeed, we live in England,' I said.

At this point he got out a Slovakian to English expression book from his pocket and began flicking through it. Sooner or later he found what he was looking for.

'Girlder-feend!' he yelled excitedly.

'Girlder-feend? Apologies, I don't comprehend,' I said. Ben investigated the word Rooballs was currently eagerly pointing at.

'Ahhh, sweetheart,' said Ben. 'Indeed, we both have lady friends. As a matter of fact, George has a wife.'

'No, no, no. Rooballs. Girlder-feend,' he said, turning out to be much more energized. 'Girlder-feend England.'

'Goodness, you have a sweetheart here in England?'

I inquired. 'Indeed, yes. Girlder-feend England.

London.'

'Extremely decent. So why you're here in Newent?' asked

Ben. 'Bus.'

'Indeed, however what are you doing here when your

sweetheart is in London?' 'Bus.'

'alright.' Rooballs began flicking through his expression

book once more. 'Telephoner,' he said, and began pointing at

me unpredictably. 'You need to give her a call?'

'Telephoner,' he rehashed, nudging me over and again in the chest with his finger.

'You need ME to phone your sweetheart in London?' I inquired.

'Indeed, indeed, yes. Telephoner girlder-feend London.'

'Errr, alright. Do you have a telephone? What do you need me to say?'

'I show book. Telephoner,' he said, waving his trusty book and showing me he had 50p for the telephone box which he was quickly pointing at through the bar window.

'alright, alright. How about we do it,' I said. 'What's her name?'

'Jenny,' said Rooballs. Ben shrugged his shoulders at me, and followed me outside chuckling away to himself. I was too anxious with regards to what I may need to say to Jenny to find the circumstance amusing.

The three of us crushed into the phonebox outside the bar and he put the 50p in the coin opening and dialed a number that he had written on a piece of paper. After a couple of rings an English young lady replied. It was extremely loud and she seemed like she was in a bar.

'Hi, is that Jenny?' I said.

'It's Jenna. Who's that? Sorry it's exceptionally loud here. I can barely

hear you.' 'I'm with a companion of yours called Rooballs. He has a

directive for you, that

he needs me to give you.'

'What's that? A message from who?'

'Rooballs. From Slovakia. He said you and he know each other?'

'Gracious, yes. I recollect Rooballs,' she said fairly reluctantly. I was starting to detect that maybe she didn't respect their relationship similarly that Rooballs did.

'Great, well he has a message that he needs me to interpret for you,' I said, while Rooballs swiftly flicked through his phrasebook.

Rooballs pointed eagerly at a word that he had found. It said, 'potrestať, pokutovať, preťažiť''. Interpretation: 'to punish'.

I gave Rooballs a curious look, however he gestured his head enthusiastically as though to affirm he certainly had the right word.

'Fail, Jenna, he says 'to rebuff'. Does that mean anything to you?' By this point, Ben had dismissed and had his temple crushed facing the glass of the telephone box. I could hear the muted wails of his giggling as he nibbled onto his fist.

'To rebuff? Rebuff what? I don't comprehend,' said Jenna.

Rooballs was occupied with looking the phrasebook for the following word, which would presumably make everything clear.

'Gracious hold tight, he will give me another word,' I said. Rooballs bungled with the book, yet as he did the telephone line went dead as Jenna hung up.

'I'm truly heartbroken, mate. We ran out of credit,' I lied.

'We could get back to?' I said, truly pitiful and confounded that the main message he had figured out how to give to his supposed sweetheart was 'to rebuff'. Rooballs shook his head and pushed the entryway of the phonebox open.

'No more cash,' he said dejectedly.

Back inside the bar I had a go at requesting Rooballs what the rest of his message was, however he didn't appear to comprehend. His trouble was before long support when I trained him how to flick a brew mat over with the rear of his hand and catch it. He yelled like a maniac.

'Right, chaps,' said Rob, who had split away from different ranchers and had approached address us. 'My people are having a grill somewhere around the stream this evening. I'm certain they'd be glad for you to come along.'

'That is amazingly sort of you, Rob. However, we would rather not interfere by any means,' said Ben.

'I demand. You're more than welcome.'

'Bless your heart. That sounds extraordinary. Yet, these are the main garments we have,' I said, pulling at my messy suit pants that I had been wearing persistently for seven days.

'Goodness don't stress over that. It's simply a lot of elderly folks individuals having a grill in a field. It will be excessively dim for them to try and see what you resemble in any case. It's the yearly party of The Severn Bore Society. It will be the greatest bore for a considerable length of time this evening,' he said.

'Cool. What's the Severn Bore?' I asked.

'A pig isn't it?' said Ben, acknowledging straight away that he had said something dumb as Rob was gagging on a significant piece of beer.

'Ha, no, it's anything but a pig. You probably knew about The Severn Bore, no?' We both checked out him vacantly. 'It's a wave that descends the stream,' he proceeded. 'In any case, I'll fill you in regarding it in a little. We really want to get rolling assuming that we will make it on schedule. Sling your bicycles in the trailer outside and I'll be out in a minute.'

'alright, splendid, is Rooballs coming, as well?' I asked.

'Errr, no, I've no thought where he's remaining. He looks cheerful enough here,' said Rob.

We said farewell to Rooballs who was all the while flicking brew mats at the table in the corner. He smiled and waved back.

Rob's trailer was stopped right external the bar and we recovered our bicycles that we had imagine locked to a close by column. We were going to place them into the trailer when I was out of nowhere hit by a dilemma.

'Hold tight, Ben, isn't this cheating getting a lift some place with our bikes?'

'What do you mean? Do you seriously think we should cycle miles to Rob's farm, in the middle of nowhere in the pitch black?'

'No, I don't imply that. I imply that we said that we wouldn't utilize some other type of transport for our bicycles, didn't we?'

'Definitely, however we additionally said we could do various things that were not on the course, as long as we rejoined the course where we left it. Like when we recruited that speed boat in St Ives.'

'I know, it's simply that Rob will presumably have heaps of other stuff to place in the trailer in the first part of the day and we may need to leave the bicycles at his while we come and help him, and afterward when we get them back and head off it implies we will not have cycled the piece among here and Rob's home, wherever

Rob's home is.' I was in any event, befuddling myself. Exactly as of now, Rob and several different folks arose out of the pub.

'alright folks?' he asked, seeing that I was holding my bicycle in mid air.

'No doubt, all is well, it's simply that, and this will most likely strong really

moronic to you yet... ' and I rehashed my punctilious worries about the legitimacy of our test to Rob.

'That is a walk in the park. I surmise assuming you're going to accomplish something as insane as this bicycle ride, you should do it appropriately,' he said. 'Here is a thought. We put your bicycles in the trailer, only for a couple of moments and drop them up at Mike's home at the highest point of the road. You would then be able to leave them at his. That is okay with you Mike isn't it?' Mike gestured. 'Then, in the morning, you can come and help me load up the trailer and come back into town to set up the rest of the stall. Then when you want to leave, you can wander up the road to Mike's house and pick up your bikes. Since his home is at the highest point of the road, you will have cycled past it as of now so you will not have cheated by any means. How does that sound?'

Rob had turned into my new
legend. 'Astonishing. Much
thanks to you,' I said.

'Glad currently?' murmured Ben as we moved into the trailer with our bikes.

'Indeed, very.'

After unloading the bicycles in Mike's back garden, Rob drove us the ten or so miles to his homestead on the edges of Gloucester.

He drove us through the huge ranch kitchen, up the steps and into a monster visitor room. A monster room, I mean, not a space for goliath guests.

'Ransack, we were anticipating that a barn or something should stay in bed this evening. Not one of your rooms. Truly, we would be completely content with the onions,' I said.

'Don't be senseless, I'm more than glad for you both to remain here.' As soon as he had vanished, I jumped for the bed.

'I'm having the bed this time,' I yelled.

'You charlatan,' said Ben.

After a fast wash and change starting with one malodorous shirt then onto the next, we went down the stairs to meet Rob.

'So have you all actually never known about the Severn Bore?' he asked, when we were in the kitchen.

'After you referenced it I understood I had known about it previously,' I said, attempting to mask my ignorance.

'I've never known about it,' said Ben, without attempting to stow away his.

'Essentially it's a wave that goes up the stream against the current. It happens two or three times each year possibly, yet the one this evening will be the greatest in 25 years they say,' said Rob.

'Cool. How would they occur?' asked Ben.

'Essentially it's the point at which there's an elevated tide and the level of the ocean becomes higher than the regular level of the estuary. The water needs to head off to some place so it sends a rush of water a few miles up the estuary. Individuals surf it here and there. Indeed this one person recently surfed more than seven miles down the waterway. In any case, we would be advised to get a break on. In case you snatch as a significant number of those sacks of grill stuff as you can in transit out that would be great.'

After around ten minutes, we maneuvered into a field in no place. We could hear the far off gab of voices and could make out the weak gleam of a fire. We followed the light of Rob's light across the boggy and lopsided field to where a gathering of around 30 individuals were accumulated around a grill the size of a pool table. It was the greatest grill I had at any point seen, built from three oil drums, and emitting a huge heat.

Rob acquainted us with his folks who were both in their seventies and very decent. They, thusly, acquainted us with their companions, who then, at that point, acquainted us with theirs and inside thirty minutes we knew nearly everyone.

After some time, a portion of the men started to put meat onto the grill. 'Would we be able to help by any stretch of the imagination?' I asked.

'Well, indeed, you can both be accountable for the grill, if it's all the same to you,' said the old person as he hacked on the smoke. 'There are two or three sets of utensils around there. Be cautious since it's exceptionally hot.' This was the misrepresentation of the truth of the century. I could feel myself carbonizing as I stood there.

'Pleasant one, George,' said Ben snidely, when the elderly person had dismissed, 'You have us a task cooking in a fountain of liquid magma. Simply think, two hours prior we were wandering the roads of Newtown, or whatever that spot was called, searching for some place to remain, and presently we're running a grill in a field for a major gathering of elderly folks individuals while we trust that a wave will come the incorrect way down the waterway. How distraught is that?'

'It's insane. It's odd to feel that assuming we had done anything differently today, like take an extra ten minutes for a break, or if we had been offered a room at that George Hotel, or if you hadn't suggested we speak to the onion stackers, then we would never have got to experience this.'

'Better believe it, or we may in any case be wandering the roads of Newtown.' 'Newent,' I corrected.

'You knew what?'

'No, Newent. The town is called Newent. Not Newtown.'

'Well, whatever, I wouldn't have any desire to go through the late evening meandering its streets.'

'Here you go, young men,' said the old person, who had gotten back with two cool-boxes. 'We have burgers, wieners, ribs, hacks, steaks and chicken legs. You should cook everything. We would truly prefer not to take any of it home.'

There was sufficient food to take care of Gloucestershire.

We set with regards to our errand of cooking the greatest amount of meat that had at any point been found in one spot. I fear to consider the number of creatures should have passed on to make the heap of pieces that we were confronted with.

There was no light other than the actual coals, so it was essentially difficult to discern whether the meat was cooked appropriately. We figured out how to acquire a smaller than normal LED keyring from one of the old women (better believe it, she was down with the children). This functioned admirably, however provided that we held it around 4cm from the piece of meat that we were investigating. This must be done at lightning rate to stop the skin on our arms rankling. In all actuality, we didn't actually have to check in case the meat was cooked. The grill was incredibly hot that the meat was charcoaled inside seconds.

We heaped the darkened food onto immense plates in clumps as we cooked it, and they were taken to a table where individuals started lining to fill their plates. 'You're working effectively,' said one woman as she passed us with a full plate of carbon. 'It possesses a flavor like a legitimate grill,' which was a well mannered method of saying that it was totally burnt.

After everybody had helped themselves, Rob came over and took the utensils from us.

'Extraordinary work, folks. You proceed to fill your plates and I'll watch out for the last couple of pieces,' he said.

'IT'S COMING!' yelled one of the gathering individuals, before long 10pm. Everybody surged towards the waterway that was presently frightfully lit by the moon.

The stream was totally still and the possibility of a 'surge of water' as we had been guaranteed appeared to be unimaginable. We were a few miles inland and

it appeared to be unthinkable that a wave could make it up that far, and I began to contemplate whether it was each of the an intricate joke. Burglarize had likewise said that we would hear it well before we would see it. In any case, aside from the structure fervor and prattle of the elderly folks individuals, I could not hear anything. Even a ripple would have made this lot gasp. My assumptions were set very low.

Just then I heard something.

It's difficult to portray the sound it made. Envision the sound that a major wave makes when it breaks close to the shore, however rather than This being trailed by the respite as the water retreats, the clamor simply proceeds. Like one major, ceaseless wave. This, as you've most likely assembled, is by and large what the Severn Bore is.

The waterway was genuinely tight at where we were standing, and we were a couple of meters from the water's edge. At the point when the drag at last came into focus it surpassed my assumptions as a whole. I couldn't resist the opportunity to heave in astonishment like the remainder of the gathering. It was, in a real sense, a surge of water very nearly two meters high going up the waterway. It was more slow than I expected yet far, undeniably more great. For reasons unknown, I had innocently envisioned that the wave would be all alone and whenever it had passed the waterway would have returned to typical. What I failed to acknowledge was that this wave was being moved by a persistent surge of water behind it. It conveyed with it enormous tree trunks and branches that it had rescued from the stream bank on its excursion. No surfers had figured out how to ride the wave this far, and to be straightforward I was somewhat alleviated. On this event it appeared to be that nature had won.

As the drag passed us, the water surged up the stream bank and overflowed the field around us. I've never seen elderly folks individuals move so quick, as they all bounced for higher ground. Ben and I, who were excessively mesmerized by the entire thing, neglected to move and the edges of the wave lapped over our feet.

The drag proceeded carefully concealed and the stream quietened down, yet in its engorged structure. The remainder of the gathering headed back towards the grill somewhere down in babble, yet we stayed awestruck on the waterway bank. I can sincerely say it was one of the most noteworthy snapshots of my life. I don't know the amount of an impact the unusualness of our evening had on the experience, however even all alone, the Severn Bore truly is one of nature's extraordinary spectacles.

Our fortune was supported when the administrator of the Severn Bore Society let us know that it was the best he had seen in north of 30 years. I attempted to consider something significant and significant to say to pass on my

feelings to the similarly awestruck Ben.

'Wonderful,' I said. 'How about we proceed to get some more meat.'

The gathering gave no indication of hailing as increasingly more wine was drank, and that's only the tip of the iceberg and more meat was eaten. They added to their liberality when the administrator gave a short discourse about our test, and gave us a check for £50 from the general public, for us to provide for the cause of our choice.

I don't recall leaving the grill. I simply recall getting up later with Ben pulling at my shirt.

'Come on, mate,' he said. 'You can't rest on Rob's feasting table. It's an ideal opportunity to go to bed.'

Vince, Bath

Jason, Harfords, Bath

Gt. Nettleton Post Office

Wiltshire, obviously

Unloading onions, Newent

Day 8 – Newent Onion Fayre

Newent to Ludlow – 46 miles

I woke up with my head beating and my mind attempting to sort out what pieces of the earlier night were genuine, which were smashed minds and which were dreams.

We directed our every day schedule of picking the most un-position of our shirts to wear for the afternoon. On this event, however, it was 6am and incredibly cold so we wound up putting on all that we claimed. Ransack was at that point occupied in the kitchen when we went downstairs.

'Grab oat. The pot's on.'

'Good gracious, take a gander at this. Weetabix GOLD!' said Ben enthusiastically plunging at an oat packet.

'What the heck is Weetabix GOLD? Have you had it previously?' I asked.

'No. I didn't realize it existed. I bet it's astounding,' he said as he arranged three of them in a bowl.

'They look like typical Weetabix.'

'Better believe it, yet I bet it's all in the taste.' There was a short delay while Ben poured milk over his Weetabix GOLD, and a large portion of the tablecloth.

'Gracious. My. God,' he spluttered. 'It's the best cereal, of all time. In the event that you thought Weetabix was great, then, at that point, you delay until you've attempted Weetabix GOLD.'

I needed to see what all the fight was about.

'It tastes very much like typical Weetabix, however with truly decent milk,' I said. 'That is new out the dairy earlier today,' said Rob as he went along with us at the table with a teapot.

'Gracious,' said Ben, 'I believe you're correct. I've recently added some Corn Flakes as well and they taste like the best Corn Flakes of all time. Furthermore these aren't Corn Flakes GOLD. Simply ordinary ones.'

'Do Corn Flakes GOLD even exist?' I asked.

'I question it, yet they ought to bring them out, assuming they're anyplace close as great as Weetabix GOLD.'

'Hold tight, however you recently said… gracious never mind.'

I later found that Weetabix GOLD was discontinued.

It was as yet dull when Rob drove us down the path to his homestead shop. This was not simply a minuscule slow down selling onions; it was a huge food retail store, complete with bread kitchen, butchery, cheddar counter, gift shop and any vegetable you could ever want.

'I thought you just developed onions?' I asked.

'No, we develop various types here. Not everything in here is from this ranch yet a large portion of it is.'

Rob was not happy with simply running a homestead and a homestead shop, he was additionally a neighborhood business visionary; consistently watching out for another dare to keep him occupied. I don't think it was even monetarily roused, as a considerable lot of his tasks appeared to be noble cause schemes.

He ran Halloween trailer rides every year called 'Frightmare', which incorporated a visit to the pumpkin fix, a spooky hayride and an excursion to a spooky house. He additionally coordinated train rides, Easter egg chases, birthday celebrations, Santa's cavern and homestead visits. My undisputed top choice was the Living Pizza Field. Loot had made a tremendous round field, and afterward split it into 12 pizza-like cuts. Each cut of the field developed fixings used to make a pizza, including wheat, onions (obviously), garlic, tomatoes, sweet corn, olives, spices and even cows, chickens and pigs. The thought was that youngsters could proceed to dive more deeply into where food came from, and how it is made. Having the field set out looking like a pizza made it more straightforward for them to identify with. Children then got to cook a homemade pizza in Rob's specially created pizza kitchen with a traditional wood-fired pizza oven. It was crafted by a genius.

We heaped the pickup and trailer high with cartons of vegetables, products of the soil. We then, at that point, needed to adjust ourselves and the produce while standing up toward the rear of the pickup.

As we proceeded back up the track, the sun was rising and had projected its morning sparkle over the fields. Now, an ostrich started running close by the pickup truck. It resembled being in Africa. Sort of.

Newent town focus was clamoring when we showed up; stallholders were wildly preparing their stuff, carnival rides were being gathered, gazebos raised, stages assembled, PA frameworks tested.

Rob left us accountable for changing a pickup and trailer heap of vegetables into an alluring and adequate market slow down. Ben respected himself with the title of Director of Vegetable Esthetics and provided me with the title of Chief Vegetable Arranger.

I before long settled that this elaborate Ben highlighting where each heap of vegetables ought to go, and teaching me to do all of the real lifting. I'm almost certain Ben didn't connect with a solitary vegetable during the whole operation.

Without wishing to brag, I before long found that I had a characteristic ability for vegetable orchestrating. It's an expertise that I had never had the chance to completely figure it out. Sweet corn husks were stacked like a block facade, carrots and leeks were spread out in grand fan shapes, and packs of onions were richly suspended from snares under the passage. Ben gestured enthusiastically and yapped orders about more onions here, and less parsnips there.

When our work was done, we set out to see what else the Newent Onion Fayre brought to the table. We were hindered by a local announcer's bell.

'Oyez! Oyez! Oyez! Great individuals of Newent, you are accumulated here today for the Newent Onion Fayre. Right away, our visitor of honor Würzel – from the stone gathering Motörhead – will perform on the principle stage.'

What was that? Würzel, from the heavy metal group <u>Motörhead</u>, was going to be performing at the Newent Onion Fayre? It was all very surreal.

What I likewise loved was the manner in which the local proclaimer had alluded to the 'fundamental stage,' as though there were a wide range of stages. There was truth be told only the one, and the word 'stage' was somewhat liberal. It was a trailer with a gazebo on it.

When the local proclaimer had completed his location we proceeded to sit down to talk with him since he looked lonely.

William Chapman was very much into his eighties yet an exuberant person who had completely accepted the job of Town Crier, which he had held for a long time. During the ten minutes that we addressed him, we found out with regards to his time in the Royal Army Medical Corps and his vocation as a paramedic. He let us know that he was one of the most established Town Criers in the nation and, get this, the most established Town Crier IN THE WORLD to have a Blue Peter identification. Indeed, you read that accurately. He was the most established Town Crier on the planet to have a Blue Peter identification. He even showed us the identification, which was stuck to his ensemble. This appeared to be somewhat odd to me at that point. Blue Peter has been going for a very long time, however regardless of whether William had got his identification during Blue Peter's first year he would have been a ways into his thirties. What kind of developed man sends drawings into Blue Peter?

'I think visitors who show up on the show likewise get identifications,' said Ben, when I voiced my interests to him later. 'They're not only for youngsters who send in drawings.'

'alright, great. That is a consolation,' I said.

I found later, that, similar to Peter the Potter in Bath, Willium had died calmly in medical clinic, matured 87, half a month after we had met him. It was extremely dismal to feel that two such energetic and vivid characters had died so before long our excursion. It was a genuine advantage to have met the two of them, and each transformed our outing in their own exceptional way.

I might want to clarify that we didn't have anything to do with the demise of both of them.

'Oyez! Oyez! Oyez! Great individuals of Newent, kindly greeting to the stage… ' said Willium, stopping to see his content, '… Würzel.'

Suddenly, Newent was changed. Brief it was loaded with grannies filling their shopping packs with onions, knitted toys and undesirable tombola prizes. The following, all the father rockers, and emos had emerged from the breaks and totally stuffed the town square before the stage.

Würzel arose timidly through the fold at the rear of the gazebo and got his guitar. He was a wispy little man wearing blue jeans and a <u>Motörhead</u> t-shirt, notwithstanding leaving the band in 1995. His hair was dark and scraggly and gave assurance to the story that he was given his moniker after his likeness to the scarecrow Worzel Gummidge.

He was joined in front of an audience by a drummer and bass-player and he mumbled a concise 'Hey,' prior to dispatching into an exceptionally engaging brief rock 'n' roll instrumental. He then left the stage with an awkward wave and the masses began to disperse. Then a voice came over the PA system that gave one of the most surreal announcements I have ever heard:

'Würzel will sign signatures at the Swan Rescue remain in with regards to a large portion of an hour.'

It was an ideal opportunity to leave Newent.

We gave our gratitude to Rob for our amazing time in Newent, and he said thanks to us for our diligent effort, and gave us both a cup of his better half's 'reality popular's onion soup and some bread.

On the exit from town, we called into a greengrocer and inquired as to whether she had several old bananas that she could save. We both felt the requirement for some organic product or vegetables (other than onions), to assist our bodies with recuperating the shock of the meat feast we had eaten the prior night. After she had found out about our test, she got so energized that she filled a transporter sack with grapes, apples, pears, peaches, plums and bananas.

'This should make a big difference for you,' she said. 'Best of luck, folks.' We ate as a significant part of the organic product as possible, and afterward balanced the remainder of the pack from The

Horse's handlebars. Ludlow was 50 miles away, and we put our focus on arriving before the finish of the day.

Soon in the wake of leaving Newent our course crossed the M50 and into Herefordshire. My insight into English districts was, and still is, dreadful, yet the bicycle ride filled in couple of holes for me. For instance, the acknowledgment that Herefordshire isn't only an incorrect spelling of Hertfordshire. Request that I name every one of the 50 US states and I could give it a decent go, yet get some information about English districts, or any British geology besides, and I am totally clueless.

We arrived at the town of Bromyard at around 2pm and halted by a bar on the edge of town. The enormous brew garden was stuffed brimming with individuals and there were Morris Dancers performing.

As they were skipping near and hitting their sticks, Ben imagined his own Morris Dancers' tune which he chimed in ideal chance to the music and the snap of their sticks: 'I'll slam yours, you slam mine. We should play willy games.'

It was a particularly immature remark, and one that had come all the way out of nowhere, however it was a few minutes before I halted laughing.

'It's simply wrong right? Developed men dressed that way, skipping around with their ringers, sticks and dumb garments. They give me the jerks,' he said.

'I concur. It ought to be made illegal.'

It worked out that Bromyard was facilitating its yearly Folk Festival, and the distinctive Morris moving gatherings were having a type of 'dance-off' to see who the best was. In our eyes, there were no victors, just losers.

A pig broil was being served, and we chose to take a shot at getting some lunch. We joined the long line of individuals and Morris Dancers (yes I know, Morris Dancers are people, as well) and held up our turn.

'What would i be able to get you?' said the fomented woman who was serving.

'Hey, we're cycling from Land's End to John O'Groats, and we... ' started Ben prior to being interrupted.

'Goodness, not this, I haven't got time for this,' she said furiously. 'Do you need any food or not?'

'Well, indeed, however we don't have any cash. Is there any work we can do in return for a bread roll or something?' said Ben, attempting to win her over.

'No, there are a wide range of wellbeing and security issues. I can't make them help back here. You'll need to attempt elsewhere.'

We had to do the stroll of disgrace past all of the self-satisfied looking Morris Dancers.

We had a very much like reaction from four different spots that we attempted in the town place, including a butcher, a newsagent, a cook and a bistro. It was not simply that we were being declined food – as this was not out of the ordinary on our test – it was that we were being checked out with certifiable disdain.

On earlier days, the reactions had consistently been happy and excited, in any event, when they had been not able to help us. In Bromyard, nonetheless, there was a clear sensation of doubt and distrust.

'I think our karma has lapsed,' moaned Ben after our fourth sequential dismissal – a new record.

'I puzzle over whether it's us, or then again on the off chance that it's Bromyard?' I inquired. 'Most certainly Bromyard. This spot is brimming with hopeless people.'

'Perhaps. Despite the fact that, we're both looking especially sad today. Neither of us have shaved in more than seven days, we didn't get a lot of rest the previous evening, and our garments smell truly bad.'

'Yet we've actually got our appeal and mind, haven't we?' 'Possibly that is hailing, as well,' I suggested.

Our incrimination of Bromyard was saved by the benevolence of one woman. Exactly when we were going to discount a whole town, the woman behind the counter in Loafers Patisserie was a beam of daylight, in a generally cloudy town. This is an analogy, coincidentally; the entire town was in reality extremely radiant when we were there. She snickered away hesitantly as we told her of our test and afterward gave us each a French-bread pizza and a pasty.

We sat on the asphalt outside Loafers and had our lunch. Similarly as we were warming to Bromyard, and lament being so disparaging of it, we saw one of the most surprising and awful sights that it is feasible to find in this world; a monster parade of all of the distinctive Morris Dancing gatherings, consolidated in one long unnerving Morris Dancing snake. Also they were moving towards us.

We jeered down our pasties, hopped on our bicycles, and left Bromyard as fast as we could.

A woman from neighboring Bishop's Frome, named Violet Eveson – the granddaughter of a nearby jump producer – kicked the bucket in 1993 leaving £47million in a trust store for nearby upgrades. At that point, this was considered the largest

at any point single gift to a cause in the UK. This isn't especially applicable. I simply needed to feature that there are (or possibly were) other great individuals in the Bromyard region, other than the woman from Loafers Patisserie.

We were before long out of Bromyard, and afterward out of Herefordshire and into Shropshire. We pushed through the town of Collington and the market town of Tenbury Wells ceaselessly and arrived at Ludlow at around 5pm.

Our visit agreed with one more celebration. The roads were loaded with revelers for the Ludlow Food Festival – our third celebration in 12 hours. There was clearly a buzz of energy related with every one of these celebrations, which was extraordinary to encounter, however the drawback was that convenience turned out to be such a ton harder to find.

We asked at almost twelve inns, bars and B&Bs around, yet were told by every one of them that they were full. Our proposals of help were additionally undesirable as every foundation had guaranteed they were completely set up to adapt to the inundation of individuals to the town.

Ludlow is a curious little town, overwhelmed by the noteworthy Ludlow Castle. The town has just about 500 recorded structures, and flaunts some remarkable middle age and Tudor engineering. Its connects to gastronomy don't end with the Food Festival either; as of not long ago, it had more Michelin-featured cafés than some other town in the UK.

We passed a house on one of the cobbled backstreets with a sign in the window which said: 'Convenience'. I thumped on the door.

A woman in her late sixties addressed the entryway. She had dazzling white hair and a major grin. We clarified that we had seen the sign in her window, and that we were searching for some place to sleep.

'Well, I do have an extra room. Yet, I seldom have anybody remaining. I don't promote, and no one will in general walk thusly,' she said.

We made it clear from the start that we had no cash, and that we didn't need her to feel under any commitment to give two odd men access to her house.

'Well, it's consistently great to have organization, so assuming you're truly frantic then I'd be extremely glad for you both to remain,' she said. Ben and I checked out one another. There was a brief delay before we turned around to the woman, and said, in amazing unison:

'We're desperate!'

The woman's name was Monica, and she had lived in Ludlow for almost 30

years. We wheeled our bicycles around to the back garden, which was a story lower than the front of her home, as it was worked onto the lofty Ludlow slope. She showed us to our room and afterward inquired as to whether she could make us anything for dinner.

'That is extremely sort of you,' said Ben, 'yet we're interfering enough all things considered. We'll have the option to get some food around, ideally. We've become very great at getting stuff for free.'

'I bet you have, assuming you've endure this far.'

'Is there anything we can get you?' asked Ben, understanding that it was somewhat of a dumb inquiry thinking about that we had no money.

'Really, indeed, hopefully you will get some milk for breakfast.'

'alright… obviously… a walk in the park,' said Ben.

Monica gave us a key to the front entryway and we set out to hit the town.

'How are we going to get milk? Are we must shoplift, or track down a cow to drain?' I asked.

'We'll figure something out. I was just being pleasant. I didn't anticipate that she should really request that we get anything. Ludlow, child!' said Ben.

We strolled back up to the palace where the food celebration was occurring. Confirmation was £5, however there was no one monitoring the entryway so we nipped inside to see, similarly as the last couple of slows down were getting together their things.

We had organized to meet our mums and lady friends for lunch in Shrewsbury the next day, and despite the fact that I had effectively sent my mum a birthday card, I didn't have any kind of present to give her.

Being a sharp foodie, I realized she would adore anything sold at a food celebration. In a mad brief asking binge I pitched my predicament to the leftover slow down holders in the expectation of certain gifts. Ben snuck outside in the shadows, humiliated by my constancy. I was compensated with the following:

Two jugs of cider
A container of elderflower
cheerful Dried cranberries
Pate
Pickled pecans
Dried blended
herbs
Sweet stew plunging sauce

In for my entire life, even at my generally liberal, I don't think I had purchased my mum a superior present.

'Oh my goodness! That is unimaginable,' said Ben outside. 'You're getting altogether too great at this blagging. How on earth did you get all that?'

'This is the thing that happens when you're not there. I'm considering
going performance.' 'You wouldn't endure a large portion of a day without
me. In any case, your mum will not need
all of that. We should have some of it now for dinner.'

'Turf off! This is my mum's birthday present. How might you like it
assuming that I ate your mum's birthday present?'

'Well, it depends what it was. I got her a CD this year, so assuming you
ate that I would think that it is somewhat bizarre, to be honest.'

'Well I would think that it is odd in case you ate my mum's
dried spices.' 'What might be said about the juice then?'

'I thought you were hungry?'

'I am, yet your mum needn't bother with two containers, isn't that right?
Also assuming that we drink one it implies you have less to convey
tomorrow.'

'What about we give a container to Monica as a
present?' 'alright, fine. Will we simply eat the pate
then?'

'No.'

Two hours after the fact, we wound up sitting in a bar off the really square
eating a plate of Paella and drinking our fourth brew of the evening.

We had got conversing with a couple in the road named Andy and Alison
and they had demanded getting us both a lager in the wake of catching wind
of our journey.

Andy and Alison were a couple in their mid-thirties, having a heartfelt end
of the week from their bustling working lives in Bristol. Regularly when we
related to individuals a portion of the encounters we had en route, their eyes
would coat over and they would wish they had never asked.

With Andy, be that as it may, he needed to know without question, each
and every detail of our trip.

'I think what you're doing is truly invigorating,' he said.

'Truly? Much thanks to you,' I said, not completely getting what the
expression meant.

'Truly, folks, I believe it's simply splendid what you're doing. There
should be some alternate way I can assist you with your excursion? What do
you still need?'

'Much appreciated, Andy, I believe we're basically completely kitted out,'
said Ben. 'Additionally, you've quite recently gotten us a lager. That is all
we need.'

Andy wasn't going to surrender that
without any problem. 'I accept you both

have helmets?'

'Well… definitely, we've somewhat got one cap that we take it in goes to wear,' I said.

'ha… ' said Andy, expecting we were kidding and afterward understanding that we weren't. 'My statement, you're not kidding? You share a protective cap? Well I do a touch of kite-surfing and I have an extra protective cap back at the inn assuming one of you wouldn't fret resembling a prat.'

'I wouldn't fret appearing as though a prat,' said Ben.

Andy gave us headings, and we made a plan to cycle over to their lodging the next morning. He then, at that point, gotten us both one more lager and figured out how to convince the man behind the bar to figure us out with a plate of paella each.

Whilst we were eating, Andy and Alison were conversing with others in the bar about us, and after we had completed the process of eating we were purchased another two pints. We at long last bid farewell and staggered out of the bar at 11.15pm toward the finish of one more important evening.

'DAMN!' yelled Ben as we lurched across the square. 'I almost forgot. We haven't got Monica any milk yet.'

Getting free milk in Ludlow at 11.15pm is definitely not a simple assignment. Every one of the shops and eateries had shut, and it was past the point where it is possible to thump on arbitrary individuals' entryways. There were no cows about, by the same token. We gave one of bars a shot the principle square however were informed that the kitchen was shut. We then tried another pub, and we were met at the door by the landlady.

'Sorry young men. We're shutting. Last requests have been served,' she said. 'As a matter of fact, we're attempting to get hold of some milk. I don't assume you've got any here that we can have?'

'Milk? Why you want milk? What amount do you want?' she inquired.

'It's a boring tale. Fundamentally, we guaranteed we'd get an old woman some milk, yet we don't have any cash and every one of the shops are shut. We needn't bother with a lot. Just a large portion of a 16 ounces or thereabouts,' said Ben.

'Great,' said the woman, 'I'll see what I can do.' She returned a couple of moments later.

'The gourmet specialist said they spent the remainder of their milk a couple of hours prior on the grounds that it's been so occupied. They've just got these, which they've been utilizing for the teas and espressos.' gave over

a transporter pack containing smaller than expected UHT milk
segments and a yogurt pot. 'I figured you could possibly purge them into this
plastic pot to make it look like genuine milk.'
    'Great. Much thanks to you, you're a lifeline,' said Ben.

In Monica's kitchen, which was down a stairway on a similar level as the
back garden, we exhausted all of the milk segments into the pot. There were
25 minimal 12ml pots, which equalled 300ml – simply over a large portion of
a pint.

Rob, Newent Onion Fayre

Onions

Sweetcorn

Wurzel from Motorhead, Newent Onion Fayre

More onions

Gee at the Newent Onion Fayre

Day 9 – Family reunion

Ludlow to Ellesmere – 45 miles

For the second successive morning, we got up in a comfortable extra room with horrendous headaches. It wasn't the way we envisioned our poor journey to John O'Groats would come to fruition, yet we were more than content with how it was unfolding.

Monica was at that point in the kitchen when we went first
floor. 'Thank you kindly again for allowing us to remain,' said
Ben.

'It was my pleasure. I trust you approved of simply a twofold bed. I would rather not assume you're gay,' she said, all the way out of the blue.

'No, we're not a couple. Ben continues to attempt to lure me however I'm not going to surrender to him,' I replied.

'Well, whether or not you're gay, it doesn't make any difference to me. Grab breakfast.'

We found a spot at the table in Monica's kitchen for almost two hours.

She had been somewhat careful about enlightening us a lot regarding herself in any case – and as it should be – yet after she understood our honest goals, she loose completely.

She filled us in regarding her life, and how she had been a medical caretaker during the conflict, and had a child with a Canadian fighter at an extremely youthful age. She had lamentably surrendered the child for reception, as she believed she was too youthful to even consider taking care of it. She afterward came to Ludlow riding a horse to visit companions who lived in the town, and had remained there ever since.

In 2005 she received a letter from her daughter – then in her fifties – who had managed to track her down. The girl lived in Canada however traveled to Ludlow straight away when Monica proposed it. The two have been very close from that point forward, and Monica has visited her girl in Canada a few times.

'That is mind blowing,' I said. 'Also how does your little girl feel about being taken on? Is there any kind of resentment?'

'None whatsoever. She totally sees how hard it was for me. Things were altogether different in those days. And besides, she was looked after by an amazing family and as far as she's concerned, they are her parents, but she has definitely found a new friend in me and we are both enjoying getting to know each other.'

'That is truly beautiful. Shouldn't something be said about you? Do you have any second thoughts?' asked Ben tentatively.

'Indeed, obviously. Never a day passed by when I didn't ponder her, and how I had parted with her. It changed for what seems like forever. That is the reason I won't ever wed. I didn't at any point feel anybody could at any point have the option to comprehend me appropriately. As I say, things were altogether different in those days – it's what I needed to do. However, we're compensating for it now. She's coming over again one week from now with her family. She has two offspring of her own. They think it is extraordinary having three grannies, as it implies they get an additional a present on their birthday celebrations and at Christmas.' Her face was loaded up with bliss as she watched out of the window, her eyes gushing as she spoke.

'And shouldn't something be said about her dad? Has she figured out how to find him? Are you still in touch with him?' I asked, anxious to discover more.

'No, no. She attempted, however I don't recall his name. Indeed, I don't recollect which officer it was that got me pregnant. There was more than one Canadian warrior during that time,' she said cheerfully. Neither of us very knew how to react to this.

'Goodness, I almost neglected. We got some juice for you from the food celebration the previous evening,' I said, fishing it from my rucksack.

Monica was charmed with her juice and satisfied that she had gone with her senses and permitted us both to stay.

'I'm the one that ought to much obliged. I feel like I've made two new companions,' she said.

After an extended pursuit we tracked down Andy and Alison's lodging – the alluring looking Dinham Hall Hotel.

'They've looked at as of now, yet they left this protective cap and this container of energy powder with me and said you would call past to get it,' said the man at gathering. He gave over the kite-riding head protector, which was fundamentally a full accident cap, yet without the visor part, and a large portion of a container of powdered Lucozade (other caffeinated drinks are accessible). Assuming that Ben planned to resemble a prat in an accident cap, basically he would be a prat loaded with energy.

'Mr and Mrs Jacobs enlightened me regarding your test,' he said. 'It seems like an extraordinary thought. The inn would be glad to offer you both breakfast.'

'Thank you, if by some stroke of good luck we'd known. We've recently topped off on grain and toast at the spot we remained,' said Ben. 'However, much appreciated especially for the deal. We truly appreciate it.'

On the exit from the inn we found Andy and Alison in the street.

Not in a real sense. That would have been very clumsy.

'Ahhh, there you are,' said Andy. 'We figured we probably won't see you before we left. We were simply triumphing when it's all said and done a last glance around town.'

We expressed gratitude toward them both for the cap and Lucozade, and Andy by and by repeated that he thought what we were doing was 'invigorating.' The more we heard it, the more we preferred it. He was basically saying that we resembled current Mother Theresas.

It was 10.30am when we left Ludlow. Shrewsbury was 25 miles away, and we were expected there for lunch.

We shrouded those 25 miles in around two hours, which was perhaps our quickest segment of the whole outing. The course climbed bit by bit for the initial eight miles along lovely little nation paths, and we traveled through the towns of Culmington and Pedlar's Rest.

'Look, Pedlar's rest. We're pedlars. I feel that implies we should stop for a rest,' gasped Ben.

'No, we're pedallers, not pedlars. Keep pedalling.'

The street at last arrived at its pinnacle a mile or so before the town of Church Stretton prior to joining an old Roman street, which followed close by the bustling A49. It was splendid to cycle along; an abandoned street extending into the distance as straight as a runway. The A-street had taken all the traffic and we were totally alone.

I cycled for almost four miles no-gave. I can read your mind; 'my god, this person is cool', and you would be correct. On that short stretch of Roman street in Shropshire, I was the coolest god-damn mofo on earth. That was, until my wheel got a pothole and I almost wound up in hospital.

I figured out how to snatch the handlebars, yet the bicycle had effectively been lost course and the front wheel had gotten the grass skirt. My right foot then slipped from the pedal and the bike skidded from underneath me and clattered down the street. I had some way or another figured out how to stay upstanding and was totally unhurt.

Ben, who had been following simply behind me, figured out how to slip to try not to hit me and ground to a halt close by, where he continued to criticize me for cycling no-handed.

Thankfully, The Falcon was additionally safe and we had the option to finish the last couple of miles into Shrewsbury without episode. I kept my hands immovably on the handlebars the whole way.

We were not ready for the cheers of six invigorated ladies as we cycled up Shrewsbury's central avenue. Briefly, we thought we had a few groupies, until we perceived the embarrassingly boisterous whoops just like those of our families. Both of our mums, sisters, my better half and Ben's sweetheart had made the excursion from Northampton to eat with us. We had just been out and about for nine days, yet it was truly inspiring to see their recognizable faces once more. They were amazed by our assets, and enjoyed extraordinary ridiculing The Falcon, Ben's protective cap and my suit trousers.

We strolled with them to a bar that they had spotted by the river.

'I bet you young men will appreciate having an appropriate dinner purchased for you,' said Ben's mum.

'Really, I don't believe we're permitted to allow you to get us lunch, I'm apprehensive,' I said. 'We concluded that it would be contrary to the guidelines to acknowledge anything from companions and family.'

'Crikey, that is unfeeling. Who made these principles?'

she inquired. 'George did!' said Ben bluntly.

'The fact was to depend on the liberality of individuals from people in general, rather than loved ones,' I said.

'Definitely, yet this is only one dinner,' said Ben.

'It is, however I would in any case feel like we cheated assuming we get purchased a supper. In case you need, you can allow them to get you a feast and I'll attempt to get nourishment for nothing, similar to we have been doing.'

'It would be great if we would all eat together, however,' said my sister.

'We'll attempt to work our appeal in the bar,' I said.

After nine fruitful long periods of gaining bicycles, garments, convenience and incalculable suppers free of charge, we were anticipating dazzling our friends and family with our skills.

'So your family will be in every way paying for their Sunday broils, however you need yours free of charge?' said the woman behind the bar.

'Indeed, I realize it sounds extremely brazen. We don't need to eat as old as. Any food that you can extra, and we're glad to wash dishes or clean tables consequently,' I said.

'We have staff to do that,' she said indignantly. There was an off-kilter mix of feet from our family behind us. Things weren't going very to plan.

'alright, I can most likely figure you out with some bread and butter,' she said.

We sat and ate our meat and potatoes while the others all got into their Sunday broils. It was merciless, however the sun was sparkling and we were both sitting in a bar garden by the stream with our three most loved ladies. Things might have been worse.

'Here, I'm not going to have the option to eat all of this. You young men have a few,' said Ben's mum, pushing a plate of dish meat before us. Ben viewed at me like he was looking for approval.

'You eat it assuming you need, mate. I'm not going to have any, on the grounds that it's actually tolerating help from loved ones,' I said.

'However these are simply extras that will go to waste.'

'Indeed, yet they are just extras since they are here eating as a result of us,' I said, attempting to make light of the amount of a fanatic for 'the standards' I was being.

'My god, you're difficult work,' said Ben. 'So it would be alright for me to eat extras from any other individual's plate in this bar, as long as they are not our companions or family?'

'Exactly.'

'He's a severe one, isn't he?' said Ben's mum.

'Enlighten me concerning it. It would be more unwinding going on a bicycle ride with Hitler. Recently he was battling up this enormous slope on his moronic minimal five-speed racer, gasping away in light of the fact that it's such a poop little bicycle, and when he got to the top I recommended he consider hoping to update his bicycle to something better to make the cycling simpler. He just cycled past and gasped 'THIS WASN'T SUPPOSED TO BE EASY'. It resembles he needs to endure as much as possible.'

The whole table burst into giggling. I could just participate. I attempted frantically to think about motivation to legitimize my conduct, however I realized Ben was correct. I figure a piece of me needed to endure, as in the harder the test that we confronted, the a greater amount of an accomplishment it is finished it.

Cycling from Land's End to John O'Groats is an extraordinary accomplishment in itself. Doing the excursion unsupported is significantly a greater amount of an achievement. Finishing the outing without spending a solitary penny is a great accomplishment, and riding a totally deficient bicycle the whole way took it to the following level.

Perhaps I was in effect somewhat masochistic, however at that point would anyone say anyone is who attempts an actual test? That is its general purpose being a test; propelling yourself intellectually and truly past your comfort

zone.

I think Ben likewise felt marginally compromised by The Falcon. He didn't simply need me to improve bicycle to speed things up; he needed me to improve bicycle to return us based on level conditions. He considered The Falcon to be something that would upstage his achievement.

I didn't see it that way by any stretch of the imagination. It was essentially an individual test of all mine The Falcon however long I could. I had needed Pinky to make it the whole way to the highest point of Scotland as well, however Ben exchanged her at the first opportunity.

Ben was not especially fit or athletic. The nearest he got to actual exercise was strolling to the bar toward the finish of his street. For him to try and endeavor to cycle 1000 miles was amazing in itself. He didn't require a lacking bicycle to make it considerably more impressive.

We bid farewell in the vehicle leave, which was shockingly passionate. Not due to the vehicle leave, you comprehend. Being brought together, but momentarily, with our family had given us both a feeling of safety and commonality. The possibility of returning into the obscure was unexpectedly very daunting.

After they had left, a woman in a long, floaty dress came stumbling into the vehicle leave towards us, as we were moving onto our bicycles. She was in her mid twenties, marginally hippyish and giggly. She was gripping an immense sandwich pack loaded with chocolate bars and sweets.

'Hi, sorry to trouble you,' she said. 'I trust you wouldn't fret, however I caught your discussion in the bar and I assemble you are cycling to John O'Groats, yet you're not permitted to spend any money?'

'Hey. Indeed believe it or not,' I said, somewhat stunned as it seemed we had our very first stalker.

'Relax, I'm not following you. My vehicle was left in this vehicle leave as well, and I needed to provide you with this pack of desserts. I figured it may come in handy.'

'Bless your heart. That is astonishing.' I said, as she ran back across the vehicle leave. The sack was full loaded with fun-size chocolate bars, hotcakes and desserts. Ben and I gawped at it like two or three kids at a fold shop.

'My pleasure. Best of luck!' she yelled back.

We ate a few bars there and afterward to compensate for our measly lunch and afterward consented to proportion the rest throughout the following not many days.

I trust what I am going to let you know fills you with as much indignation and dissatisfaction as it did me.

Let me set everything up for you. It is Christmas Eve, very nearly three months after we finished the outing (Dammit! I trust I haven't spoilt the consummation for you). Ben and his family have been welcome to my folks' home for supper. We as a whole had an incredible evening and drank an excessive lot of when the discussion went to our bicycle ride. Somebody referenced the day that we as a whole met in Shrewsbury and afterward Ben and I thought back with regards to the hippy young lady and the sack of desserts. Now, my mum burst out chuckling and afterward immediately put her hand over her mouth.

'What's so interesting?' I asked.

'Nothing. Simply snickering concerning what fun we had that day,' she said. 'For what reason did you giggle when I referenced

the hippy girl?'
'Did I?'
'Yes. You did.'
'Gracious, no
reason.'

She chuckled again and afterward clenched down on her clench hand like she had recently placed her foot in something. Allegorically, obviously; my mum's rug is very clean.

'Well, concerning that sack of desserts. I sort of gave it to the young lady to provide for you,' she said.

'You did what?' I said, not accepting what I was hearing.

'I carried those chocolates with me to provide for you, however when I heard how truly you were taking 'the standards' I figured I would give it to another person to provide for you.'

'When? How? I actually don't comprehend.' I could experience a displeasure rising within me.

'I saw her in the vehicle leave before we left and perceived her from the bar, so while you were all talking I let her know you doing and inquired as to whether she could give you the desserts when we had left. Apologies, I figured you would appreciate it.'

'obviously we liked it, yet that is on the grounds that we thought it was from an irregular, agreeable more odd, not my own mum,' I said, angrier than I had addressed my mum since being a teenager.

'I figured you would perceive the chocolates just like similar ones I regularly buy?'

'What? Giggles? Better believe it, mum, since you're the main individual on the planet who might purchase them?'

'They weren't Snickers. They were Racers – Aldi's own-image Snickers.'

'Well you're by all account not the only individual on the planet who shops at ridiculous Aldi, either.'

There was an awkward quiet around the room and some abnormal clamors from Ben, who was gotten between needing to concur with me and not having any desire to scrutinize my mum.

I realize her aims were great, yet I felt that she had subverted all that we were attempting to accomplish. She recently chuckled and said I was being sensational, yet assuming I had slipped her some carbs during one of her freaky weight control plans, or slipped some sugar into her tea during Lent then I would be formally abandoned in no time. Mums don't generally know best.

So the writing is on the wall. We fizzled. The entire test totally debased by an honest pack of desserts given by my own mum. I can guarantee you that until that second on Christmas Eve, neither Ben nor I had a solitary piece of information that our test had been messed with. In case you can pardon us this one mix-up, I can guarantee you that it was the first and keep going of such examples on the trip.

The curiosity benefit of cycling in thick woolen suit pants had worn off before long leaving Land's End, and after nine days I had developed to loathe them with a passion.

I had moved every advantage the extent that my knee, which circulated air through my lower leg, however the detriment was that it made a tight, thick band of texture that scoured and abraded, and totally fixed in the top portion of my leg. It could be said, my leg was cooking in an encased pack of hot perspiration. I like that this isn't the most delightful of depictions, however it's the main way I can pass on the discomfort.

To exacerbate the situation, as the pants were around eight sizes too enormous for myself and must be attached with bailer twine and turned over at the abdomen band a few times, they cut into my tissue like the string on a joint of pork. In the rankling sun, my uncovered cushy layers had become pork scratchings.

Regardless of the inconvenience, we had a simple evening time's cycling with the landscape seldom adjusting from its even level. However, the disposition was dismal. We both concurred that gathering our families had been a poorly conceived notion, looking back. It was extraordinary to invest energy with them, however it had broken our concentration. Following nine days without such contact, we had become used to not knowing who we would meet every day, where our next dinner would come from and what kind of encounters we would have. Having that short insight back in ordinariness caused us both to feel undeniably more secluded and forlorn than we had before.

'I stop for a minute,' said Ben, 'it's made still up in the air than any other time to get

to John O'Groats when possible.'

'Me as well. It's discouraging to imagine that they will be in every way back home currently, sitting on the couch, drinking tea, making whatever they like for supper. Here we are, perched on a grass skirt by the roadside in screw knows-where not understanding where we're resting tonight.'

'interestingly, from what they were all colloquialism at noon, it seems like they are altogether extremely desirous of what we're doing and would like to be here than at home on the sofa.'

Fortunately, this snapshot of dejection just went on around two hours. As we began to eat up the miles through the enchanting Shropshire open country, things abruptly felt much better.

It was evident that convenience would be elusive as civilisation was practically non-existent. The town of Little Ness was, as you would anticipate, very little, and Stanwardine-in-the-Fields ought to be renamed One-house-in-a-Field.

About 20 miles past Shrewsbury we arrived at the modest community of Ellesmere. It was 7.30pm and simply on the edges of town we passed a tight boat marina.

'For what reason don't we attempt to blag a boat for the evening?' proposed Ben, grinding to a halt by the gate.

'Without a doubt the boats in the marina will be brimming with individuals? How about we simply head into the town and attempt and track down some place there,' I said.

'Goodness continue, it merits an attempt. There may be some vacant boats.' 'Okay,' I sighed.

There were a few boats restricted in the marina yet no indication of something going on under the surface either ashore or water. Ben thumped on the entryway of a house that appeared to serve as the marina's office.

'There's no one in. We should go,' I said.

'Hold tight. Allow them an opportunity. See, somebody's coming.'

A little man with a managed silver facial hair growth and trimmed silver hair addressed the entryway. He appeared to be indistinguishable from Mr Hankey – my GCSE Media Studies instructor. What? You mean you don't have a clue what Mr Hankey resembles? That is a disgrace, since this man might have been his twin brother.

'Hi?' he said questioningly.

'Hi. I apologize for disturbing you, yet are you accountable for the marina here?' asked Ben.

'Uh huh,' he nodded.

'Incredible. We're cycling the length of the country without going through any cash whatsoever, and we were contemplating whether there is any shot at us dozing in a boat tonight.'

'For what reason would you like to rest in a boat?' 'That is the thing that I asked him,' I said.

'Well we've been going for nine days at this point and we've dozed in B&Bs, individuals' homes, stables, all sort of spots. At the point when we saw this spot we figured it very well may be amusing to rest on a boat.'

The man messed up his face and squeezed his palms against his temple.

'Fellows, chaps, chaps. It's almost 8pm. I'm simply eating and settling down
before the television and afterward both of you messy buggers turn
up on my doorstep.'

'I know, we're truly heartbroken. We'll take a shot around. Sorry for irritating you,' I said.

'No, no, no, it's alright. I would like to help you all out,' he said, looking somewhat less hopeless. 'I'm simply working out how I can.'

He stopped for a moment.

'Okay. I want to figure you out with a boat for the night.'

The sun was setting as Neil – the marina supervisor – strolled us along the bank of the marina. It was a truly lovely second. The entirely still water mirroring an ideal orange sky, and we were being given our own boat for the evening. Ben had increased present expectations at this point again.

'Move on board!' said Neil. 'I must drive her back to the opposite end so I can attach you to the mains.'

'Don't stress over that, Neil. We wouldn't fret not having power. We simply needed some place to rest,' said Ben.

'Nah, don't be senseless. You will not have the option to completely see the value in life in a limited boat without electricity.'

As well similar to a marina for exclusive boats, Blackwater Meadow Marina likewise had an armada of recruit boats, one of which Neil had allowed us to have for the evening. He continued to apologize lavishly that it had not been completely cleaned.

I had never been on a trench boat and I was absolutely stunned when I descended through the incubate. I'm not misrepresenting when I say it was more extravagant than my own home. It had a parlor region with a level screen TV,
DVD player and hello there fi; a feasting region with seating for a considerable length of time; a completely fitted kitchen that incorporated a dishwasher; a washroom with a genuine shower, and two rooms – one of which had an en-suite. It was seemingly the most rich convenience of the trip.

Ben guaranteed the twofold room, as the boat thought had been his, and I took one of the single beds in the other bedroom.

After providing us with the visit through the boat, Neil vanished back to his home and got back with a jug of red wine, four jars of lager, some teabags and a large portion of a 16 ounces of milk.

'I'm apprehensive my cabinets are vacant right now,' he said, 'any other way I would have offered you some supper, as well. The town is just a brief stroll not too far off, so I'm certain you'll find something effectively enough there.'

Neil had turned into a main competitor for the 'most pleasant individual that we met' grant. There was no such thing as this honor, incidentally, yet assuming it had then Neil would have been a main contender.

We drank a jar of brew each and strolled the five minutes into Ellesmere town focus. I don't intend to propose that we really wanted the Dutch boldness just to wander into the town place. Ellesmere is truly not that intimidating.

We called into an Indian café in the wake of being tricked in by the smell. The youthful server let us know we would need to return on Tuesday to address the administrator. It was Sunday. Sitting tight two days for the chance of getting a free curry was a little impractical.

We had one more dismissal from a focus point however at that point a caring man from the kebab house provided us with a huge piece of chips to share.

'If by some stroke of good luck we had some bread,' I said, 'then, at that point, we could have chip butties and wine back on our boat.' That was a line I never figured I would hear myself say.

'Extraordinary thought. I'm certain we can get some flat bread from the Co-operation around there,' said Ben.

Ben was not recommending that Co-operation is infamous for selling old bread. He implied that shops that sell bread are probably going to have excess stock toward the day's end that they are compelled to toss out. It was 9.30pm, by this point, and the shop was 30 minutes from closing.

'We don't will quite often have an excess of bread left by the day's end yet I'll surely search for you,' said the woman in Co-operation, who had the face and way of an amicable lollypop-lady.

'Here you go. Is this okay?' she said, holding out a little portion of newly prepared storage facility bread. At the point when I say 'newly prepared', I mean newly heated a couple of days previously.

'That is awesome. Much obliged without question,' I said. 'We figured out how to get a few chips not too far off, so we will make chip butties.'

'What a smart thought. You surely are on an experience. Do you have any margarine and ketchup?'

'No. Much thanks to you. We'll approve of simply chips and bread,' I said.

'Don't be senseless. You can't have an appropriate chip butty without spread and ketchup. Can you?'

'No, I assume not.'

'Stand by there, I'll be back in a moment.' She returned a moment later with a bundle of spread and container of Heinz Tomato Ketchup.

'Goodness, you're stunning. Be that as it may, how did you... ?

'Shhhhhh,' she intruded on, putting her finger to her lips, 'breakages.'

We had expected to see some component of liberality from the little autonomous foundations that we requested blessings at, yet we had expected the inverse from the large companies. We had expected that the measure of organization engaged with the bigger grocery stores would limit their capacity to show liberality. Nonetheless, we had been discredited on a few events. It seems that even working for a large corporation allows some element of free will. And if rules can't be bent, then there will always be 'breakages'.

If, similar to me, you were interested with regards to the beginning of the word 'ketchup' (No? Just me?), I will fill you in. It is believed that the word comes from the Malay word kēchap, which was likewise a sauce. Yet rather than being tomato based, it was produced using fish brackish water, spices, and flavors (not ideal in a chip butty). In the eighteenth and nineteenth hundreds of years the word was utilized as a conventional term for all vinegar based sauces and it was not until the twentieth century that the word became inseparable from the pureed tomatoes that we know today. Much obliged to you, Wikipedia.

Back on the boat we each gathered two tremendous chip butties, and opened the wine. It was an exquisite warm evening so we sat on the little deck at the rear of the boat.

Before our excursion began I envisioned a wide range of potential situations of where we may go through every evening and what kind of food we would eat. Sitting on the

deck of an extravagance narrowboat with two chip butties and a jug of wine had never at any point entered my perspective. Staying there with the splendid, brilliant Shropshire sky and the delicate lapping of the water on the boat, was the most substance I had felt in a long time.

The boat felt like it was influencing a ton, however when I ventured momentarily onto the land to beware of the bicycles the ground kept on influencing. We moved inside at about 12 PM and made some tea, to attempt to counterbalance the a large portion of a container of wine and two lagers that we had both consumed.

'What are you doing?' I asked Ben, who had been in the kitchen for some time.

'I'm simply washing my jeans,' he slurred. 'Alright. Why?'

'Cos they haven't been washed for days.'

'So you felt that 12 PM on a waterway boat would be the best an ideal opportunity to wash them? Have you not gained from my errors? How can you go to dry them?'

'You'll see. You'll see.'

I stayed there with some tea in one hand and the remaining parts of my brew in the other and paid attention to an Elvis Costello CD that we found in the pantry. I was upset by a recognizable murmuring noise.

'Are your jeans in the microwave?'

'That's right, they sure are. Two minutes ought to do it.'

'That is virtuoso,' I said, bouncing from my seat and joining Ben in the kitchen.

It was extremely odd to stand and watch some Union Jack fighter shorts pivot on a microwave plate. It's not something I had at any point done, nor something I can at any point envision doing in the future.

DING.

'They're done!' said Ben excitedly.

He removed the fighter shorts from the microwave.

'Crap!' he said, tossing them to me. 'They're wicked hot.'

'Arghh,' I said, getting them, 'and they're not dry. It resembles an outrageous adaptation of those hot towels that you get in an Indian eatery. But, I'm not cleaning up with these. What's this earthy colored stain on the arse?'

'That wasn't there previously!' yelled Ben.

'It's a consume mark! You've consumed your jeans and presently you have a super durable pallet blemish on your arse.'

Day 10 – A Welsh puncture

Ellesmere to Up Holland – 58 miles

We were welcomed in the first part of the day by Neil with a tremendous heap of toast and jam.
After a long, comfortable breakfast at hand, we were out and about by 10.30am.

'What the heck? Why the street signs are in Welsh? When did we enter Wales?' said Ben, slipping to a halt.
'Hold tight, I'll check,' I said, pulling the day's headings from my pocket.
It was too hard to even think about cycling while holding the course book, so each morning
I would record the directions for that day onto a piece of paper which I then, at that point, kept in my pocket. This entire cycle took no less than ten minutes.

'It says here: 'Among Ellesmere and Penley, the visit momentarily enters Wales

– the primary sign being the street signs'. Well they were correct with regards to that. Indeed, apparently we are in Wales.'

'Cool. Britain tick,' said Ben.

'Indeed, however we'll be back in England soon. We can't get to Scotland through Wales, you div.'

'No doubt, I realized that. I was simply saying.'

We were going to set off when I peered down and saw a colossal thistle standing out of The Falcon's front tyre.

'I think we have a slight issue,' I said, taking out the thistle and holding it up to Ben.

'Gracious, bollocks. Is it level? What are we going to do?'

'It's totally level. I surmise we simply walk and ask at the principal house that we check whether they have a cut fix kit.'

'For what reason did you need to proceed to get a cut in no place?' 'I didn't decide to get a cut here did I?'

'No, I'm trying to say that your wanky bicycle has caused us no limit to problems.'

'It's a cut, for the good of god. It might have straightforwardly happened to your strong bike.'

'However it didn't, did it? It happened to that heap of crap.'

'You're being somewhat absurd. We've cycled almost 400 miles and this is our first cut. That is very great going, right? It's simply a cut. It's no large deal.'

Half an hour of strolling later we arrived at a gathering of three houses. There was no reply at the main house. Or on the other hand the second. In the long run, following a couple of moments, a man with a grin that filled his whole face addressed the entryway of the third house. He chuckled when he saw us, like he had been expecting us.

'Hellooo,' he said, 'have you come to look round the house?'

'Fail, no,' I said, 'Sorry to trouble you. Are you anticipating individuals?' 'No, no, it's fine. How might I help you?'

'We're on a bicycle ride and we have a cut. I don't assume you have a cut fix unit and a siphon that we could borrow?'

'Oooh, that will be the thistles,' he said. 'They're cutting the hedgerows today and there are thistles all around the road.'

'I let you know it wasn't my issue, Ben.'

Ben was too bustling gazing in dismay at the one who had addressed the entryway. In spite of living in Wales, he had a particular Yorkshire complement. His enlivened face was loaded with character, remembering a special triple bended dimple for his jawline. I can just expect that this was a truly mind-blowing aftereffect of grinning and snickering. He resembled a friendly figure of deformity, and I half anticipated that water should spray from his mouth.

'I think I've presumably got a maintenance unit in the carport. I'll proceed to view you. All that's a cycle muddled right now as I'm currently moving,' he said, highlighting the For Sale sign toward the finish of his carport. 'I have somebody coming to check out any moment now. That is the reason I was somewhat befuddled when you went to the entryway. I go by Peter, by the way.'

Peter was a certified person. He arose out of the carport with an unopened cut fix pack and a powerful tire pump.

'Here you go,' he said. 'I realized I had one some place. Not certain why, as I've not possessed a bicycle since I was a child.'

Peter had resided in Wales for a very long time, and was intending to move to a more modest house right over the boundary in England. During the ten minutes that we spent fixing the cut in his carport, he didn't quit chuckling. It was exceptionally invigorating, and was the ideal counteractant to Ben who groaned ceaselessly about The Falcon. He unhesitatingly guaranteed that he could eliminate the internal cylinder from The Falcon's tire with his uncovered hands and that 'tire switches are for losers'.

'How about you simply get two or three teaspoons out of the excursion set?
It
would be much speedier,' I said.

'No, I can do it. It's simple. Just you watch,' he said, gritting his teeth and becoming marginally purple as he pulled and attempted to prise the internal cylinder from the tyre.

'You appear as though you're battling. How about you simply provide me with a few teaspoons? I could've had it off by now.'

'Hold tight!' he snapped, becoming blue. 'What use are teaspoons going to be anyway?'

'To use as tire switches. What did you think?'

He kept on endeavoring, so I ventured into his backpack and took out several spoons while he wasn't looking. After ten seconds, the inward cylinder was out and I hadn't needed to become blue.

'Gracious, I didn't figure it would be that simple,'
said Ben. 'Have you at any point really fixed a cut?' I
inquired. 'Well no, yet I realize they are annoying.'

Being raised in the country, I was accustomed to having penetrates as was genuinely skillful at fixing them. Ben, then again, was a cut fix virgin. He watched, in certifiable profound respect, as I set to work.

'What amount of time is it will require?'

he inquired. 'Five minutes.'

'Five minutes? I thought we would have been hanging around for ridiculous hours. I didn't understand it would be so quick.'

'I asked why you were so miserable.'

Peter remained over aside, watching us and chuckling the whole time.

'Both of you resemble a wedded couple,' he said.

Just as we were getting together, the bequest specialist maneuvered into the carport for certain forthcoming purchasers. Their countenances looked marginally muddled at seeing two oddly dressed men and their assets tossed across the driveway.

'We'll move. Much obliged such a great amount for the entirety of your assistance, Peter. Best of luck with the house move,' I said, as we wildly crushed everything into our backpacks and pushed our bicycles not too far off and out of sight.

'I'm exceptionally intrigued by your bicycle specialist abilities,'
said Ben. 'Much obliged. I can't really accept that you've never
had a cut in your life.'

'We don't get numerous thistles in London. In reality, I got a cut once, yet I was unable to be tried to fix it.'

'So what did you do?'

'I just purchased another bicycle instead.'

After Peter had referenced the support cutters, it ended up being undeniable that the street was canvassed in thistles. Just to play it safe, and to keep Ben glad, we pushed our bicycles for a large portion of a mile until the street was clear.

After only five miles in Wales we crossed once more into England, and the area of Cheshire. It was extremely fitting that in spite of the fact that it made up a minuscule part of our absolute course, Wales actually influenced our excursion by providing us with our main cut of the whole outing. What's more in spite of the fact that we didn't meet any certified Welsh individuals in Wales, the one Welsh occupant that we met was totally extraordinary; a fine envoy for the country.

We went through the town of Farndon, which has the National 24-hour Cycling Championship. The champs will quite often pile up mileage of north of 500 miles in a 24-hour time frame. This is very astounding considering we were covering around 60 miles in an eight hour day. The possibility of doing three of these stretches one after the other, at multiple times the speed, was boundless. I disdain legitimate competitors. They make most of us simply look rubbish.

We arrived at Chester and were somewhat disillusioned to find that its tenants didn't all seem as though the cast of Hollyoaks.

On the events that we went through other town places en route, we had both felt a slight sensation of claustrophobia and a longing to get once more into the open country. This was mostly in light of the fact that cycling in metropolitan regions is a great deal more requesting, and furthermore in light of the fact that individuals in towns would in general be more reluctant and dubious of us. Chester felt distinctive in some way. The actual town is exceptionally hitting with its combination of Roman, Medieval, Victorian and Tudor design. The roads were likewise loaded with travelers strolling the roads erratically, so we fitted in perfectly.

Chester was the last English town to tumble to William the Conqueror, and it has the most ridiculously complete city dividers in Britain. Two realities that I am certain you will be excited with.

Regardless of the entirety of the set of experiences and culture on offer, we had hunger issues purported into Subway to take a stab. Craig, the amicable South-African administrator, offered us a foot long sub and a beverage each. We ate half there and afterward, and reserved the other half away to eat out and about. I imply that allegorically, obviously; we didn't eat our food off the tarmac.

On the exit from town, we called into a bicycle shop called The Bike Factory, where a man mercifully oiled our bicycles and fixed Ben's brakes.

'The cycling's genuinely terrible among here and the Lake District,' he cautioned. 'You're going solidly into the core of all the business around Merseyside. Be cautious, in light of the fact that the vehicles don't possess a lot of energy for cyclists around there.'

Just a couple of moments subsequent to leaving Chester we were back in the excellent open country, with the revolting spread of the modern Ellesmere Port apparent in the distance.

'Perhaps our course evades all that terrible stuff,'
recommended Ben. 'I trust so,' I said, 'however I don't
think it does.'

'I frantically need a few shorts,' I said to Ben. 'My balls are horrendously uncomfortable.'

'No joking. I don't have a clue how you've endured for such a long time in those silly pants. I just dealt with a few days in those tracksuit bottoms and they were very comfortable. You should've cut the legs off those long ago.'

Ten days of wearing thick woolen suit pants had at last incurred significant damage and the perspiring, abrading and tingling had become excruciating.

'I likely should cut them off, yet that wouldn't stop them being awkward. I want some genuine shorts or my balls will deteriorate,' I said.

'Much obliged for that psychological picture,' said Ben, 'I just sicked up a touch of my Subway.'

We arrived at the town of Frodsham, where the town sign gladly brags its honor 'North West in Bloom – Best Small Town 2001'.

Ben detected a sign for Frodsham Leisure Center and we followed the street towards it in the desire for observing some to be deserted shorts. The Leisure Center ended up being a school, as well. The primary entryways were locked, yet we grabbed the eye of one of the women in the workplace who went to the entryway and opened it hesitantly.

'Would i be able to help you?' she asked, finding us and down.

'I trust so. Do you by any possibility have a lost property?' I

said. 'Have you lost something?'

'Not actually. We are watching out for some shorts.'

'Sorry, no. I don't approach the lost property cabinet I'm apprehensive.'

She had not been especially inviting, yet we could barely fault her.

We were a couple of peculiarly dressed men, on school property, requesting to have a scrounge through the lost property. It's no big surprise she didn't invite us in with open arms.

We plunked somewhere near a divider and attempted to empty a portion of the Lucozade energy powder into our water bottles. The breeze had gotten and the white powder blew surrounding us, similar to we were important for a revolting snow globe.

The entryway was opened a couple of moments later by a huge jock measured man, wearing a running vest and shorts. He had a very much tanned face and he gave us a harsh look, like he was going to thoroughly demolish us. His running vest was a gift shirt for the Coniston 14 street race in 1998. I preferred that he, alongside the remainder of the town (North West in Bloom – 2001), was holding tight to the recollections of the wonder days.

'Would i be able to assist you with anything, men of their word?' he asked in a compromising manner.

'Sorry, we're simply leaving. We're simply attempting to top off these caffeinated drinks,' said Ben.

'Goodness, is that what it is?' he chuckled. 'The women inside could see you on the CCTV and they thought you were accomplishing something with drugs. They requested that I come and investigate you.'

'Good gracious. Sorry. It's simply Lucozade, I guarantee,' said Ben.

'No concerns. It's simply that being a school and all we need to investigate these things. I think they thought you planned to have a go at managing to the children.' He ventured from the entryway and strolled towards us with his arm outstretched and a comforting grin on his face.

'The name's Mr Smiddy. I'm the head of PE. You can call me Martin.'

'Much appreciated, Mr Smiddy. I mean Martin. I apologize for being an annoyance, we'll be on
our way,' I said.

'You take as much time as is needed. No surge. All in all, they said you needed to examine our lost property? What's the arrangement, are you destitute or something?'

'Actually no, not exactly. We're cycling the whole length of the country without going through any cash, and I'm watching out for some shorts, rather than these suit trousers.'

'That sounds pretty insane. Why you didn't simply wear shorts from the start?'

'We had nothing toward the beginning. Simply some fighter shorts. We didn't have bicycles,' said Ben.

'You're joking?' he said. 'So you figured out how to blag all of this stuff from
individuals en route?'

'Yes.'

'That is astounding. You folks are frantic.' He shook his head, incapable to take everything in. 'I can figure you out for certain shorts. Accompany me. We'll see what else we can find for you both. You all break me up.'

He drove us down a couple of hallways and into the PE evolving rooms. It was whenever I first had been in a school changing room in ten years and it was satisfying to find the recognizable smell of sweat, mud and Lynx deodorant.

Mr Smiddy opened the store cabinet and rootled around inside. (As it turns out, the word 'rootle' doesn't get utilized sufficient nowadays). After he had completed the process of rootling, he arose with his arms loaded with dress and other irregular items.

'The main shorts I've found are for youngsters and they won't fit you. However, don't stress I'll figure you out with a few. Is any of this of utilization?' he said, discharging the substance onto one of the benches.

Never before had two developed men been so energized at seeing a heap of others' dismissed clothing. Mr Smiddy watched on with his arms collapsed, charmed to see our excitement.

'A belt. Astounding,' I said.

'Goodness, a Frodsham School shirt. Looks somewhat retro.'

'Here you go, Ben. Shades. You've been whining about getting flies in your eyes.'

'You are a legend, Mr Smiddy. Can we truly have these?' asked Ben.

'obviously, grab any of that. None of it has been asserted all year, every year. I'll proceed to attempt to get you some shorts.'

Mr Smiddy (it appeared to be off-base calling a PE educator by his first name, particularly as we were in the school evolving rooms), returned a couple of moments later conveying some the skimpiest running shorts I had at any point seen. They were produced using a velvety blue material and were cut along the edges to permit full leg movement.

'Amazing, much appreciated. Those look... errr... vaporous,' I said. 'Where did you get them from?'

'These are mine, however you're free to have them.'

'That is exceptionally kind, yet I would rather not take your own garments. I can attempt to get some shorts from elsewhere.' I should call attention to that this was an alternate pair of shorts to the ones he was wearing. I don't need you to think he had whipped off his shorts before us there and then.

'Trust me, I figure my children would be pleased to see the rear of these. Continue, attempt them on.'

'I think I'll need to give them a shot later. I'm... errr... going commando at the moment.'

'You haven't got any jeans, either?'

'Well, we have one sets each, however mine are broadcasting right now.' 'Pah, both of you are something different,' he snorted.

Frodsham was heaven contrasted with what we were confronted with straightaway. Soon after leaving the town, we joined the terrible Runcorn to Widnes street which is fundamentally a motorway that it is legitimate to cycle along. More vehicles ignored us the following not many miles than the whole rest of our excursion joined. I didn't count them all, so I can't make certain of this reality, yet I think it is very likely.

There was a hard shoulder which ought to have made things more secure, yet this was covered with vehicle sections and broken glass. We thought we were over the most exceedingly terrible of it, however at that point we saw the scary sight of Runcorn Bridge. The scaffold is formally called 'The Silver

Jubilee Bridge' trying to make it sound beautiful and curious. It's not. It's totally terrifying.

The actual extension would look very alluring, assuming that they moved to an alternate region of the planet, painted it an alternate tone and shut it to everybody except cyclists. It is, be that as it may, light green, arranged in a rambling mass of industry and utilized by north of 80,000 drivers a day.

The extension was opened in 1961 to cross the River Mersey and the Manchester Ship Canal. It is the main course across, albeit swimming appeared to be ideal. We showed up at the scaffold at the pinnacle of busy time and headed over to the roadside to design our attack.

The northward roadside, which we were on, had a very thin piece of asphalt, close to a foot wide, which appeared to fill no need at all. The Falcon would have been smooth and limited enough to float along this, yet had Ben endeavored to cycle along it on The Horse, his handlebars would have taken up portion of the left hand path, too.

Our course book referenced a 'walker walkway' on the contrary side of the extension, which was simply noticeable. It was a tantalizingly wide asphalt shielded from the street by a metal accident obstruction. The main issue being that among us and it were four paths of tenacious traffic.

Remember the PC game Frogger? All things considered, endeavoring to go across this

stretch of street, at busy time, with our bicycles would have been more enthusiastically than the last degree of Frogger. What's more we didn't have the advantage of having three lives. There was no decision except for to remain out and about that we were on, and simply go for it.

'Right, after this one,' said Ben, half-on board The Horse. 'No, no, stand by, after this one... No hold tight, prepared? After this one.' And so it went until ultimately we both limited onto our bicycles in wonderful synchronized fashion.

What followed was around five of the most frightening minutes of my life. The paths of traffic on the scaffold are really limited that there is no space for vehicles to give cyclists any opportunity. On two events Ben's handlebars were cut by passing vehicles. We lost count of the quantity of irate drivers who blared their horns at us like we were a genuine irritation to them. We kept our eyes zeroed in solidly out and about ahead and cycled as quick as we could.

Once clear of the scaffold, we were welcomed with more perspectives on beautiful compound plants and vehicle destroying yards.

After another ten miles, the course ultimately left the A-streets and reemerged the open country. We went through the towns of Eccleston and

Crank as the breeze began to get, and the scene turned out to be more undulating.

Not since Cornwall had we needed to get off from our bicycles due to a slope, however right away before the town of Skelmersdale, Ben conceded rout. I accepting this as a welcome greeting to walk, too.

'It's my lower leg muscles. They're truly throbbing today,' said Ben. 'What's your excuse?'

'I needn't bother with a reason. I can't be tried to cycle up this slope.' 'That doesn't seem like you. Regularly you like to suffer.'

'Better believe it, well we've languished enough over the beyond few hours.'

On arriving at the top, we maneuvered into a field and fell in the grass for a break. Shockingly, it was one of the most beautiful perspectives on the whole outing. We had a broad cornfield straightforwardly underneath us, which prompted more fields and afterward in the far distance the dim spread of Runcorn and Widnes. The far off murmur of traffic and industry was overwhelmed by the ensemble of birds, and during the 15 minutes we lay there, not a solitary vehicle passed.

'I'm prepared for bed,' said Ben. 'Me too.'

As if to insult our bed-prepared spirits, the principal fabricating that we went over, only a couple of moments later, was an extremely upmarket looking lodging – The Lancashire Manor Hotel.

'Thank you, God. See, it's predetermination,' said Ben, pulling over.

'It's somewhat out of our association, right? We've not remained in anything like this so far.'

'Worth an attempt right? They may have staff quarters or something that we can rest in.'

Within the inn didn't coordinate to the appeal of the outside, yet it was as yet far better than whatever else we had remained in. The gathering was unfilled, however a woman showed up from the back room after we rang the ringer, and we gave her our now all around practiced discourse. I won't exhaust you with it again.

'I'm heartbroken, we can't offer you a room, though it pains me to say so. We can offer you a rebate, yet the lodging is important for a chain and we can't simply give free rooms like that.'

'You don't need to tell them,' kidded Ben. 'We'll even tidy up the room a short time later. You will not realize we'd been there.'

'I'm grieved. I can't help. We wouldn't have the option to allow you to accomplish any work it is possible that, though it pains me to say so. There are a wide range of wellbeing and security and protection implications.'

We could detect that she needed to help, so chose to utilize our unmistakable advantage; the unfortunate, defenseless faces that prevailed upon Mrs Rogers.

'I can approve nothing myself, however I'll call my region supervisor and see what she says.' She hurried into the administrative center and afterward returned a couple of moments later.

'My administrator needs to know whether the inn will get any openness or media inclusion assuming we let you stay. That is to say, are you composing a book about it or anything?'

'Indeed, indeed, obviously. I will compose a book about it,' I shouted. 'What's more I'll make certain to say how extraordinary this inn is.'

'alright, amazing. I will not be a moment,' she said, getting back
to the workplace. 'I didn't realize you planned to compose a
book,' said Ben. 'Neither did I.'

We were both giggling when she returned.

'Right. I have you a space for the evening. Breakfast is 7am until 11am in the first part of the day. Supper is served until 9pm. What time will I book you a table for?'

'Supper?' Ben said.

'Breakfast?' I said.

'Yes. You eat and breakfast on us, as well. Will we say 8pm? That
gives you an hour.'

'Goodness. Much appreciated. Indeed, 8pm is awesome. Thank you.'

'They better have a pool,' kidded Ben as we strolled to our room.

'See us!' said Ben hurling himself onto one of the beds in our room. 'We've blagged an opulent hotel.'

'Don't you have a blameworthy outlook on the way that we just got this is on the grounds that they believe they will receive exposure in return?' I asked.

'Nah, course not. They'll disregard us in two or three days.'

'No, I don't mean blameworthy about deluding them. I mean don't you feel guilty about the fact that it's the first time we've got something just on the basis that they thought there was something in it for them? We are supposed to be testing people's natural generosity but the hotel was only generous because it thought it was going to get publicity.'

'Indeed, I guess you're correct,' said Ben. 'You're the person who said you were composing a book. However, she needed to help us. That is to say, she was a great individual yet couldn't do anything as a result of the bureaucracy.'

'I know. Relax, I'll deal with it. It simply feels somewhat like we cheated, that is all.'

'Good gracious, this shower is fucking stunning,' I yelled to Ben from the washroom two minutes after the fact. 'I bleeding love hotels!'

It didn't take me long to move past the liable feeling.

She really want not have tried booking us a table. We were the main individuals in the whole restaurant.

Dinner was extremely great yet somewhat awkward. It was weird enough having a conventional supper reclined across from Ben, when our discussion on the bicycles was normally based around who could do the most intense fart. It was additionally somewhat odd having a server that plainly needed to be anyplace other than serving us.

In the inn bar thereafter, Jaime-Lea – the server – was something else entirely. The second her shift got done, every last bit of her sharpness and antagonism disappeared and she was extraordinary amusing to talk to.

'So is it genuine that you both don't have a penny among you, and you have this way rummaging off of individuals?' she asked.

'Fundamentally. Yeah.'

'Reasonable play to ya,' she said subsequent to necking 33% of her half quart of ale. 'Assume you could do with a fuckin lager then?'

'Aww, much appreciated, however you don't have to get us drinks,' I said.

'I realize I don't, yet I want to. In any case, Gav behind the bar's had bugger all to do each and every evening. Should give him something to do.'

Like the eatery, the bar was totally vacant. 'Is it generally like this around here?' I asked.

'Better believe it, essentially,' said Jaime-Lea. 'We have meetings and weddings here some of the time, yet it's dead a large portion of the time.'

She took one more taste of her pint.

'Moronic spot to fabricate an inn, if you were to ask me,' she mumbled. Jaime-Lea got us another two pints, and Gav the barman got us a fourth. I'm not totally certain that both of them were really paying for the beverages, as we didn't see any cash go into the till. In any case, it's the prospect that counts.

'Haven't you got a home to return to?' Ben asked Jamie-Lea.

'Nah, I live in a level over the inn. There's no getting away from this grisly spot. I'm here day in and day out, even on my days off.'

She was practically sleeping on the bar when we stumbled down the passageway to our beds.

I take tremendous take pleasure in remaining in inns. It doesn't occur frequently, so when it does I am quick to take advantage of my visit. I stare at the TV in bed, since I can. I flick through the entirety of the diverse satellite stations, since we just have the essential ones at home. I drink whatever number of the various teas and espressos could be expected under the circumstances. I even beverage the home grown teas and have been known to eat the sugar sachets since they are there. I utilize the woolen clothes. I wear a shower cap. I use bubble shower and lotion. I wash my hair with cleanser AND conditioner. I dry my hair with the hair dryer. I now and then even read the Gideon Bible.

On this event, in any case, I disregarded each and every one of these extravagances and climbed straight into bed and rested. On account of the idea of our bicycle ride, every night's convenience was obscure until late into each evening. The nature of our lodgings became unimportant. All we really wanted was some sanctuary, and regardless of whether this came as a cow shed, a waterway boat or a visitor house, we were still as grateful. Things were stripped down to rudiments; a rich lodging was presently not an opulent inn, it was just some place to rest around evening time. During our visit at The Lancashire Manor Hotel, the TV wasn't turned on, the shower cap and lotions remained in their parcels, the tea and espresso plate stayed immaculate, and the Gideon Bible

stayed in the bedside drawer.

Day 11 – Singing for sandwiches

Up Holland to Milnthorpe – 67 miles

Jaime-Lea was serving at breakfast and she had returned to her zombie-like work persona. She dealt with a bashful grin as she brought us both an espresso, yet offered nothing in the method of conversation.

I found that the Lancashire Manor Hotel shut down before long our visit. Not as a result of us, I should add. It was a pitiful, yet some way or another anticipated end. How such a major inn had made due in such an arbitrary area for such a long time was an amazement in itself. Here I am surrendering them the compose that I guaranteed and it's presently all useless. Having said that, I haven't provided it with the most sparkling of surveys; plastered servers, stealing bar staff, an abandoned café, and its nearness to Runcorn. I do trust that the staff all secured positions somewhere else, however, and that Jamie-Lea found elsewhere to live.

Mr Smiddy's shorts were crazy. They were skirting on disgusting and scarcely legitimate. In contrast to most running shorts, these didn't have any kind of covering and were cut as far as possible up to the abdomen on each side. This implied that a segment of my Union Jack fighter shorts at the highest point of every thigh was on long-lasting showcase each time I moved my legs.

However, they were amazingly stimulating. I felt free. I felt freed. I felt stripped. Contrasted with the suit pants, they were mind blowing. I could feel the air on my legs – just as more close places. I unexpectedly felt more athletic, as well, similar to I had been wearing the pants pre-rivalry to keep warm, and presently I had changed into my legitimate sporting equipment. My legs in a split second felt more grounded, my body felt more empowered and I was chomping at the bit to go.

Soon subsequent to leaving the lodging we found ourselves miserably lost.

We had arrived at the town of Up Holland and it gave the idea that there was just a single street out of the town, which we had taken. It turns out there is an elective street that we missed. It was four miles and a long tough stroll before we understood this.

Ben and I accused one another, thus scarcely represented the whole morning.

When we talked, it was to complain about the navigation.

'However i'm not sure how you could pass up a great opportunity such an essential course on the course,' said Ben.

'Well you can do the exploring from this point forward on the off chance that you like. Do you think I

appreciate spending ridiculous ages replicating out the course onto an idiotic piece of paper each morning?'

Ben paused.

'There should be a superior way. Wouldn't we be able to get somebody to copy the page of the course book for us every day, so that we have the specific headings you actually don't have to convey the entire book while cycling,' he said.

It was stressing that it had required eleven days for two apparently smart men to think about this straightforward thought. It was so astute, yet such an incredibly clear arrangement, that up to this point we had both neglected to consider it. It was a disclosure. It was the response to our concerns in general. I felt like a new man.

'I guess we could try it out, assuming you need,' I said to Ben, not having any desire to show him any gratification.

We arrived at the town of Garstang and Ben effectively got a copy of the following not many pages from a nearby bequest agent.

'Sorry for being in a particularly foul disposition earlier today,' I said. 'I was simply getting truly baffled with the navigating.'

'No concerns. I realize that you've been great at doing everything. I do see the value in it. I'm glad to try it out if you want.'

'Sure. Lead the way.'

Five minutes later...

'Goodness, bollocks to this! I bleeding disdain exploring. I favored it when you were in control,' he said, giving me the headings back.

We had covered the length of Garstang high road multiple times, Ben actually couldn't conclude which bearing we should leave by.

The nearby Co-operation provided us with a tremendous pack of semi-wounded bananas and we set off again with me exploring, a changed companionship, and a potassium over-burden. We joined the bustling A588 and followed it as far as possible into Lancaster town focus fully intent on doing a spot of sightseeing.

The traveler data was shockingly occupied for a work day in September. I couldn't help thinking that Lancaster was not an optimal spot for a traveler to visit, however I was ready to be convinced otherwise.

'Well there's the palace,' said the accommodating woman in the Tourist Information, 'that is definitely worth a visit, yet it's shut today. There's a going thing on in the Crown Court, I think.'

'The palace has a Crown Court?' I asked.

'Goodness yes. It's as yet a completely working jail, as well. Or on the other hand you could... let me

think... you could go to the Maritime Museum. I've never been nevertheless I'm certain it's brilliant. Or on the other hand there's the theater, in spite of the fact that there will not be anything on during this season of day. What else is there? There's the church, that is great. Or on the other hand the Priory Church. There's such a lot of you could see. Gracious, I almost neglected, there's the Lancaster Leisure Park.'

'The Leisure Park sounds great,' said Ben, having begun to float off to rest during her other suggestions.

'Indeed, it is. It's a shopping town with a major collectibles place. I believe there's a youngsters' play region there, too.'

'Goodness, maybe the Leisure Park doesn't sound ideal after all.'

Lancaster Castle is genuinely amazing to take a gander at, but since of the way that pieces of it are as yet utilized as both a jail and a court, admittance to guests is exceptionally confined and it is beyond the realm of possibilities to expect to visit the pinnacles, keep, towers and prisons. It appears to be a disgrace that it is just hoodlums and suspected crooks that get to partake in Lancaster's best vacationer attraction.
'Will we try the Maritime Museum out?' asked Ben once we were outside.
'Are you serious?'
'obviously I'm not. I can imagine nothing I would prefer to do less. Lancaster's junk isn't it?'
'Better believe it, it is a little, in spite of the fact that assuming somebody came to Northampton Tourist Information, the best guidance they would get is to go to the Shoe Museum.'
'I know. Northampton's far more detestable. However, that is the reason I moved to London.' 'The shoe gallery's entirely great. Have you at any point been?' 'No. I'd prefer visit Lancaster's Maritime Museum.'

We wheeled our bicycles down into the downtown area. In transit we passed a busker who was playing a gravely tuned guitar joined by a severely tuned voice.
'Even the buskers in Lancaster are poop. We could sing better compared to that,' said Ben.
'Really, that is not an ill-conceived notion. We could do some busking for our lunch.' 'Better believe it, very funny.'
'I'm serious. Why not? We don't need instruments; we could just sing and get people to give us food instead of money.'
'You're not kidding aren't you?'
'Better believe it, why not?' I said, turning out to be progressively invigorated by the thought. 'What
about Christmas hymns? We both know the
words.' 'It's September.'
'I know. We would be proactive.'
'You're frantic. However, sounds enjoyable to me. We should do it.'

We tracked down a vacant cardboard box close to a dustbin and opened it out to shape one huge piece of card. Ben then, at that point, figured out how to get a marker pen from a confounded shop partner and we set to work planning our sign.
We expected to ensure individuals comprehended that we didn't need

cash. However enticing as it seemed to be to busk for cash and afterward spend it on anything we desired, we had made it clear from the beginning that we wouldn't utilize cash by any means, regardless of whether it was given to us. We chose the following:

WE DON'T NEED
MONEY WE JUST NEED
FOOD

We scribbled our message onto the cardboard in large capital letters and set our bicycles by a wellspring in an interesting cobbled square off the central avenue. There were heaps of individuals lounged around on the edge of the wellspring and the means of a neighboring structure. What was more significant with regards to the area of our 'fix' was that it was outside a part of Greggs.

It had appeared as though a great thought when I proposed it, yet when we were really remaining in Lancaster town focus going to dispatch into a cappella form of O Little Town of Bethlehem, I understood I was staggeringly apprehensive. I used to sing in a band and was very glad to remain before hundreds (several) individuals and sing rock melodies, however the prospect of busking unexpectedly filled me with fear.

Ben didn't keep down. He dispatched into the principal section like a prepared master. I was dumbfounded by his voice. His talking voice is marginally noisy and bothering, and I anticipated that his singing should be a melodic form of this. I was unable to have been all the more off-base. He seemed like an elegant elderly person, with long stretches of involvement singing with a congregation ensemble. He sang with an impacted baritone voice that overwhelmed me totally. The tone and volume were remarkable. I put forth a valiant effort to contend, yet I was no counterpart for him.

Neither of us realized what followed the line, 'the quiet stars pass by,' so we just rehashed the primary piece. Everybody just gazed at us in bemusement.

'For what reason are you singing Christmas tunes in September?' asked a woman who drew closer us.

'We are assisting individuals with getting into the Christmas soul early,' said Ben. 'Well I'm a dedicated Christian and I think that it is extremely hostile that you are

singing songs so early. You ought to both be embarrassed about yourselves. It's viewed as exceptionally misfortune.' And with that she put her nose turned up, turned and stepped off up the street.

'She wasn't extremely Christian for a Christian, was she?' I

said. 'Hopeless cow. How might this reason offense?' asked
Ben.
'What difference does it make? On the off chance that there is a divine
being then I question he would be irritated with regards to us singing a
portion of his hits too soon in the year.'
'His hits?'
'You know what I mean. Holiday songs are HIS tunes aren't they?'
'Indeed, no, he didn't think of them. Do you think he gets eminences each
time
individuals sing them?'
'No, yet he ought to. He wants a superior lawyer.'

One young lady, matured around four, begun moving directly before us
before her mum snatched her by the arm and drove her away murmuring
'senseless boys.'
Our tirelessness in the long run paid off.
'Do you not have anything to eat?' asked a grinning moderately aged
woman. 'No,' said Ben.
'Are you destitute?' she asked.
'Not by and large, no. That is to say, we are for half a month. We're
cycling to Scotland without spending any money.'
'Gracious. Alright. What kind of sandwiches do you like?'
'That is exceptionally sort of you, however we're not anticipating that
people should get us sandwiches. We figured individuals may have food that
they don't need or will discard,' I said, furtively charmed by the possibility of
a sandwich.
'Well I'm going into Greggs to get my lunch, and I'm glad to get you both
a sandwich. What do you like?'
'Aww, thank you,' said Ben. 'We'll eat without question, anything.
Anything that's cheapest.'
She gotten back with two packs of sandwiches (one ham and one cheddar,
on the off chance that you were pondering) and a portion of bread.
'There you go. They said you could have this portion of bread, as well, as
they planned to toss it out.'
'Thank you,' I said, 'that is truly kind. What's your name?'

'Susan,' she said. 'Well you both appear to be several truly pleasant
young men, and I most certainly accept that superbness achieves excellence.
Best of luck with the remainder of your journey.'
Before eating the sandwiches we attempted a version of Silent Night in
German that I could in any case recall from grade school. A person on a
bmx, in his mid thirties, drawn closer with a little paper sack from Greggs.

'Howdy folks. You can have these two doughnuts assuming you
guarantee to quit singing.' 'You have yourself an arrangement. Much
appreciated, mate,' I said.

Toby, the BMX man, was a truly fascinating person. He was on a half-
hour break between his two distinct positions. He worked in an industrial
facility toward the beginning of the day, and a café the entire evening and
evening. He was attempting to set aside cash to change over a room in his
home into a recording studio. Ben, being an artist with a home-studio, stood
and talked for a long time about blenders and 8-tracks, condenser mics and
advanced samplers. I stood gesturing eagerly however long I could, prior to
letting them have at it and lurking off to sit on the means of the exhibition
hall that lines one edge of the market square. Sadly, it wasn't the Maritime
Museum, if not I would have been in like a shot.

Ben went along with me sooner or later and we got into the sandwiches.
We were before long drawn nearer by an unusual looking teen with a wreck
of brilliant light hair, school coat, untucked shirt and a half-scattered tie. He
was around 17 and was flanked by two or three chuckling adolescent young
ladies. He remained there with a colossal smile across his face and a
transporter pack in his right hand.

'We were snoopping on your discussion a couple of moments prior,' said
the kid, with a marginally camp, rich northern complement. 'We've gotten
you a pack loaded with food and stuff, however there's a condition.'

'Errr… alright,' I said.

'You both need to sing Take on Me, by A-ha.'

'Would you say you are not kidding? You need us to
sing that here? Presently?' 'Yes.'

'I just know the ensemble,' said Ben.

'Me as well. No one knows the words to the remainder of the melody.
We'll simply do the theme. Is that alright? What's your name?'

'Bounce. Think about the desserts,' he said, pulling his cell phone from
his pocket and pointing the camera towards us. 'I will stick this on
YouTube.'

'Abhorrent charlatan,' murmured Ben.

The finish of the melody peaked in an ear-penetrating cry like a large

Alsatian had gotten our balls in its teeth. A gathering of pigeons that had been
searching on the ground close by completely took off on hearing our
aggravation. Passers-by recoiled as they rushed past. Bounce anyway still
smiled and pointed the telephone at us.

'That was awesome. I think you've procured this,' he said, returning the
telephone to his pocket and giving us the transporter pack. It was full

brimming with treats, peanuts, chocolate bars, bubbly beverages, jam desserts, crisps and extra-solid mints. This was one of the greatest single demonstrations of liberality on our entire outing, and it had come from a messy young person. Our test never neglected to hurl surprises.

'I think you would be advised to give me those doughnuts back,' said Toby – the BMX desperado – who had returned as though by magic.

'Huh? Alright. Why's that?' asked Ben, giving him the pack of donuts.

'The arrangement was that you got the doughnuts assuming you quit singing, and I just heard you singing.'

'Goodness poo, sorry mate. We completely neglected. This person came and paid off us with a major pack of desserts assuming we sang to him. I thought you simply needed us to quit singing Christmas carols?'

'I'm fucking joking, folks,' he chuckled, giving back the doughnuts. 'I'm not going to remove your doughnuts. At any rate, I don't think what you were doing considered singing. It was painful.'

'Are you all destitute too, then, at that point?' said a voice from further up the gallery steps to our left.

We went to see a man in his mid twenties, wearing a couple of old tracksuit bottoms, and enormous unsanitary puffer coat. His eyes were red and tired-looking and an inconsistent facial hair growth covered his endured face. His dried lips clung firmly to a little moved up cigarette.

'No. We're not destitute,' I said, timidly, understanding the meaning of the utilization of 'also' in his inquiry. 'Indeed, we don't have anyplace to remain today, yet we do have homes to go to. Are you folks homeless?'

His name was Paul and he had been residing harsh for quite a long time, here and there. We clarified about our excursion and why we were busking for food. He appeared to be truly entertained by it all.

'You should believe we're genuine simpletons doing this outing when we have homes to go to. I trust you're not annoyed by it?' I said.

'Outraged? Nah, not under any condition mate. I think what you're doing sounds wicked, man. It sounds considerably more fun that seven days in Butlins or highest point. Anyway, if you have to sleep in barns and stuff like you have, then it will make you appreciate how lucky you are when you get back to your houses.'

'That is so obvious. Furthermore meeting you causes us to acknowledge how fortunate we are. We stress when we miss a supper or then again in the event that it begins getting dim and we have no place to remain. You need to go through that each and every day.'

'That's right. We sure do.'

'What is Lancaster like for vagrants?' asked Ben.

'It's very great. That is the reason there's such large numbers of us. These parcel are largely destitute, as well,' he said, highlighting a gathering of around eight individuals towards the opposite side of the means. 'I come from Manchester initially, however I expected to leave. A mate let me know Lancaster had great inns and poo, so I came here with regards to eighteen months prior and I've been here since. There are one or two asylums and spots to get food. Indeed, you folks could remain this evening, I'm certain. There are normally two or three extra beds.'

'That is truly sort of you, however I think we'd feel like fakes assuming we took up a bed in a destitute haven,' said Ben.

'Okay, suit yourselves,' he laughed.

'It's been great to meet you and I trust things straighten out for you soon. You appear like a truly nice chap,' said Ben.

'Definitely, you both are, as well. Relatively few individuals sit and talk to us parcel as you do. Reasonable play to you both. Best of luck getting to Scotland.'

'We're never going to get this food into our packs,' said Ben as we strolled back to our bicycles. 'For what reason don't we give some of it to those guys?'

'Smart thought. They merit it significantly more than we do. We can get food at whatever point we need just by singing Take On Me.'

We crushed a bundle of treats, dry-simmered peanuts, extra solid mints and the beverages into our backpacks and took the transporter pack with the leftover crisps, treats and desserts to Paul.

'Here you go, mate. We've not got space for all of this in our sacks. We thought all of you could possibly take care of us,' I said.

His face lit up.

'Much obliged, folks. Thankful,' he said.

On out of Lancaster we passed a bicycle shop.

'How about you check whether they can effectively fix The Falcon here? It's getting strange. The chain is tumbling off each couple of hundred meters,' said Ben.

'Fine. In case it quiets a little longer.'

We wheeled it into the shop and the man consented to investigate The Falcon's chain.

'Nah, I can't fix that. You will require another back derailleur,' he said.

'Nothing but business as usual,' mumbled Ben.

'Do you have any of those?'

'No, not for a bicycle like this. I could attempt to arrange one, however they're difficult to get hold of and it would require a few days to arrive.'

'Is there whatever should be possible to it, to make it last somewhat
longer?' 'Not a chance. It's appropriately broken.'

'I believe it's an ideal opportunity to begin searching for another bicycle,
George,' said Ben priggishly. 'I don't think we've truly got time to begin
chasing after another bicycle today. For what reason don't we simply
continue onward and assuming we see some place that appears as though a
chance en route we can stop,' I proposed, with no goal of
halting whatsoever.

'Except for we're in a major town now. Definitely this is the best
spot to attempt?' 'No doubt, however I'd prefer get moving. The
chain's not that bad.'

'IT FALLS OFF EVERY FUCKING MINUTE!' he shouted.

'However I'm the one that needs to put it on. It just requires a couple of
moments. I'm not dialing you back so for what reason does it trouble you?'

'It irritates me that you're proceeding to ride such a piece of poo when we
could get a good bicycle,' said Ben as he cycled off.

'It was adequately hard to get these bicycles. The Falcon has made it from
Cornwall to Lancaster so it can't be doing too badly.'

I moved onto The Falcon and accelerated after him. The chain tumbled off
straight away.

'Continue onward!' I yelled. 'I'll get you up!'

The course followed the bustling A6 for a large portion of a mile prior to
turning onto minor streets through the lovely towns of Nether Kellet and
Over Kellet. We arrived at the little market town of Milnthorpe at around
6pm. I was befuddled regarding the reason why a few towns are portrayed as
'market towns' the point at which others don't brag with regards to the way
that they have a market. I did some broad examination (Wikipedia) and it
appears to be that the expression is a lawful term starting in bygone eras,
which gives a specific settlement the option to hold a market. It doesn't mean
they need to. But they can if they want.

It was 6pm on a Tuesday and there was no indication of a market in
Milnthorpe.

But it might have had one, you know, in case it needed to.

We arrived at the principle square, which was likewise apparently known
as the 'market square', as it appeared as though the kind of open space that
could have a market, should Milnthorpe conclude it needed one. The square
was abandoned separated from a gathering of five young Goths crushed onto
a seat. They growled at us as we drew nearer. As a matter of fact, it was all
the more an innocuous chuckle, yet a growl appeared to suit their picture

better.

'Yo, fellows,' said Ben, attempting to be cool, 'do you are aware of anyplace around we could remain this evening... for free?'

They all smiled at one another. Apologies, I mean snarled. They all snarled at each other.

'No. Why? Are you jaunts?' requested one from them.

'No. We're cycling to Scotland and we're not permitted to go through any cash,' said Ben.

'That is screwed up, man,' said one of Goths.

'Better believe it man, completely,' said Ben, sounding
absolutely lame. 'Would we be able to remain with any
of you folks?' I asked reluctantly. 'Nah, man, my
cushion is excessively little,' said the head Goth.

'You mean your mum wouldn't let you,' said one of the young ladies. 'You don't have your own pad.'

'No doubt, whatever. Nor does none of you.'

'Okay, home slices. Keep it genuine. Word to your moms,' said Ben, going to leave. As he did, he got his leg on the pedal of The Horse and staggered a couple of feet prior to becoming caught in the bicycle's casing and going totally gaga onto the cobbled asphalt. Only seconds prior, he had attempted to be all 'down with the children's with a gathering of youngsters and afterward, directly before them, he had figured out how to terrifically fall while pushing his bicycle along an asphalt. As Ben lay folded in a store with his bicycle on top of him, I looked on, incapable to inhale as I was chuckling so hard. The Goths cried with giggling. I mean in a real sense cried. Like werewolves. At the moon. That is Goths main event, right?

'Okay, applauds helping me out,' said Ben snidely when he was back on his feet.

'Sorry, I couldn't breathe.'

'Better believe it, well I'll recollect that. Fast, we should escape here.'

The Cross Keys Hotel was a monumental structure that stands on the
corner
of the primary junction in the town.

Ian the director couldn't offer us a bed for the evening, however said that we were free to set up a shelter in the vehicle leave, assuming we could track down one. He likewise offered us a pizza each on the off chance that we returned later.

About 20 meters not too far off, a woman was cleaning her front windows. The house fronted straightforwardly onto the road so we needed to stroll around her to pass.

'Excuse me,' said Ben, 'this will seem like a truly peculiar inquiry, yet I don't assume you have a tent that we could acquire for the night?'

'You need to get a tent?' she asked.

'Indeed, it's a tedious account, however fundamentally Ian from the inn up the street said that we can set up a shelter in his vehicle leave in case we can get one.'

She paused.

'Well, I have a tent, yet how would I realize that I'll get it back?'

'I can guarantee you that we'll take incredible consideration of it and return it to you first thing,' said Ben. She considered this for a moment.

'Great. I'm not sure what difference would it make. Stand by there, I'll take a quick trip and check whether I can track down it.' She headed inside and returned a couple of moments later with a tent, and her significant other, whose work it was to remain in the entryway and look scary, in the event that we had any questions about returning the tent.

'I really want it back tomorrow by 8.30am. That is the point at which I go out to work,' she said.

'You have an arrangement. Much thanks indeed.'

'Hello there Ian. We've figured out how to get a tent. Is the proposal of your vehicle leave actually open?' I asked in the Cross Keys, five minutes later.

'Blimey, that was speedy. Where did you get that?'

'From a woman directly in the distance. She was the main individual we asked.'

'I'm exceptionally dazzled. You folks are great. Indeed, obviously you can set up your shelter in the vehicle leave. If it's all the same to you, I would lean toward it in the event that you could delay until it gets dull. It very well may be somewhat strange assuming you're putting a tent up while everybody is as yet showing up at the bar. I'll present to you several pizzas when I get a minute.'

'Would you say you won't be somewhat cold in the tent?' asked Ben.
'For what good reason? Is it accurate to say that you are asserting the hiking bed AGAIN? I haven't utilized it once
yet.'

'You can utilize it in case you need, yet it scents of me now.'

'I couldn't care less. I almost stuck to death at Mrs Rogers' house.'

'Fine. You can have it then, at that point. Yet, I'm cautioning you, it might have a couple of tacky patches in it,' he laughed.

'Gracious, you're a debilitated fucker. Keep the bleeding camping bed. I will proceed to ask at that other bar across the street in case they have a cover or something I can borrow.'

The bar across the street couldn't have been more unique. It looked precisely as old as would have done during the 1950s; heaps of metal, not many lights, and – based on the three elderly people men at the bar – presumably the equivalent occupants.

'I have a duvet you can get,' said Chris, the man behind the bar. He was in his mid-thirties with spiked hair, pierced ears and a fluorescent shirt, directly from a 1980s disco.

'That would be great. Much thanks to you. I'll drop it back in the first part of the day assuming that is alright,' I said.

'My pleasure,' he said, pushing me in the shoulder coyly. 'Assuming you want anybody to keep you warm in the evening, you know where to come.' The men at the bar laughed.

'Much appreciated, however I'm as of now imparting the tent to another man.' 'Far better. Trio!' he laughed.

'I think I would be wise to lay down with one eye open this evening with you directly across the road.'

'no doubt,' he said with a wink.

When it was dull we begun to set up the tent. I'm trash at setting up tents. Even in daylight. There is just a single individual on the planet more terrible at setting up tents than me, and tragically he turned out to be in the bar vehicle leave with me. In obscurity, we were totally incompetent.

Ben and I verged on choking each other during the tent's erection. Allow me to reword that, as it seems like a sadomasochistic form of Brokeback Mountain. We verged on choking each other over the span of setting up the tent. There, that is better.

'What are you doing?' shouted Ben.

'I'm placing stakes in. What does it look like?'

'Try not to fix the internal piece. Simply stake the flysheet.'

'However at that point the flysheet and the inward will contact and we'll get wet.' 'Bollocks. That is a metropolitan myth.'

'No it's not! It's a reality. I've been in a lot of tents that have released.'

'That is on the grounds that you're so poo at putting them up.'

'For what reason are you being so parsimonious with the stakes?' 'There's no good reason for utilizing stakes for it.'

'alright,' I said, and afterward fixed the inward tent at any rate, while he was attempting to fix the zip.

After around 45 minutes, we had tangled the tent into some type of fundamental safe house. Fortunately there was no wind, and downpour appeared to be far-fetched. I had attempted to join the person ropes for good measure, yet Ben had grabbed them away saying, 'there's no chance are we having fellow ropes.'

I won't ever get exhausted of the fervor of moving into a tent. It is one of those minutes that achieve outrageous sensations of energy and sentimentality. In the completely dark, we bumbled our hiking beds, duvet and assets into some kind of request and set down to go to sleep.

Day 12 – The hitman

Milnthorpe to Carlisle – 50 miles

We stirred to the sound of drilling.
'What the heck is that clamor?' asked Ben.
I fixed the zip and jabbed my head out of the tent. Four laborers were boring into the landing area of the vehicle leave under three meters from the tent. The person with the drill recognized me with a cause a commotion yet continued with his work.
'A few workers are penetrating right external the tent,' I said to Ben.

'It seems like my head will detonate.' It was generally very strange. We rested in a tent, in a bar vehicle leave and woke up in the center of a structure site.

'How could you rest?' I asked.

'Splendid. Didn't awaken once. What about you?'

'Not extraordinary. I needed to overlap the duvet in half with the goal that I wasn't resting on the tent floor however at that point my feet jabbed out the bottom.'

'In any case, you should've traded for the hiking bed. On the off chance that you were given a four-banner bed and a plume duvet, you'd in any case whinge regarding how severely you slept.'

We brought the tent down in record time and crushed it back into the pack, similarly as it down-poured. *'There's nothing more regrettable than a wet tent,' or so my father claims.*

Ben restored the tent to the woman not too far off, while I returned the duvet to my admirer in the adjoining bar. Fortunately, he was still sleeping higher up when I called, so I left it with a woman who was cleaning the bar.

We then, at that point, went to recover our bicycles and express profound gratitude to Ian.

'Why not both come in and have some morning meal in the lodging?' he asked as he opened the cabinet that housed our bicycles. 'Simply proceed to prepare a table at whatever point you're. Request anything you desire off the menu and tell whoever serves you that it's been cleared with me.'

We felt quite nibbled awkward in the inn café. The tables were loaded with sharp looking older couples getting ready for a day's visit through the Lake District. We were found a seat at a table in the corner, unwashed and bristly, wearing a similar garments we had been wearing for 11 days.

'What would i be able to get you?' asked the waitress.

'I'll have the Full English, please,' said Ben.

'I think I'll go for the kipper and poached egg please,' I said.

'Kipper and poached egg? What the hell?' addressed Ben when she had left.

'I just idea I would go for something somewhat unique. We've eaten such a lot of poo this outing I don't figure I could deal with another fry-up.'

'You'll think twice about it. I'm not going to give you
any of mine.' sufficiently sure, I thought twice about it
deeply.

For some explanation, I half anticipated that Ben should be the jealous one, yet it turned out there was no contest. For reasons unknown I believed that 'Kipper with Poached Egg' would be something other than a kipper with a poached egg. I don't have a clue what I was anticipating. Possibly two kippers. Or on the other hand maybe three. What is the aggregate thing for kippers? At any rate, I was given a kipper and a poached egg. Very much like it said. It was exceptionally delicious, yet I have never felt more noteworthy jealousy than I did at seeing the plate of steaming oily bacon, frankfurter, beans, seared bread, hash earthy colors, mushrooms, tomato, egg and dark pudding that Ben was served. I approached crying.

Thirty seconds after the fact I had eaten mine, and I then, at that point, needed to sit and watch Ben climax over his Full English. Not in a real sense, obviously. That would have been revolting.

We set off on our bicycles, not long before 9am, at the pinnacle of busy time. Busy time in Milnthorpe comprised of an old woman while heading to the greengrocers, and a rancher fixing the ties on his trailer. Envision how bustling it gets assuming that Milnthorpe chooses to have a market. Since it can in the event that it needs, you know.

Milnthorpe sits right on the edge of the Lake District. When the buzz of that little 'market town' had blurred, we were encircled on all sides by 'the loveliest spot man hath never found,' as indicated by William Wordsworth.

It seemed like we were on vacation. In fact, we were on Day 12 of our vacation, however this was whenever that we first genuinely felt it.

For the following 15 miles we saw close to about six vehicles. The downpour had halted, however the air was as yet moist with thick low-lying cloud. It made the view look much more awesome. Dry stone dividers weaved their way across fields prior to being gobbled up by the fog. Spooky abandoned stone outbuildings were incompletely noticeable, and sheep got like apparitions across the hillside.

There is likewise something impactful in the way that amount of what makes the Lake District so delightful is man-made. I don't mean the sheep and the mists – I'm almost certain man didn't make those. I mean the staggering dry

stone dividers, the forsaken horse shelters, and the image postcard towns that intersperse the region. The actual scene is clearly fantastic, yet it is man's increases that truly give it its character.

We went through the towns of Brigsteer and Underbarrow which appeared to both be snoozing. I stopped immediately to take a gander at the directions.

'For what reason do you need to continue halting to check we're going above and beyond?' asked Ben. 'There is just a single street in the Lake District and we are on it.'

'Assuming there is just a single street, then, at that point, why we are at a junction?'

'That street up there doesn't count. That is somebody's drive. It must be down along these lines.' He set off down the slope through the town and I collapsed up the headings and followed him without twofold checking.

'This is apparently less than ideal, Ben,' I said, a couple of moments later. 'You disdain it when I'm in control don't you?'

'Well, yes. Particularly when I'm the one with the bearings and your ability to know east from west has been demonstrated to be shit.'

'That is false. I have an incredible internal compass.'

'No doubt, you're similar to a homing pigeon,' I said mockingly. 'Well you're similar to a homo pigeon.'

I contemplated the route.

'You realize that street that you said was somebody's carport?' 'Yep.'

'Well as indicated by this present, that is the street we wanted.'

We walked back up the slope peacefully and afterward took the right road.

Our course book cautioned us about a slope after Underbarrow that would 'most likely require getting off'. All things considered, not for two finely tuned competitors like us. We traveled up without breaking sweat.

Actually, Ben had said that it was 'absolutely impossible that The Falcon planned to make it up the slope,' which made it the main test I had at any point confronted. Ben was then compelled to react by driving The Horse up, as well. We imploded in a load at the top, sweat-soaked and exhausted.

The following three miles were all declining into the town of Bowness-on-Windermere, which sits, obviously, on the banks of Lake Windermere – England's biggest lake.

After 15 miles spinning through the curious nation paths, Windermere was a major shock to the framework. It looked pretty – from a good ways – however was genuinely terrible. The asphalts were slithering with mentor parties visiting the overrated shops, purchasing overrated tat, and filling their appearances with overrated food. The streets were clogged with through-traffic, vacationers and coaches.

We tracked down a spot of grass close to a shabby booth selling frozen yogurts and keepsakes. Ben recognized an external tap by the booth and went to top off our water bottles.

'UH, EXCUSE ME! You can't utilize that tap. It's for clients just,' yelled a voice through the stand's hatch.

'Goodness, apologies. We're simply topping off a few drinking bottles. Is that alright?' 'No. They're for clients as it were. Are you anticipating purchasing anything?' 'Sorry, we don't have any money.'

'No tap then, at that point,' he said.

Soon subsequent to leaving Windermere we saw a sign admonition us of something that we had been fearing since getting hold of our course book: Kirkstone Pass.

The course that our book itemized took us over Kirkstone Pass, which is the most elevated mountain pass in England and would be the 'hardest move of the visit'. The street acquires 1,300 ft in six difficult miles, and vowed to be not normal for anything we had ever attempted.

As a general rule, it wasn't really awful. By this, I imply that We didn't need to get off and stroll at any stage. We did, in any case, quickly take off our shirts after the principal half-mile battle. A very much planned break after around four miles separated the excursion pleasantly, as well. We sat against a stone divider along the edge of the street and ate our lunch.

Using the old bread that the woman had given us in Lancaster and the packs of crisps from Bob – the understudy – we assembled two epic fresh sandwiches each.

The last two miles passed with next to no episode, and on arriving at Kirkstone Inn – which denotes the highest point of the pass – we needed to inquire as to whether we were really at the top.

We halted to take in the view, which was shocking toward each path. The street behind us wound its direction back down the valley towards Lake Windermere, and afterward past us toward Scotland. The sun was out and the perceivability was fantastic. It is clearly normal for End to Enders to arrive at Kirkstone Pass and not have the option to see anything on account of fog.

We could see a lake at the lower part of the valley toward the path we were going and it provoked us with its shining, cool, invigorating quality. Hot,

sweat-soaked, got dried out and on the highest point of a mountain, the landscape was abruptly of little interest. We were in urgent need of a swim.

The plummet from Kirkstone Pass was without a doubt the quickest I have ever experienced a bicycle. It was perhaps the quickest that man has at any point voyaged, in any type of transport.

If The Falcon had wings, I swear she would have taken off. It was one of the most frightening, however most invigorating things I have at any point done. Slowing down wasn't actually a possibility for me, as The Falcon's brakes possibly had any slight impact when going at an absurdly lethargic speed, or uphill. I just yielded and let The Falcon do what she was best at doing – not stopping.

There was shockingly little traffic one or the other way, which implied that we had the option to take the 'hustling line' through the many curving twists. Vehicles would be probably not going to arrive at such paces on such a twisting downhill stretch, so it implied that we didn't need to fight with any vehicles attempting to surpass us. I went by Ben, who turned and almost had a cardiovascular failure when he saw me pass.

The street gradually evened out at the lower part of the valley, and I guided The Falcon up a grass skirt to halt. It was something like ten seconds before Ben came to me.

'How in the world did you go such a great deal
quicker than me?' 'I told you. The Falcon is a
world class dashing bike.'

'No, you're on a bad kid's bicycle. I didn't slow down once down there yet you actually went by me.'

'Keep in mind The Falcon.'

'This is a result of your weight advantage,' said
Ben. 'What do you mean?'

'Well, you're fatter so you get more force down the hills.'

'Shut up. You're simply sluggish in light of the fact that the enormous handle on your head makes bunches of wind resistance.'

'Well your man boobs fold around like plane propellers giving you extra speed.'

Conversations among Ben and me were seldom more experienced than this. We did once have a conversation about governmental issues, however it was based around the impossible situation that we needed to shag either John Prescott or Margaret Thatcher to save humanity. We both hesitantly settled on Maggie.

We arrived at the town of Glenridding at around 3pm. We alluded to it as 'Glen-free a-ding-ding' since we thought it was entertaining. Thinking back, it is less so now.

Glen-free a-ding-ding is a little town on the edge of Ullswater – the second biggest lake in the Lake District. Many individuals believe Ullswater to be the most excellent of the lakes, and Wordsworth depicted it as, *the most joyful mix of magnificence and loftiness, which any of the lakes affords.'*

As well as the bait of Ullswater, Glen-free a-ding-ding (perhaps it will get more clever assuming I rehash it) is additionally a famous base for explorers, as it sits at the lower part of one of the famous courses up Helvellyn – England's third most noteworthy top, behind Scafell and Scafell Pike.

The town (Glen-free a-ding-ding, that is) was a wonderful combination of conventional structures and current comfort, with an open air store, gift shop and a traveler information.

We stopped up on a fix of grass just past the town, and stripped down to our fighter shorts. We then waded into the water up to our waists. It was ball-clenchingly cold. Inside nanoseconds my balls had withdrawn up within me and my Glen-free a-ding-ding had withered to the size of a cigarette butt. I screeched like a girl.

'Looks decent in there?' said an old woman who was strolling along the keep money with her husband.

'It's... ok... ok... surely... ok... ok... reviving,' said Ben.

'You should go along with us,' I said.

'Perhaps sometime later,' she laughed.

The Glenridding Mini-Market was a fantastic shop. It was pressed to the roof with all that you might at any point need to purchase, and a lot of stuff that you could never need to buy.

'We get some odd-bodies in this shop, however we've never had individuals doing what you're doing?' said the woman behind the counter, after we recounted her our story.

Her name was Avril and she seemed as though she was destined to run a town shop. I don't imply that in a deprecating manner. She just appeared as though precisely the kind of individual that you would need to purchase your day by day paper or arrangements from; a warm and amicable grin, a quieting loosened up way and all the persistence on the planet to stand and pay attention to two messy youngsters ask for food from her. She resembled a more youthful Mrs Goggins from Postman Pat.

'Would you like one of these pies? I'm probably not going to sell a lot more of

these, as time's slipping away in the day. We have a huge chicken pie here... this current one's a steak pie... what's more that one is apple.'

'That is exceptionally liberal of you,' said Ben. 'Which one will we have, George?'

'Gracious continue, take each of the three,' she said. 'I'm certain you'll track down space for them.'

It was almost 6pm when that we left Ullswater.

'Where are we going to remain this evening?' asked Ben.

'Not certain,' I said, investigating the course book. 'We've just done around 25 miles today so it would be great to attempt to do however much we can in the time that is left.'

'Yet it'll be dim in an hour.'

'Taking a gander at this, it appears to be that there's nothing among us and Carlisle, which is another 25 miles away.'

'Carlisle? However, that is in Scotland isn't it.'

'No,' I said unhesitatingly, simply because I had the book before me and had the option to check. 'Not exactly. I figure it may have been essential for Scotland once, maybe.'

'We'll never do another 25 miles today. Particularly with these knave hills.'

'As per the book, there's a short segment of uphill coming up, and afterward it's declining the whole way. We should give it a go.'

'Okay, yet I would rather not wind up dozing in a wicked field tonight.'

The course left the Lake District and finished country roads the towns of Greystoke, Little Blencow and Hutton-in-the-Forest, following corresponding to the M6. The course book had not lied; it was downhill the whole way and it caused us to feel like legitimate cyclists interestingly. Indeed, it would have done, had I not needed to shut down like clockwork to reattach The Falcon's chain.

It was dull when we arrived at Carlisle.

'Wicked hellfire. For what reason did the English battle for this spot? The Scots can have it back assuming that they need?' said Ben.

'Definitely, it seems as though somewhat of a dump, yet perhaps we've recently come in on its most exceedingly awful side.'

Within the initial five minutes of showing up in Carlisle, we had been told we

were 'several fookin bicycle poofs', were inquired as to whether we needed to purchase any corrosive, and afterward lectured by a brought back to life Christian. This was three separate episodes, coincidentally, not only one insane person with his finger in numerous pies.

We did a couple of laps of the town community on our bicycles to attempt to get some motivation of where to pursue convenience. Carlisle was by a wide margin the greatest town we had attempted to remain in, and we didn't actually have the foggiest idea where to start.

At the top finish of town we strolled past an incredibly elegant looking inn called the Crown and Miter. It was opulent that it had a custodian. I have never remained in an inn with a doorman.

'Excuse me. Is it alright in the event that we bring our bicycles into the hall?' Ben asked the custodian. He gazed back at Ben with a look that didn't say no, yet didn't say yes.

'Or would you mind simply watching out for them for two or three minutes assuming we left them outside?'

He proceeded with a similar gaze and didn't let out the slightest peep. We wheeled them up the means and into the stylish foyer.

The assistant gazed upward from her PC with the robotized grin that she would welcome all visitors with, yet this before long dropped and her eyebrows raised with a look that said, 'how could you move beyond security?' Ben gave her our spiel.

'No, we will not have the option to help you, I'm apprehensive,' she said, before he had finished.

'Gracious, alright. Would it be feasible to address the administrator by any stretch of the imagination, just to check?'

Her face didn't adjust. 'No, I don't think so.'

'For what reason did she see us like that?' asked Ben when we were outside. 'I surmise since we resemble two or three tramps.'

'No doubt, however we could've been moguls, for all she knew.'

'Yet we resemble a few vagrants, and we were requesting a free room.'

'Valid. However, even so.'

We attempted another inn – The County Hotel – and got a comparable reaction, though this time cheerfully. The secretary was working alone and brought no position to the table for a free room without a supervisor's assent.

Not at all like at the Crown and Miter, obviously in the event that she might have helped, she would. We then tried the Ibis on Botchergate, which seemed to be Carlisle's main

business road. The secretary was staggering; blonde, Swedish (likely) and had a name that neither of us could even endeavor to articulate. The more we saw her name identification, the more it appeared to be that we were gazing at her bosoms. She thought the entire thought of our test was insane, and continued to get some information about it.

'So you rested in a stable with a bull?' she asked in wonderful English however with a trace of Scandinavian hotness. 'You all are hilaaaaarious.'

'Do you figure you could possibly assist us with anyplace to remain this evening? We don't require a room. We could rest in the cleaning cabinet,' I said.

'Hang tight, I'll check for you.'

'The administrator says everything he can manage is £30 for you two,' she said. 'The typical cost would be about £60 so this is an excellent deal.'

'Thank you,' I said 'That sounds like an awesome arrangement. Sadly, we don't have any cash whatsoever. We're not permitted to spend a solitary penny.'

'Hang on. I will attempt him once
again.' A couple of moments later, she
returned.

'He said he could offer you both a space for £11. This is the staff rate, I think, with an additional a rebate added.'

Ben and I checked out one another with a similar sensation of defenselessness. We were being offered a room in a brilliant, spotless, comfortable, new lodging with hot showers, enormous beds, and no workers penetrating meters from our heads, for just
£11.

We said goodbye to the Swedish magnificence, and she waved us off and wished us great luck.

It was 9.30pm and we were all the while remaining in Carlisle town focus. It started to rain.

'Eleven sodding pounds. We were so close. We could be having a shower in our lodging at this point,' said Ben. 'I feel like I could cry. I love the Ibis.'

'I would prefer to be standing apart here in the downpour, than having a shower with you,' I said.

'I didn't mean together, you bellend. What's the arrangement now?'

'What about we go to a bar and simply inquire as to whether we can proceed to remain at theirs?'

'It doesn't seem as though we have numerous other options.'

Walkabout is a chain of Australian themed bars. In addition to any old Australian themed bars, they are OFFICIALLY the coolest Australian themed

bars this side of the planet. Indeed, that is as indicated by their site at any rate. I don't know that I've at any point been to an Australian bar in Britain that was not a Walkabout, so the opposition isn't huge.

There were outdoor tables outside the front of the bar, and a couple of gatherings of individuals were sat under parasols in the downpour watching Manchester United play a Champions League game on a screen through the entryway. We reviewed the gatherings of individuals and settled on our arrangement of assault. We headed towards a gathering of chaps who resembled students.

We inquired as to whether any of them would put us up for the evening, yet no one was impending. We attempted similar methodology at one more table of folks who were too invested in the football to try and recognize that we were addressing them.

'Yous can rest at mah hoose,' said a Scottish voice from the opposite finish of the table. We went to see a man in his mid seventies, with firmly trimmed silver hair, a gravely moved cigarette dangling from his mouth and a woolen jumper that seemed as though it had been weaved by somebody with serious visual weakness. His eyes were wild and puncturing. They were amplified by a couple of severely sellotaped glasses that made him look really startling. I question he had at any point lost a gazing rivalry in his life.

'Truly? Alright, fantastic. Much obliged. That is exceptionally sort of you,' I said, checking out Ben for some indication of acknowledgement.

'Much appreciated, that is great of you. Yet, we truly don't have any desire to put you out,' said Ben.

'Affirmative, it's nae trouble. Yous both need some place to rest. I have space. It's th' leest ah can dae. Nae trouble,' he said, thumping back the shot of whisky that sat close to his half-completed 16 ounces of Guinness.

'However we may be a couple of chronic executioners,' kidded Ben.

'That is stunningness ceremony. I'm a chronic executioner tay,' he said blazing us a look that made Hannibal Lecter seem as though a teddy bear. He then burst out laughing and we laughed, too, although somewhat less convincingly.

'The name is Mick. Here, go get yerselfs a small beverage,' he said, giving over a £10 note.

'That is exceptionally liberal of you, however we're
alright,' I said. 'Let's go ya pussies. I demand. Get
me another 16 ounces, too.'

'This will sound truly inept,' I said, 'yet we're on this test to cycle the length of the country without spending any money.'

'Uh huh,' said the man. 'Aam askin' you ta spend mah money.'

'I know, I know, yet a piece of the arrangement is that we're not permitted to utilize cash by any means – considerably others' money.'

'Ah for screw purpose,' he said, getting the arm of a person sat watching the football. 'Proceed to get these small chaps a fecking drink. What's more one for myself and yous, as well.' He bumbled in his pocket and gave the person £20 instead.

The youthful understudy didn't have a clue what to say. He was simply being requested to proceed to purchase drinks by an alcoholic Scottish man. You could see him gauging it up in his mind, and afterward it out of nowhere clicked that he was getting a free drink.

'Okay. What will it be then, at that
point?' he said. 'Two pints of Guinness
please,' I said.

'Ack, now we're in business,' said Mick. 'Yous need to quit being such southern nancies.'

What followed was, regardless, the most unusual evening of my life.

We sat conversing with Mick on the seat outside Walkabout for one more hour. During that time, he sent the youthful chap toward the finish of the seat to purchase one more round. It unfolded that Mick had been a heavy drinker for a long time. He had figured out how to remain 'evaporate' for a very long time until the day we met him. Toward the beginning of that day he had been to the specialist to get the aftereffects of certain tests. He was informed that the disease that he was being treated for had spread all through his body. Mick then arrived at Walkabout just as it was opening, and had been there ever since. Ten hours of strong drinking had made his words slur somewhat, however it hadn't hampered his energy or his memory.

'Aam the best living English-talking writer in th' world today,' he declared.

'You're an artist?' I

inquired. 'Ok huh.'

'Cool,' and before I even got an opportunity to ask him, he dispatched into a presentation. Likely arousing a lot of inconvenience for the other drinkers.

'This current one's known as The Gargoyle,' he said.

The Gargoyle
Has wings… of stone
He's separated from
everyone else and
feeling All those
things
No human animal realizes
The garments, of dreams
He shows

As however to appear to intend to
see. Conviction – in dream – be
fact
And showcasing its
part The rain
Wears out his tears
With lethal hostility
Yet he prevails to be
Totality
And passes,
impermanent Man.

I was truly astounded. I don't have a clue why, however I had anticipated that his poetry should be, all things considered, poo. I didn't completely comprehend the sonnet whenever I first heard it – I'm as yet not certain I do – but rather the manner in which he recounted it from memory with his conspicuous Scottish inflection, extreme gaze and impeccably estimated conveyance was unimaginably captivating.

Mick then took us to the pub across the road, and we took a seat by the window so that we could keep an eye on our bikes that we had pretend-locked to a lamp post just outside. The spot was colossal, yet practically unfilled, aside from a gathering of around 15 guys remaining on a generally abandoned dance floor. The music was really clearly that Mick's Scottish intonation turned out to be much more hard to comprehend. He got us both a dose of whisky and another 16 ounces, and furthermore requested us a burger and chips each, without us having the opportunity to protest.

The more he drank, the more he focused on himself to us. He let us know that he was gay, yet had never uncovered this to anybody for the duration of his life, nor had any kind of relationship with anyone.

'When ah was yoong you could be pit in prison for being a buftie like me,' he said. 'Ye ken whit aam sayin? Aw mah life I've hud tae imagine aam somethin' aam nae.'

He jabbered about 'God's will', as well, and he gave us the feeling that he was embarrassed about his homosexuality, and felt that he had deceived God.

'Ah dornt extravagant either ay ye, by th' way,' he said, necking his whisky. 'Why not?' asked Ben, somewhat insulted. 'What's going on with us?'

'Well you ah not my sort, and his legs ah excessively furry,' he said highlighting my uncovered white thighs.

'I've killed individuals,' he then, at that point, said some time later. 'I've killed bunches of people.'

This was a discussion plug like no other.

'It was mah work,' he said after a long interruption. 'Aam nae glad 'session whit ah did.'

'What do you mean it was your work?' I asked hesitantly.

'Ah worked hide th' english government killin' psychological oppressors. IRA for the most part.' 'Doubtlessly that is a splendid work?' said Ben.

'Yes, you would think things being what they are, wooldnae ye? All mah life I've hud aw thes responsibility inside me abit th' things I've dain an' th' things I've seen. I've never talked aboot this tae anybody. Aam nae assumed tae. But after whit happened at th' doctor's this morn, ah cooldnae give a fuck anymore.'

He enlightened us seriously regarding the spots he had lived and the things he had done. At a certain point he began talking in Russian – a necessity for one of his missions, clearly. Ben and I were both completely grasped by his accounts. We had met some intriguing characters on our excursion, however Mick was in a class of his own.

We were then confronted with the snapshot of returning and rest at his home. We abruptly ached for the simple, pleasant nature of the others that we had remained with – Monica in Ludlow, or David and Annie in Nanstallon – rather than confronting the vulnerability of a night with Mick.

He drove the way back to his home which was a brief stroll from the bar. He was stunning all around the asphalt and sporadically needed to clutch a divider or light post to recover his equilibrium. In spite of his age, and helpless dress sense, he looked genuinely fit and had an amazing athletic build.

'Are you certain this is a smart thought?'

murmured Ben. 'Better believe it, we'll be fine,' I

said, not completely convinced.

'I'm totally pooping myself. We're returning to rest on the floor at a prepared executioner's home, who is totally shitfaced. Are we insane?'

'When you put it that way, it sounds somewhat inept, yet he appears as though a truly decent chap who simply needs to take care of us. What's the most terrible that can happen?'

'Errr, that we get freeloaded or killed, or both,' said Ben.

Mick lived in a little gathering level on the edge of Carlisle. It had not been brightened since the 1960s. Either that or Mick was into retro-styling amazingly. A couple of pitiful belongings dabbed his receiving area; library books, a radio, a spilling over ashtray, and, to some degree shockingly, a windowsill loaded with seedlings.

'If ye move those seats outta th'way ye can rest on the floor,' he said. He vanished into the kitchen and arose with a jug of whisky and three glasses. 'Time for a small measure before bed?'

This was to a greater extent a proclamation rather than an inquiry, as in spite of our affable decays we were both given an immense slick whisky. Ben tasted at his like an epicurean, and I brought down mine with the expectation that it would make me rest better. Mick drooped into his rocker and seconds after the fact he was asleep.

'Poop! What do we do now?' asked Ben.

'I don't have the foggiest idea. We can't simply rest with him stayed there can we?'

'No. However, I'm not going to attempt to wake him and put him into bed. Are you?'

'No way.'

'I'm so happy I have the camping cot. In any event in case he awakens you'll be the more straightforward one to assault,' said Ben.

'Quit gloating about your ridiculous camping bed. Also, on the off chance that he awakens in the evening and attempts to assault or murder us essentially I'll have the option to make a fast escape while you'll bounce round the room like you're in a sack race.'

We both began chuckling at the idea, however at that point halted rapidly when Mick began squirming. Mick snoozing was definitely less unnerving than Mick awake.

Ben moved into his camping cot and I covered my legs with my towel and we lay on the floor aching for the morning.

We had hushed up for around ten minutes when I chose to deliver a fart. Presently, I'm a genuinely productive farter – I would even go similar to saying that I'm an expert – yet this didn't resemble anything I had at any point done. It went on for around ten seconds and its vibrations thundered through the sections of flooring, reverberating round the whole room. We investigated towards Mick who rearranged in his seat, sat ahead, opened his eyes momentarily, and afterward returned to sleep.

Ben practically wet himself with chuckling and I needed to place my clench hand in my mouth to stop myself yelling. It was exactly what we expected to break the tension.

'Good lord,' said Ben, 'we're dozing close to a plastered executioner and you proceed to let out something to that effect. I've heard nothing like that before.'

'It was most certainly one of my best. I believe it's a blend of the Guinness, the burger and the fear.'

It's reasonable for say it was not one of my greatest night's sleep.

I floated all through awareness, kept conscious by the presence of Mick drooped in his seat a couple of feet away. He would swear boisterously at himself at standard stretches for the duration of the evening – apparently in his sleep.

Sooner or later in the early hours of the morning, Mick hurled himself up from the seat and lurched down the passage to what we assumed was his room. Ben then pushed the sitting room door closed behind him, so that we would at least get some sort of warning when he returned.

The temperature dropped extensively and the breeze and downpour battered the feeble committee level windows. I put on my suit pants yet they did essentially nothing to keep me warm. Ben lay conceitedly close to me in his resting bag.

Me and The Falcon, Kirkstone Pass

Ben before the summit of Kirkstone Pass

Ben, halfway up Kirkstone Pass

The Falcon

The road up Kirkstone Pass, from Ullswater

Day 13 – Welcome to Scotland

Carlisle to Dumfries – 39 miles

'Guid mornin', campers,' said Mick as he burst through the entryway. He remained in the entryway skipping around on his toes informal sparring. He was ready for business and excitement, and was unmistakably not feeling any eventual outcomes from the earlier day's drinking.

'Ah heard voices comin' frae in here an' it took me a small while tae recall ah hud broom ght ye home.'

'Definitely, it took us some memorable time where we were, as well,' I said. 'What did ah tell ye mah name was?' he asked.

'Mick,' said Ben.

'Ach, noo. Ok say 'at tae fowk ah dunnae kinn. Mah genuine name is Ronnie.'

Ronnie offered us breakfast however at that point found he didn't have any food in the house. Rather he made us an espresso and bested them up with the rest of the whisky. He then sat back in his arm chair and spent an hour retelling most of the stories about his life that he had told us the night before. Neither Ronnie nor his level appeared to be so overwhelming in the daytime.

From his parlor window, you could see into the back garden which was imparted to a line of six different pads. Ronnie, it unfolded, was the assigned head gardener.

'No other person aroond here gi'es a jobby abit plants,' he said.

He had done a brilliant job. It wasn't going to win any awards at Chelsea, but you could tell he had put a lot of time and effort into the garden. It was fascinating to witness the two extreme sides to Ronnie's personality. Part of him was an angry, bitter, cynical, former killer. The other part was a generous, thoughtful, kind, nature-loving old man.

Shortly after completing the trip (damn it, I've spoilt the ending again), he sent me a lovely long letter saying how much he had enjoyed us both staying with him, and to thank me for some audio books that I had sent him. He enclosed a couple of poems – including a new one, which he said he wrote about me.

Out of your eyes
The love of life appears
Seeking liberty to feel

The actual, the real.
Your solitude absorbs
So gladly...
Knowing and yet unknowing me
I've no need to explain
The want of wanting
The haunting of you shall be me
And love completely
But teardrops on the windowpane

Of experience this is youth.
And I passing through your life
Hope to stain that glass... with
truth. And leave it with you.

When I tell people of our experience with Ronnie, I admit that his stories
do sound far-fetched. Out of all the people in Carlisle, we happened to end up
with a drunken hitman, who was in his final weeks of life. Most people laugh
and say that it sounds like a load of bullshit. Ronnie's story, that is, not my
version of events.

I don't consider myself a very gullible person. In fact, I tend to be very
suspicious of people. Especially those that I don't know. But in Ronnie's
case I never doubted anything he said. Looking back, this seems a little
naïve.

I have been told on a couple of occasions since, that it is a classic sign of
senility, that people will have delusions about a fabricated heroic past. In a
way, I hope that Ronnie was just a delusional old man and that none of his
shocking past life actually happened. I would be comforted, to some extent,
if it turned out he had spent most of his years holed up in that council flat
tending to plants and listening to the radio.

Minutes after leaving Ronnie's we were caught out by a torrential
downpour. The raindrops battered the road surface like machinegun fire, and
within seconds the gutters were full. The torrent of water elbowed its way
down the high street looking for its escape. We did the same, and found
refuge in the doorway of a shop. The window was well stocked with random
household things, such as varnish and carriage clocks, but there was also a
random selection of bike accessories.

'Surely there are some bike bits we could ask for while we are here?' said
Ben.

'Like what?'

'I don't know, but your bike is rubbish. It must need some new bits.'

'It probably does, but I've got no idea which bits would make it less
rubbish if we replaced them.'

Ben stared at The Falcon as though the answer would appear to him at any
moment. 'Hold on, I've got an idea. Wait there,' he said, propping his bike
up and disappearing into the shop.

I stood there wincing at the thought of him asking the bemused
shopkeeper for a free derailleur, tyre, brake cable or inner tube, just for the
sake of it. He emerged from the shop with a big grin on his face and two
black bin bags in his hand.

'The latest in waterproof cycling gear,' he said.

'You are a genius.'

We tore a hole in the bottom of each bin liner for our head and a hole in each side for our arms. The bin bags were big enough to cover our rucksacks, too, and keep our few belongings sheltered from the rain.

As we set off again, it felt like we were on a movie set. Despite it being 9.30am, the streets were eerily deserted. The rain was so dramatic that the film director would have asked to tone it down because it was too unrealistic.

We had no idea where we were going. I had left the day's route in my rucksack, which was now inaccessible because of the bin liner. We cycled in the direction which our instinct told us was north. Two weeks on the road had given us an acute natural awareness of our location and direction.

Or so we thought.

'This is the road we came in on last night. We need to be going in the opposite direction,' I said.

'I thought it all looked a bit familiar,' said Ben, as we turned around and retraced our steps.

Less than a mile north of Carlisle on the A7 we passed a branch of Morrison's – the supermarket (other supermarkets are available). We both agreed that cycling in such horrendous conditions was particularly unpleasant, so decided to stop and try and get some breakfast.

We entered the supermarket followed by the glare of several exiting shoppers, who seemed a bit confused by our attire. The fashion of knee-length bin bags and skimpy shorts had apparently not taken off in Carlisle.

'Shall we try and get some bread and butter like we did in Ellesmere Port?' I suggested.

'I really fancy a fry-up. What do you say we try our luck at the café?'

We approached the lady at the till and tried our well rehearsed routine.

'Ye want a free breakfest? Ah cannae authorize 'at. Yoo'll hae tae gang an' spick tae th' stair manager. Gang ower th' the customer services desk.'

Everyone in Carlisle seemed to be Scottish. And not just a bit Scottish, but extremely Scottish. It was almost like they were pushed out of Scotland for being too Scottish.

'What the hell did she just say?' asked Ben as we walked away.

'I'm not sure but I think she told us to go and ask the store manager.'

We eventually located him at the Customer Services desk. He was Scottish.

'Sae ye want a free breakfest?' he said. 'Och aye, Ah hink we can sort 'at it fur ye. Whit will it be? Two full Englishes? Or shoods ah said Scottishes,' he said with a cackle.

'Two Scottish breakfasts would be amazing. Thanks so much.'

'Nae problem. gang an' tak' a seat an' i'll gie a body ay th' kimers tae sort ye it.'

'Ok,' we said, without the faintest clue as to what he had said.

Five minutes later, we were brought two large fry-ups and a pot of tea. If the Scots in Scotland were even half as nice as the Scots in Carlisle then we were in for a treat.

The rain had not relented by the time we braved it back outside, almost two hours after we entered. Our bikes, which we had unsubtly pretended to chain to the trolley depot, were still there. On this rare occasion, I secretly hoped that the bikes would have been stolen. That way, we could have abandoned the whole trip – due to circumstances beyond our control – and then headed home to our warm dry beds and home comforts. There would be no shame in admitting defeat, having made it so far, only for our trusty steeds, that we had worked so tirelessly to acquire, to be taken from us by a couple of pesky Carlislians.

Unfortunately, nobody had seized the opportunity, and the bikes remained where we had left them, ready for us to climb aboard with our damp, bin-liner-coated arses.

Reaching Scotland was certainly an anti-climax.

A bridge across the River Sark marks the border and we were greeted with a brown 'Scotland Welcomes You' sign in the town (if you can call it that) of Gretna.

Gretna is of course famous for its registry offices. In Scotland, the 19th century law that allows 16 year olds to marry without parental consent is still taken advantage of. The first building you see after entering Scotland is one such registry office. The 'First House in Scotland Marriage Room' or 'Last House in Scotland' – depending on which direction you approach it – is a single storey white and black building, right next to the main road. I've definitely seen more romantic wedding venues, but it did have a certain charm.

It was noon and still raining heavily. There was no sign of any brides or grooms, but I got quite excited by the idea of a couple turning up for a spontaneous marriage, and urgently requiring two witnesses. Unfortunately, nobody did. The only way that a wedding by the side of a busy road, on a wet Thursday in Gretna could have been less romantic, would be if Ben and I had been the witnesses.

'Have you ever been to Scotland before?' asked Ben as we stood hugging the 'Scotland Welcomes You' sign (this is a compulsory rite of passage for anyone that enters Scotland by bike or on foot).

'Yes. This is my second time,' I said.
'When was the other time?'
'About five minutes ago.'
'Eh?'
'I had to nip back into England a few minutes ago because my route instructions blew back over the border.'
'You're a moron. So you've never been to Scotland before today?'
'No.'
'Me neither.'
'Rubbish, isn't it?'
'Yes. It never stops raining.'

We posed for a photograph by the sign (again, compulsory), and then set off again. We followed a fairly quiet road that ran parallel to the busy A75, but the cycling was incredibly unpleasant. The rain had collected on the road so much that we were cycling through an inch deep puddle that stretched all the way from Gretna to Dumfries.

'Ben, do you remember that ear stud that Eric gave me back in Cornwall?' I said as I cycled alongside him to avoid being sprayed by his back wheel.
'Yeah, why?'
'I've lost it. It's been attached to my t-shirt all this time, and now it's gone. It must have got knocked off by the bin liner.'
'Oh well. It looked stupid anyway.'
'That's not the point. He gave it to us for good luck.'
'And?'
'Maybe our luck has run out.'
'Cheer up. You're becoming as miserable as me.'

On the way into Dumfries a car pulled out of a side road right in front of me. I applied the brakes, which were ineffective at the best of times. In water, and at high speed, they were completely useless. I was half off the bike by the time I hit the car. The Falcon's pedals and frame slammed into the back driver-side corner of the car, leaving a hefty scratch and a slight dent. Most of the skin was missing from my right knee, but other than that, The Falcon and I had come away quite lightly. The lady's car (I'm not being sexist – she was a female driver) definitely came off worse. She pulled to a stop and got out of her car to inspect the damage. Not to me, but to her car.
'What have you done, you idiot?' she shouted. By this point I had picked The Falcon up off the floor, and was cycling as fast as I could down the hill to catch up with Ben. Yes, technically I was leaving the scene of an accident, but there is no doubt that it was her fault. After all, she did pull out in front of

me. But I also knew that my bike didn't have adequate brakes, and when it comes to driving they say that if somebody hits you from behind, it is always their fault. I assumed this probably applied to cyclists, too, but I didn't want to hang around to find out.

'What happened to you back there?' asked Ben as we pulled into a side road.

'I just had a bit of a run in with a car. I told you our luck had run out.'

'If your luck had run out then you would have come off a lot worse. Are you ok?'

'Yeah, I'm fine thanks,' I said. 'It was a bit scary. I think that's my first ever bike accident involving a car.'

'Really? I've had plenty of them. If you think Dumfries is bad, you should try cycling in London.'

'So what's the deal? Whose fault would it have been, and should I be responsible for getting her car sorted?'

'I've no idea. I've never hung around to find out either.'

We happened to have stopped right next to Robert Burns House, which is 'one of Dumfries's most notable tourist sights'. Or so our route book claimed. Robert Burns, or Rabbie Burns, or Scotland's favourite son, the Ploughman Poet, Robden of Solway Firth, Bard of Ayrshire or just plain old Bob, as I like to call him, is Scotland's most famous poet. I'm sure most of you know this already, but for those – like me – whose history is missing a few key events (such as everything that happened, ever) then I think it's sometimes helpful to give a bit of historical background. Where was I? That's right... Robert Burns is Scotland's most famous poet. He wrote poems, and he... errr... he did something with Liberalism or Socialism or both. And I think he probably invented Burns night, too. That's all I know, I'm afraid.

'Shall we go and have a look around Robert Burns House?' I asked Ben.

'We might as well, I suppose. At least it will be dry in there.'

'I was thinking more that it would be good to learn a bit more about Robert Burns and where he lived.'

'Yeah, of course. That too. But mostly because it will be dry in there.'

Robert Burns House is a small sandstone house just outside Dumfries city centre. It is where he wrote many of his most famous poems, such as that one about the thingy, and that other one about that place.

The man who worked there – the only other person in the building – was very nice and did his best to generate enthusiasm, but in truth, we were both much more interested in the electric heater that sat in the corner of the gift shop. We lurked beside it for a few minutes, pretending to read leaflets and look at postcards, until we had regained feeling in our lower legs and feet.

'Please, feel free to have a wander around the rest of the house. There are lots of interesting things to look at,' he said.

We did. There wasn't.

Don't get me wrong, I understand that Robert Burns was a remarkable man and that his work gives happiness and inspiration to many people, but that doesn't make the house that he grew up in any more interesting.

Robert Burns didn't live a particularly showbiz life. His house looked like any person's house from the 1700s. It had bedrooms, with beds in. A kitchen with a table in it, and a desk where he wrote. There were also windows that you could see through, and doors that both opened and closed.

I can see the appeal in looking around a house such as Graceland, with all its extravagance, or even Michael Jackson's Neverland, but Robert Burns' house just looked like a house. And a fairly unremarkable house at that.

I think my distain for unnecessary 'places of interest' stems from my visit to the Henry Ford Museum, just outside Detroit, Michigan. Henry Ford was… how can I put this politely?… a complete freak. He created, during his lifetime, a model village of significant buildings and things that had influenced his life. This sounds fair enough, but then you discover he had a favourite text book when he was at school, so he located the birthplace of the author of that particular book, and had her entire house shipped to his model village. That's not a normal thing to do. Still, at least Robert Burns House was dry and warm.

'If that was one of the best things to do in Dumfries, then I don't think there's much hope for this place,' said Ben, once we were outside. 'I would rather go to the Northampton Shoe Museum.'

A little further down the road we came across a shopping centre. There was nowhere suitable for us to leave our bikes, so we wheeled them into the shopping centre. Within seconds we were apprehended by a security guard.

'Ye cannae brin' those bikes in here,' he said.

'I know, sorry. It's just that we don't have any way of locking them up. We've just come in to get something to eat.'

'Whaur ur ye gonnae eat?' he asked.

'Wimpy!' I said, spotting a Wimpy close by.

'Awe rite. Weel jist prop yer bikes up by th' dyke thaur ootwith. an' dornt gang ridin' them aroond in haur.'

'Did you get that? What are we supposed to do?' I asked Ben.

'I'm not sure. I think he told us to leave our bikes by this wall and not to ride them inside.'

'Dammit! I've always wanted to ride my bike around a shopping centre. Why did you tell him we were going to Wimpy?'

'I just saw it here and thought he might let us bring our bikes in if we weren't going far. Also, I was genuinely excited about seeing a Wimpy. I thought Wimpy became extinct in the 1980s.'

'Me too. But how are we going to get free food here?' asked Ben.

'Same way we have for the last thirteen days, I guess.'

Pam, the manager, was a large, jovial lady in her late thirties. She had a huge mane of black hair and an even bigger smile. We tried to win her over by telling her about the appalling weather and how kind and generous all Scottish people that we had met had been.

'Are ye takin the pish? Ye want free burgers?' she said with a laugh.

'Errr, yeah, I guess so. I know it sounds cheeky, but we're decent blokes, I promise,' I said hopefully.

'Alrecht. Tak' a seat an' I'll brin' them ower tae ye,' she laughed.

Not only did she bring us a burger each, but fries, milkshakes and a couple of bags of crisps. She stood chatting to us for a while as we ate.

'Ae ye boys got any sort ay raincoat?' she asked.

'We've got a couple of bin-liners that we got in Carlisle this morning,' said Ben.

'Hang oan thaur. I'll gie ye some e'en bigger ones,' she said, and disappeared back behind the counter. Ben and I smirked at each other convinced that there was no way she could trump the bin-liners we already had. We were wrong.

'Hoo abit these bad jimmies?' she said, holding up the most ridiculously big bin bags we had ever seen.

'Oh my god. What do you use bags that big for?' I asked.

'I've got nae idea. They sent us them frae heed office, but they're far tay big e'en fur th' wheelie bins 'at we use. Ah hink they might be body bags.'

'Let's hope not,' said Ben. 'Thanks, Pam. These are amazing.'

We sat and drank our milkshakes as slowly as possible, to delay our return to the cold, wet world outside.

It was 3.30pm by the time I suggested that we leave.

'Do we really have to do more cycling today?' asked Ben.

'We've only done about 35 miles today. We were hoping to do at least 70.'

'But it's been pissing it down all day. It's no fun cycling when the weather's like this.'

'I know, but it would be good to do a few more miles today, because then that's less we have to do for the rest of the trip.'

'How many miles are you thinking?' asked Ben
dejectedly. '20-25?.'

'Oh bloody hell. You're such a masochist. Where will another 20 miles
take us?'

I looked at the route book, and it was clear that there was very little in the
way of civilisation until Kilmarnock, which was almost 70 miles away.

'I'm not sure. There looks like there are plenty of places we pass through,'
I lied. 'How about we aim for the town of Moniaive, which is less than 20
miles away?'

'Give me that!' said Ben, snatching the book from me.

'There's bugger all on the route for bloody miles. We'll end up getting
stranded in the middle of nowhere in this pissing weather,' said Ben,
becoming increasingly frustrated with my stubbornness.

'Let's at least get to Moniaive. Tomorrow you'll be glad you did it.'

'I don't care about tomorrow. I care about today, and I don't think we
should go any further. Look what it says here about Moniaive in the guide
book: 'Moniaive has a marker post in the main street dating from 1638.'
That's all it says. What makes you think we'd even find somewhere to stay
there?'

'I just think we're better off trying to get as many miles done today as
possible.'

'But why? It's not like we're in a race, as you keep reminding me. We've
done 35 miles today. Let's just consider the rest of the day a write-off.'

I knew Ben was right, but the idea of calling it a day at 3.30pm when we
had planned on a big day's cycling just seemed wrong.

'How about another ten miles then as a compromise?' I suggested.

'What about NO? Truly, why? We can simply do those additional ten
miles tomorrow. If you want to do more cycling today then fine, but I'm
staying in Dumfries tonight. You continue and remain in that inept spot with
the moronic wooden post.'

I hesitantly consented to punch out and remain where we were for the
night.

Dumfries, that is, not Wimpy.

We sat peacefully for an additional ten minutes prior to saying thanks to
Pam, recovering our bicycles, and wandering back outside into the rain.

'Are you going to pout the entire day?'
asked Ben. 'I'm not moping,' I said
sulking.

'Yes you are. Trust me, you'll say thanks to me later.'

We observed a bar further up the street and chose to ask inside whether there were any inns or B&Bs around.

The structure was extremely odd. It was anything but a bar, accordingly, however it was anything but a bar or a functioning men's club by the same token. It was more similar to a local area room that ended up having a bar in it. It was 4.15pm on a Thursday and there were somewhere around twelve men in there. The odd thing was that no one was talking and each and every one of them was sat confronting a little TV screen in the corner that was showing Deal or No Deal.

The pressure in the room was terrible. At that point, I didn't actually comprehend the program – I've since become snared, as well – and it was puzzling to watch a gathering of men with such concentration and fixation in their appearances. Even the barman didn't take his eyes off the screen as we walked to the bar. We got some information about convenience – in murmured voices, so as not to ruin the occasion – but rather he actually kept his consideration on the television.

'There's a couple of lodgings doon 'at way ye coods attempt,' he said, guiding his arm toward his right, however not changing his gaze.

'alright, thank you,' I said, and we sneaked from the bar.

'Arrangement, YOU IDIOT! Bargain! TAKE THE BLOODY MONEY!' one of them yelled at the TV in transit out.

We attempted a B&B and afterward an inn. The originally was full, and the second couldn't help. We then, at that point, coincidentally found the Aberdour Hotel.

'How might I help you, fellows?' said the man at gathering. We clarified our circumstance and he provided us with the vibe of a dean giving a detainment. 'Is this some kind of thing for a noble cause, since I've been misled before?'

'No, it's not. That is to say, certain individuals have supported us, however that is not what's going on with it,' I said.

'I've been misled before by individuals saying they're working on something for a noble cause and afterward they simply take advantage.'

'We totally comprehend. Indeed, the place of this excursion is that we're doing whatever it takes not to take advantage of individuals' liberality by utilizing charity.'

'So you're not doing it for charity?'

'No. We're doing it as an analysis to perceive how kind and liberal individuals of Britain are,' said Ben.

'Yet you said that individuals have supported you?'

'Indeed, certain individuals have, however simply because they demanded it.'

'So you are doing it for a noble cause then, at that point? Cos I've been stung before by individuals guaranteeing they were working on something for charity.'

We were wasting time. He thought briefly 'Hang
tight there briefly, and I'll see what I can do.'

He returned a couple of moments later with a key in his hand.

'I will take a risk, since you appear to be two or three nice folks. I apologize for sounding so dubious, however I've been stung before by individuals professing to work on something for charity.'

'obviously, we totally comprehend,' I said, not actually understanding. I was uncertain whether or not he needed us to be fund-raising for a noble cause, however I realized that we had been straightforward with him, so left it at that.

Seeing two clean lodging beds was a much needed development to Ronnie's lounge floor. We removed our spongy shoes, shorts and socks and balanced them on the radiator. We then lay on our beds drifting in and out of sleep. Following a couple of moments there was a provisional thump on the door.

'Come in,' said Ben instinctually, failing to remember that we were both lying on our beds, in matching sets of Union Jack fighter shorts and that's it. It was Colin – the director. He did a twofold take and afterward looked very embarrassed.

'Sorry,' I said. 'We were simply drying a portion of our garments on the radiator.
We don't actually have any extras, which is the reason we're in our pants.'

'Right. Alright,' he said. 'I simply needed to tell you that I've had a word with the cook ground floor, and you can have whatever you like off the menu for supper. I've likewise left £10 behind the bar so ensure you have several lagers each, too.'

Scotland was ridiculous brilliant.

Colin bid farewell, however at that point returned a couple of moments later to provide us with a couple of tracksuit bottoms that he had rescued from lost property.

'I think I better have these as you have your suit pants and some shorts,' said Ben, having a special interest in the tracksuit bottoms immediately.

'alright. However, you had a couple of tracksuit bottoms previously. Keep in mind? Also you chose to simply cut the legs off them.'

'Better believe it, well I will not be cutting the legs off these children,' he said as he pulled on a couple of dry, comfortable tracksuit bottoms. I sat on the bed in my clammy jeans looking on enviously.

After supper and two or three lagers we got back to our room. It was just 7.30pm and we had convenience and were showered, taken care of and watered. Most evenings we would in any case have been out and about at this time.

'What will we do now?' I asked.

'I don't have the foggiest idea. We could simply have an early night?'

'We should have a meander around Dumfries. This is our first night in Scotland after all.'

Dumfries didn't have a ton making it work during the day. There was even less occurring around evening time. To be reasonable for Dumfries, it was a wet Thursday in September. I'm not exactly certain what we expected.

We then, at that point, detected an old film down one of the back roads. 'Extravagant the film?' recommended Ben.

'I can not imagine anything better. We should try.'

We checked the postings board outside. There was only the one screen and it was showing a film called John Tucker Must Die.

'I think I've known about that,' said Ben. 'It should be poo.'

'Well it doesn't seem as though we have much choice.'

The hall was vacant, and the young lady behind the counter didn't look mature enough to see a PG all alone, not to mention work in a film. She was messaging on her telephone and wrapped keeping in touch with her message prior to turning upward to recognize us.

We gave her our sob story about how it was our first night in Scotland, and how we wanted to relax etc. She just shrugged her shoulders and said: 'Whatever. Doesn't make any difference to me. Just go on in.'

I can't recollect anything about John Tucker Must Die. I've seen trailers of it on YouTube since, and nothing about it looks recognizable. I didn't nod off, yet I just totally drafted off and my psyche shut down totally. It was two of the most loosening up hours of my life.

That's not a support for the film, incidentally. It was only the first time in quite a while that I had the option to simply totally turn off and not need to converse with anybody, or ask anybody for anything, or stress over where we planned to eat or sleep.

There was likewise something relieving about being at the film. It was something that 'not unexpected' individuals did. Individuals with cash. Individuals who had a great time. Not that we hadn't been having a great time, but rather every snapshot of the day was busy with a type of actual effort or mental and enthusiastic test. *John Tucker Must Die required none of this.*

I could perceive Ben felt the equivalent way.

As we left the film behind an older couple who had been the main other two individuals at the appearance, Ben did a little skip along the road.

'That was exactly what I really wanted. I feel extraordinary now,' he said.

'Me as well,' I said, and skipped close by him, affectionately intertwined, past the old couple back to our interesting little visitor house.

Scotland sign, Gretna

Day 14 – A place of our own

Dumfries to Neilston – 83 miles

'Ensure you have some morning meal before you go,' said the woman in the workplace, who we ventured to be Colin's better half. 'Colin has needed to go out today, yet he said to give his all the best and to ensure you both had something to eat prior to heading off.'

It was a brilliant, bright day and we both felt such a great deal better compared to we had the day before.

'Great call getting us to stop when we did yesterday,' I said to Ben, during breakfast.

'I told you. I'm in every case right,' he said. 'Scotland doesn't look really awful in the daylight does it?' He was right, for once. It didn't look really awful at all.

The street climbed progressively for twenty miles after Dumfries along the pleasant B729. We went through the towns of Dunscore and Moniaive and in 20 miles we saw close to twelve vehicles. Moniaive, it ended up, had minimal more than the wooden post and it would have been a genuine battle to track down some place to stay.

We had been informed that the Scottish high countries were wonderful, yet the landscape north of Dumfries shocked us totally. Everything looked much greener than anything we had gone through, and the moving scene was dissipated with little hedges of pine trees and an intermittent antiquated ruin. In some other country these would be made into vacation destinations. Scotland has so many of these, that the vast majority of them go unnoticed.

There was very little in the method of civilisation among Dumfries and the town of Dalmellington where we halted for lunch. Dalmellington was a quiet, however tragic looking town. Iron and coal were found in the close by slopes during the 1800s, and for more than 100 years it was a flourishing mining town. Iron creation finished during the 1920s and the coal mineshaft shut during the 1980s, and presently the town feels somewhat neglected.

We called into a bistro on the central avenue. I say 'central avenue', however I think there was just the one road. We were especially aware of requesting free food in a spot that was unmistakably battling, so we demanded that we accomplish some work in return for something to eat. The woman behind the counter demanded that we didn't have to effectively help, and furnished us with a

hotdog bap and some tea.

As an illustration to show exactly how tranquil and quiet Dalmellington was, I was almost run over by a man in a wheelchair.

I was cycling down the central avenue, when he pulled out before me to go across the street without looking. I figured out how to steer far removed without a second to spare however my foot got the floor as I attempted to recapture balance and the pedal turned and smacked against my shin, right away prior to touching the rear of my leg seriously on the fundamental machine gear-piece. I pivoted to see the man in the wheelchair proceed to the opposite roadside without even an acknowledgement.

I assumed the best about him, accepting that he had some type of mental weakness, just as physical, however at that point looked as he occupied with an uproarious discussion with a companion once he came to the next side.

We followed the occupied (by all accounts) A713 to Patna, which was another weird looking town. Patna is essentially a major lodging domain plonked squarely in the center of some lovely Scottish open country. The town was worked in 1802 to give houses to the laborers of the close by coalfields.

Patna pulled in travelers for some time when a close by estate transformed its grounds into a troop park. This ultimately shut in the last part of the 1990s, and the procession park became vandalized, in the end bringing about the lodge being burned to the ground and left as a ruin.

We called into Costcutter to attempt to get another thing to eat. The young lady behind the counter was in her teenagers, and she grinned when we recounted her our story, like it was the most intriguing thing that she had at any point heard. She had lived in Patna every last bit of her life, so the odds are it most likely was.

'Aight, that is bleeding evil, folks,' she said. 'I'll get yers some food. I ought to presumably check with mama director first yet a cannae be pestered and she'll never see in any case. Yous stand by there.' She got a shopping crate from the entryway and started scouring the racks, passageway by path, searching for things to give to us. She filled the crate with bread rolls, a bundle of ham, a square of cheddar, tomatoes, a tin of heated beans, some stomach related bread rolls, two steak pies, apples, pears and two drinks.

'Will this make a big difference for you?' she asked, giving the bushel over. We stood open-mouthed.

'Un-be-lieve-capable,' said Ben. 'Many thanks. Are you certain you're ready to give us all of that?'

'Definitely, grass it. It's presumably all previous its best-before date in any case,' she said, realizing beyond any doubt that it wasn't.

We generally appeared to coincidentally find liberality in the most impossible of spots. It was minutes, for example, this that our confidence in human benevolence was given its greatest lift. Patna, as it ended up, was a damn fine place.

We ate the steak pies and an apple each, and stuffed the rest into our packs to have for dinner.

The street move in the wake of leaving Patna, and afterward dropped for around eight magnificent miles through rich farmland. We arrived at the town of Drongan and halted for a speedy break. I paused for a minute to check our advancement in the course book. There was a tad of data about Drongan. It said:

'... another mining local area whose fortunes endured when the nearby pit shut in 1986. The town's childhood supposedly have a solid nearby competition with adjoining Coylton.'

We didn't stick around extremely long. For the following twenty miles we didn't stop. Not on account of the Drongan packs, obviously. That would have been senseless. Just on the grounds that we were quick to cycle however many miles as we could to compensate for our miserable distance of the past day.

We went through the town of Tarbolton, which has some relationship with Robert Burns, yet chose not to stop to discover what. After our involvement in Robert Burns in Dumfries, we realized we would not be missing out.

The climate was incredible, we had an excess of food, the inclination of the street was in support of ourselves, and Scotland was amazingly lovely. Yet, there was still only one little issue: the Falcon couldn't oversee in excess of a fourth of a mile without the chain falling off.

I had turned into a prepared professional at reattaching it, however it was still extraordinarily baffling. I could sense Ben's anger increasing each time, and he would always mutter an 'oh for fuck's sake' or a 'here we go again' under his breath. Assuming it happened when I was behind him, I would attempt to reattach it subtly and afterward get him up without him taking note. I was effective on a few events, however more often than not he would look back and see me bumbling with the bicycle. He would then try halting to allow me to get up to speed, to make sure he could mumble something like: 'I let you know we ought to have supplanted that piece of poo back in Bath.'

'Don't pay attention to him,' I said, stroking The Falcon's handlebars. 'You're just about as screwed up as your bicycle,' said Ben.

'Well, you're huge... what's more... errr... enormous and inept like your bicycle,' I said. It wasn't one of my best comebacks.

We showed up in the town of Kilmaurs not long before 6pm. The Falcon's chain had tumbled off once more, and Ben was near isolating it totally and folding it over my neck.

'Good gracious,' said Ben, 'I don't accept it.'

'I know, I know. I receive the message,' I said as I attempted to reattach it. 'No, I'm not discussing the bicycle. Investigate there.'

Just across the street from us was a bicycle shop called Walkers Cycling.

'Would you trust it? It's a bleeding bicycle shop. It's destiny,' said Ben. 'We've got to take a quick trip and check whether they can do anything regarding that bicycle. I can't go on like this.'

'alright,' I said, 'yet all at once it's 5.55pm. I figure it'll be closed.'

It was open. We were welcomed inside by an unshaven man, who looked more like an amicable maths instructor than somebody who should work in a bicycle shop. I clarified what we were doing, and that we were having a couple of bicycle issues, and inquired as to whether they had any tips or guidance on how we could delay the existence of The Falcon.

'No issue. I'll get one of my folks to come and investigate it,' he said.

We were joined outside by two youthful mechanics who went through no less than ten minutes oiling and tweaking the back derailleur and chain.

'We've halted at several bicycle shops en route as of now and the two of them let us know that it was totally broken and that there was no expectation,' I said.

'That is not in the soul of your experience,' said John, the unshaven man, who claimed and ran the shop with his significant other Susan.

'So you've truly come this way without going through any cash whatsoever?' asked Susan.

'Yes.'

'And you've figured out how to get some place to rest consistently, and a lot of food?'

'We've gone hungry a couple of times and we have needed to rest in a couple of odd spots, however we're doing ok.'

'We get a great deal of End to Enders bringing in light of the fact that Kilmaurs is by all accounts on large numbers of the famous courses,' said John. 'But I think in all the years I've been working here that you two are the craziest.'

'Without a doubt,' giggled part of the gang, who was all the while seeing to The Falcon. 'These tires are level, as well. You should presumably put some more air in

them on the off chance that I were you.'

'We don't have a siphon tragically,' I said.

'You're kidding? You are cycling 1,000 miles and you don't have a siphon. What might be said about a cut fix pack?' asked John.

'No,' I said, feeling like I was being told off.

'What occurs assuming you get a cut in no place?' 'We got one.

In Wales. We needed to stroll to the closest house.'

'You all are totally crazy. Susan, proceed to snatch these young men a siphon, cut fix unit and whatever else that you figure they may require. What's more what the heck were you doing in Wales, anyway?'

'I don't actually have the foggiest idea,' I said.

Susan returned a couple of moments later with a siphon, cut fix pack, a 'Walkers Cycling' drinking jug and holder, and a modest bunch of energy bars.

'There you go,' said the one who had been taking care of The Falcon. 'You ought to have the option to receive a couple of more miles in return now.'

'You mean The Falcon isn't broken?' I asked excitedly.

'No, The Falcon is a long way from broken. It simply required a touch of adoration and affection.'

I needed to embrace him yet I figured out how to contain myself.

'Doesn't your back hurt riding something so little?' asked John.

'Indeed. A considerable amount,' I said.

'He LOVES torment,' said Ben.

'Thank you all such a great amount for your liberality and excitement,' I said as we moved back on our bikes.

'Not in any manner,' said John. 'We ought to much obliged. You've made our day.'

All four of them remained on the landing area before the shop and waved us off. If you are ever in East Ayrshire – or further afield – and have bike problems, then I would wholeheartedly recommend Walkers Cycling. Despite the fact that, I think the vast majority need to pay for their provisions and repairs.

Interestingly, John Dunlop – the creator of the pneumatic bike tire – was conceived only a few miles west of here. As a matter of fact, on re-understanding that, it isn't exceptionally fascinating at all.

I might want to add that, in the wake of leaving Kilmaurs, The Falcon's chain never tumbled off again.

We were in such positive feelings that we neglected to see that we had been cycling uphill for ten miles.

'Will this fuckin slope at any point end?'

said Ben. 'I trust so,' I panted.

'Will we search for some place to remain in the following town that we get to?' 'Better believe it. There's a spot called Neilston in another ten miles.'

'Ten miles? Are you messing with me?' asked Ben.

'Blunder, no. It doesn't resemble there's whatever else before there anyway.

We've done all around well today. I figure we'll have done more than 90 miles.' 'WHAT? My god, you are such a slave master. Assuming I'd realized we had done

anything close to that amount, I would have halted for the day a very long time back.' 'I know. That is the reason I didn't tell you.'

The street kept on moving for quite some time and afterward slid steeply for one more three miles into the town of Neilston. Our initial feelings of the town were not very ideal. It was 8pm and a young lady in her initial adolescents was being debilitated external the Chinese important point on the primary street.

Ben recommended that we attempt to go through the night in the congregation, yet the congregation entryway was locked. We thumped yet there was no response.

'That resembles the vicar,' I said, detecting a man strolling not too far off away from the congregation. We pursued him.

'Excuse me,' gasped Ben. 'Are you the vicar for that congregation up the street?' 'Indeed, I am. Is there an issue?' he asked suspiciously.

'No, a walk in the park. We were... ' Ben stopped, attempting to slow down and rest, 'we were puzzling over whether there was any chance of us dozing in the congregation tonight.'

'Dozing in the congregation? Whatever for?'

'We're cycling the length of the country without going through any cash and we really want some place to rest tonight.'

'Sorry, I can't help you.'

'We needn't bother with beds or anything like that. All we really want is some type of sanctuary,' I pleaded.

'No. I can't help, I'm afraid.'

'Do you know anybody that could possibly help us?' asked Ben.

'No, I don't think so. Goodbye,' he said, and strolled away.

Somewhat not too far off we saw him stroll into his home – a gigantic mansion.

'I never figured I would say this,' said Ben, 'yet that vicar was a complete cock.'

'I know. Check out the size of his home. It should have somewhere around five bedrooms.'

'They're presumably generally loaded with bound and choked ensemble boys.'

I might want to bring up that this vicar may don't really work in Neilston. The current vicar is presumably an exceptionally pleasant individual, and I'm certain they would have invited us into their congregation with open arms.

Towards the base finish of the town we detected a bar called The Traveler's Rest. We concealed our bicycles around the back by the canisters and headed inside. It was a warm, comfortable bar that would not have watched awkward on a cold mountainside in Germany; loads of wood framing, angrily lit, an energetic environment, and heaps of individuals wearing lederhosen. I lied about the lederhosen.

There were around twelve individuals in the bar, and the vast majority of them encompassed the pool table where a man wearing decorator's overalls was taking on some youthful challenger. The decorator strutted around the table like Paul Newman, and continued to pot four reds in succession prior to continuing in the white off the dark. The remainder of the gathering cried with chuckling and the youthful challenger raised his prompt over his head in victory.

There was one solitary man sitting at the bar, and we remained there for a couple of moments until the barman appeared.

'Sorry chaps. I don't figure I can help you, I'm apprehensive,' said the landowner after we had gotten some information about the chance of some place to rest. 'We do have a couple of rooms accessible for lease, however I can't actually give you one of those.'

'We wouldn't require one of your legitimate rooms. Would we be permitted to rest here in the bar?' asked Ben. 'We would be no trouble.'

'Sorry, no, I can't allow you to remain in the bar, though it pains me to say so. It would repudiate our protection policy.'

'Are you truly going all that way without going through any cash?' asked the man at the bar, who had been paying attention to our request.

'Yes. We've been out and about for two weeks.'

'Reasonable play to you,' he giggled. 'Allow me to get you both a beer.'

Alec lived south of the boundary and was only up in Neilston short-term for business. He was very obscure with regards to the sort of business that he did, so we didn't pry. He asked us a wide range of inquiries about our excursion, and afterward demanded getting us another brew. It was 10pm when we recalled that we

had no place to sleep.

The pool-playing decorator's name was Jim, and he was a joiner, rather than a decorator. In spite of the fact that, I don't know how somebody who fits wood together can get such a lot of paint on their garments. Jim The Joiner – as his companions called him – was in his forties and very loquacious. He was clearly 'the man' of the Traveler's Rest, and potentially the entire of Neilston. Promptly after conversing with him he had requested the barman to get us both a brew on him.

'I wish ah coods help ye wi' some place tae stay,' he said mid pool shot, 'however our hoose jist isn't enormous enaw, aam afraid.'

'Rest is exaggerated at any rate,' said Ben. 'The brew is better.'

'Yoo have an extra hoose, haven't ye, Les,' called Jim to one of different men in the group.

'Extremely interesting, Jim,' chuckled Les. We didn't comprehend the joke, however snickered along anyway.

We spent the following hour drinking all the more free brew, playing pool and eating soup and bread that one more of the men had requested for us. We were sitting in a warm bar on comfortable seats, drinking free lager and eating broccoli and stilton soup with crunchy bread. We didn't have any worries whatsoever. That was, until we recollected that the probability was that we would go through the night on the streets.

'Anyway,' said Ben, 'our karma was because of run out at some point. Basically we are full and drunk.'

'I actually think we'll track down some place to remain. We could stroll down towards Paisley. It's a couple of miles. It's a lot greater and there will undoubtedly be a lot of spots to remain,' I suggested.

'It's basically impossible that I am going any further this evening. I'd prefer rest in the bar vehicle leave than walk any more. I'm knackered.'

Midway through our fifth 16 ounces – as we stood watching Jim The Joiner get beaten at pool once more – Les moved toward us holding a lot of keys. He was a tiny man in his forties, with a cordial face and an English articulation. He had resided in Neilston for quite a long time and considered Scotland 'home'.

'I will face a major challenge here, chaps,' said Les. 'These are the keys to my home. It's practically vacant right now as I'm currently selling it, yet you can both proceed to rest there this evening, if you like.'

'Would you say you are not kidding? So you truly have an extra house?' I said, unfit to clear the smile off of my face.

'Well, indeed, I surmise that actually I do. It actually has all of my office gear there and PC stuff, which is the reason I'm taking somewhat of a bet. I like you both, however, and I think you are certified. Kindly don't let me down.'

He gave us bearings to the house which was about a fourth of a mile back up through the town. We said our gratitude to everybody, and afterward wheeled our bicycles shakily to Les's.

We had dozed in a waterway boat, a luxurious lodging, and an independent level, however we had recently been given our own special current, three-bed semi-segregated house in a peaceful circular drive for the evening. We had increased present expectations at this point again.

Before heading to sleep, we made cheddar, ham and tomato rolls from the provisions we were given in Patna. I lay on the rug canvassed in a towel. Ben, typically, was utilizing his dozing bag.

Ben and The House, near Dalmellington

Ben, somewhere in Scotland

Me, somewhere in Scotland

Walkers Cycling, Kilmaure

North of Dumfries

LEE Neilson

Day 15 – Another food festival

Neilston to Crianlarich – 42 miles

We arose to the sound of something falling through the letterbox. We had just been in our new house for one evening, and right now individuals were sending us post. I staggered down the stairs in my jeans and found a dispersing of five dispensable razors and a gel bicycle seat lying on the doormat.

'Ben?' I yelled higher up. 'Why has someone posted razors and a gel seat through the door?'

'Huh? Gracious, that can't avoid being that person from the previous evening. Dave, I think his name was
– the chap who got us soup.'

'How would you know?'

'Cos he said we were looking messy and he planned to give us a few razors so we could shave.'

'Goodness. What might be said about the gel seat?'

'That is for you. He went to view our bicycles by the receptacles the previous evening, and afterward said he was unable to accept you'd been riding a particularly awkward looking bike.'

We got our things together and figured out how to clean up the wreck that we had made in the kitchen similarly as Les showed up to mind his home. We expressed gratitude toward him for his massive liberality and requested that he give our gratitude to all the others at The Traveler's Rest.

We were out and about at a decent 9am. It was a cold however clear morning. The initial three miles were downhill as far as possible, and we freewheeled into Paisley keeping watch for breakfast. Paisley is a town in itself, however it has continuously been gobbled up by adjacent Glasgow.

At the time, we were both very disillusioned with Paisley town focus. We cycled around for 15 minutes searching for any indication of something going on under the surface, yet couldn't track down a solitary shop or bistro that was open. It was like it was the apocalypse, however somebody had neglected to tell us.

Having since done some Googling, I have found that Paisley does truth be told have a town place with a decent looking pedestrianized shopping road. This in some way figured out how to escape us.

As we were leaving town we ran over a bistro called Korner Kitchen. Inside, there was a line of three laborers generally sitting tight for their breakfast.

The bistro was controlled by two noisy, grinning women. We looked as they flipped bacon, singed eggs and poured tea with a veritable love and excitement for their
work. When it went to our chance to be served, they had as of now timed us and had caused a stir at our garments. We did vary marginally to their typical demographic of heater suit clad workmen.

'What would i be able to get both of you studly chaps?' said the more youthful of the two ladies.

We clarified our test and inquired as to whether there would anything say anything was we could do in return for some free food.

'Oooooh, what do you figure, Jan? Should we give these two tying youthful fellows any food?' she said to her colleague.

'Better believe it, what difference would it make. Assuming that one with the meager shorts shows us a touch more leg,' she laughed.

'That'll be you then, George,' said Ben. This was an amazing failure. I was being made to display my body in return for food. I felt objectified. I felt modest. I loved it. I lifted up the side of my scanty blue shorts, and uncovered my heavy white thighs.

'Phwoooooaarr,' said the two women as one, preceding emitting into giggling. 'What about a frankfurter bap, some tea and a custard doughnut each?' she said.

By the time we had completed our morning meal it was 10.45am, and our solid beginning had disappeared. We followed the A726 out of Paisley and crossed the Erskine Bridge. For span lovers out there, the Erskine Bridge is a 524m, link remained, box brace span, worked in 1971 and planned by William Brown. It interfaces West Dunbartonshire with Renfrewshire. For those less intrigued, the Erskine Bridge is a major extension that crosses a river.

We halted most of the way across the scaffold to respect the staggering perspectives on the River Clyde. Public phones and adverts for The Samaritans were introduced at ordinary stretches along the scaffold's railings, and our disposition took a solemn turn when we understood that we were remaining at one of Scotland's most infamous self destruction spots.

We had a choice to make when we arrived at the opposite finish of the extension. We could either follow the bustling A82 to Loch Lomond, or take the more drawn out course which followed a cycle way and minor streets portrayed by the course book as: *'gravely surfaced' and passing 'behind metropolitan regions not suggested for solo cyclists.'*

'We most certainly take the A82,' said Ben resolvedly. 'Why? We're not independent cyclists,' I said.

'No doubt, however it sounds dodgy. At any rate, the A82 will be much quicker.'

'It will not be dodgy. I bet we're substantially more liable to be harmed on the fundamental street than on a cycle path.'

'Assuming I will get harmed I would prefer to be hit by a vehicle than wounded or shot.'

'You truly are a screwball,' I said. 'How about we take the tourist detour. I'll ensure you.'

'Fine, well I'm not going to secure you and assuming you get cut then, at that point, it's your own fault.'

The Clyde and Loch Lomond Cycleway, as it is formally called, is a cycle course that broadens 20 miles from the focal point of Glasgow to the shores of Loch Lomond. It was totally splendid to cycle along. Despite the fact that we had followed moderately calm streets all through the outing, we actually must be aware of the possibility of different vehicles. The cycleway was generally our own and it was very freeing. I even pulled a wheelie.

There were a couple of areas that strayed through marginally summary lodging bequests, however there was never any danger of risk. Ben had a slight a showdown with a fly that flew into his mouth, however they figured out how to determine that between themselves.

We showed up in the town of Balloch at around 2pm, during one more food celebration. The Loch Lomond Food and Drink Festival occurred in the vehicle park of the Loch Lomond Aquarium.

Most of the slows down offered free tastings, which ought to have fit us impeccably. It was in reality more problem that it was worth, notwithstanding, as we needed to pay attention to a dreary attempt to close the deal about the advantage of Scottish olives over Greek olives, and gesture away energetically for ten minutes in return for a solitary Scottish olive. We then had to endure the same for a morsel of Scottish cheese, and again for a Scottish chipolata. It was not the best return for 30 minutes effort.

We chose to turn to our attempted and tried genuine methodology. We actually had a touch of cheddar and a few tomatoes from the earlier day, so just required somewhat more for lunch.

Ben figured out how to get a little portion of bread, and I was given some sun-dried tomato focaccia.

'My god, you are a particularly working class blagger. Foccacia? What the hell?' said Ben.

'Check out you with your worker bread,' I said. 'I'm humiliated to even know you.'

Cycling along the shores of Loch Lomond had vowed to be one of the features of our excursion; 25 miles without a solitary slope, the shimmering lake on one side and the battered mountains on the other. The course book caused us to salivate at the prospect:

'The A82 north from Balloch is a wonderful road.'

It isn't. In principle it ought to be, yet it's really a genuinely horrible street. The A82 fills in as the fundamental course connecting the swamps and the western good countries, which implies that pretty much every individual going among Glasgow and the north passes along this road.

We embraced the skirt intently, as a steady stream of mentors, vehicles, bands and motorbikes snarled along the thin street. Concerning the view, that likely would have been great assuming we had the option to see it. During an intermittent break in rush hour gridlock the view was darkened by a thick boundary of trees that developed along the shore.

The most baffling issue, notwithstanding, was the real street surface. It was anything but an issue with potholes, in that capacity. For reasons unknown – potentially intentional – the whole surface is finished like a cheddar grater. It was totally debilitating to cycle along. We ought to have had the option to cover the distance quickly, as there was no inclination, yet it seemed like a genuine exertion just to keep going.

In rundown, the A82 ought to be a wonderful street. All it needs is finished reemerging, to be shut of any remaining traffic, and to have some genuine deforestation.

We at last arrived at the villa of Ardlui at the northern finish of Loch Lomond. It was 7pm and we were prepared to tap out. Ardlui has an inn and a camping area however we had no karma tracking down convenience at either.

'There's a couple of spots in Crianlarich – that is the following town – that you could attempt,' said the man at the campsite.

'alright, much obliged. How far is
that?' I inquired. 'Ooooh, it's just
another 3-4 miles.' 'Crianlarich,
child!' said Ben.

Crianlarich was more like ten miles further up the street, and every last trace of it was uphill. Both of my hands were crude from scouring on the handlebars and my back felt like I had been snapped fifty-fifty. It was one of the most incredibly excruciating day's cycling of the excursion, and it was exacerbated by the conviction that it

should be our easiest.

I realize that it's a banality, however cycling – and any remaining proactive tasks, besides – is totally dependent on being in the right mental zone. All together for your body to accomplish its maximum capacity, you should have the option to concentrate all of your psychological energy into removing yourself from any aggravation, uneasiness, and the acknowledgment of the test that you are confronting. I'm not talking for a fact here, coincidentally; I'm citing from a book that I read. I have never arrived at this psychological zone and each type of actual exercise I have at any point done has caused extreme measures of torment and discomfort.

It was practically dull when we arrived at Crianlarich. We followed signs to the Crianlarich Youth Hostel, which we felt certain would have the option to take care of us. Our expectations were run by a grinning, hairy man, who told us, cordially, that there were no rooms accessible by any means, and that no we were unable to rest on the floor, or rest in his office, and no he didn't have a tent that we could acquire. All things being equal, we got into a significant discussion with him about CAMRA (the mission for genuine beer), however I don't know why, for sure the importance to our outing was. But if you are ever in the area and want to talk to someone about beer, then the guy at the Crianlarich Youth Hostel is your man.

'We're buggered,' said Ben, when we were outside. 'Assuming that a Youth Hostel won't allow us to remain, then, at that point, what chance have we got of finding somewhere?'

'Relax. We say this consistently. That chap at the camping area said there were heaps of choices here. We'll find somewhere.'

'No doubt, however that chap likewise said it was only several miles up the road.

And he neglected to make reference to that it was mostly up a wicked mountain.'

We pushed our bicycles once more into the town and called into Londis to request some food. The man behind the counter said he couldn't help, however recommended that we attempt the Ben More Lodge for some place to remain, which was simply out and about out of the village.

Whilst we were outside, the man from Londis came out. He emerged from the shop, I mean. He didn't declare to us that he was gay. That would have been very random.

'Here you go. I viewed as these for you. Two fish pasta prepare prepared dinners, and two spag bol prepared suppers. They are largely past their best-before date, yet I'm certain they'll be fine,' he said.

'Awesome. You are a star. Much thanks to you,' I said.

They were microwave dinners. All we wanted was a microwave.

The Ben More Lodge is a solitary story long white structure, encircled by a couple of wooden chalets. The spot had a beautiful comfortable feel to it, with a thundering log fire. One of the white dividers of the bar region had been totally canvassed in spray painting. Not a demonstration of careless defacing, but rather many little messages written in pen from guests to the Ben More Lodge. Most were from individual cyclists or climbers who had gone through on their excursions. Phrases such as '*Pain is just weakness leaving the body*,' '*Scotland Rules*,' and '*Ease the chaffing*,' were scrawled all over the wall and it was fascinating to think of all of the different groups of people who had undertaken challenges of their own and shared similar moments of pleasure reading the tales of others.

We chose to add our own message. Subsequent to going through a few minutes attempting to consider something clever or inspiring to compose, we agreed to 'LEJOG – with no cash. *George and Ben.*' *Truly inspirational.*

The administrator strolled over to us following ten minutes. His name was Graham and he was in his mid thirties, stocky with spiky dark hair.

'I comprehend you are searching with the expectation of complimentary convenience this evening as a feature of some test,' he said, in a scarcely observable Scottish accent.

'Indeed, believe it or not,' said Ben.

'Well that is not something I can approve myself. I would have to check with the proprietor. Is that good with you both?'

'Indeed, obviously. Thank you.'

'She's not working today so I should call her at home, yet she may not be back for one more hour or thereabouts. I'll acquire you over a free brew the meantime.'

'60 minutes?' murmured Ben, when the director had left, 'We can hardly wait for 60 minutes.'

'Why not? We've got nothing else to do, and he's bringing us a beer. What could be better?'

'What occurs on the off chance that he addresses the director and she says no. It'll be gone 10pm by then, at that point, and we'll be in the Scottish mountains with no place to stay.'

'I hadn't considered it like that. I surmise we'll stress over that assuming it occurs. Hopefully she says yes.'

It was a staggeringly long and restless hour. Disregard A-level outcomes day.

Forget your nation being 1-0 down in the World Cup Final with five minutes of injury-time added. Disregard holding on to check whether Jack Bauer will save the world once more. This was genuinely tension.

Just before 10pm, Graham stepped over to us. His face was completely emotionless.

'I've recently addressed the proprietor,' he said, 'and she said that I can't allow you to have one of our rooms or cabins, I'm afraid.'

'Gracious, alright… ' I said.

'Yet,' he intruded on, 'she said you are free to have one of the bunks in the staff bunkhouse. Is that good with you?'

Ben and I checked out one another and afterward laughed.

'No. As a matter of fact, that is not adequate, Graham. We need your best hotel or nothing by any means. Obviously that is alright, you're an outright legend,' said Ben, standing up and giving him a colossal hug.

I did likewise, and we had an off-kilter bunch embrace for a couple of moments. Graham's face remained totally unfeeling. I envision he would have presumably appeared to be identical on the off chance that he won the lottery or when he was having intercourse. Not that I have envisioned him engaging in sexual relations. That would be weird.

'When you said 'bunkhouse', I thought you planned to show us to some rodent plagued shed. This is astounding,' I said.

'Well, it's not The Ritz, but rather ideally it's sufficient for you both,' said Graham.

The bunkroom had six beds and an en-suite washroom. We were the main inhabitants so had the pick of any of the beds.

'It's above and beyond, Graham,' said Ben. 'I believe I'm the most joyful man on the planet at this moment. I thought we would have been dozing in a chilly Scottish field tonight.'

'Great, well I'm happy we could help. Is there whatever else I can help you with?'

'Really, there is something,' I said. 'We were given these microwave suppers from Londis up the street. We don't have a microwave, clearly. Is there any possibility that you could warm these up for us, or let us utilize a microwave, please?'

'That is a walk in the park. I'll proceed to figure that out for you. Return over to the bar region shortly or so.'

'We repeated the experience, Georgie Boy. See this spot, it's great. Bagsie having this bed,' said Ben, plunging onto one of the base bunks.

We both had a speedy shower – not simultaneously – and put on the most un-slutty of our shirts prior to getting back to the bar.

'I figured you could save those suppers for one more day,' said Graham. He was conveying a plate with two major dishes of soup, two plates of chips and two buttered baguettes.

'Hell, I was truly anticipating my outdated Londis microwave supper,' I said sarcastically.

'Graham, you really are my saint. I may need to give you another embrace,' said Ben.

'No. That truly will not be fundamental. I'll bring you over one more several brews. Goodness, incidentally, you can eat toward the beginning of the day. Simply let the individual know who is working that you cleared it with me.'

Korner Kitchen, Paisley

Ben, Loch Lomond Food & Drink Festival, Balloch

Day 16 – The highlands

Crianlarich to Fort William – 42 miles

'Where are those razors that Dave gave us?' asked Ben.

'In the lower part of my sack, I think. Why?'

'I will shave. It's time.'

Whilst Ben was shaving, I went to keep an eye on our bicycles which we had concealed around the rear of the hotel. The Falcon's rear wheel was extremely level. I had seen it the other day yet it was a lot of more awful. Because of our new siphon and cut fix unit this was of little worry by any stretch of the imagination. I acquired a cleaning up bowl loaded with water from the eatery kitchen and afterward set to chip away at The Falcon.

Ben rose up out of the bunkroom a couple of moments later resembling a 12 year old kid. The facial hair had really made him look more experienced, yet in a filthy, trampy way, and presently he had returned to his pre-pubescent self.

'How would I look, eh?' he

inquired. 'Energetic,' I said.

'You should give it a go.'

'No. I can't actually be tried to be straightforward. Wasn't it excruciating shaving that much facial hair off?'

'Yes. I went through four of those razors. What's new with the cleaning up bowl and cut kit?'

'I was simply checking The Falcon's tire for an

opening.' 'Why?'

'In light of the fact

that it was level.'

'Did you fix it?'

'No, on the grounds that there wasn't a hole.'

'So you have a bicycle whose tires go down without

penetrates?' 'Yes.'

'My god, that bicycle is such a heap of crap.'

We gobbled porridge and a cook for breakfast and set off presently before 10am. The just a tad subsequent to leaving Crianlarich prior to dropping to Bridge of Orchy; a villa comprising of a lodging, a railroad station, and a several houses. Goodness, and an extension,

of course.

The course book referenced that the BrIdge of Orchy Hotel served a 'incredible banoffee pie', which we fantasized about as we cycled past. As it turns out, an awesome companion of mine cases that his Grandma developed banoffee pie. I

don't accept him.

Just after Bridge of Orchy we passed Loch Tulla – a mirror-like lake encompassed by windburned heather and a dissipating of old pine trees. It was starting to seem as though the Scottish good countries that I had envisaged.

The climate was as yet dry, however the sky in front of us was dark and we realized that downpour was inescapable. The street climbed steeply through a bend that appeared to continue for a significant distance. We were presently in obvious Braveheart country. Except for the street, there was no indication of civilisation in any direction.

Unfortunately, bank occasions and streets make a deadly blend. The traffic was determined, and a continuous downpour of motorbikes dealt with the street like Brands Hatch. In addition to the fact that it made cycling terrible, and possibly perilous, however the clamor was horrendous. It resembled having a mosquito caught inside your eardrum. It was not how we envisioned the distant Scottish high countries would be.

Just before the culmination, we arrived at a lay-by where we halted for a break. There was a frozen yogurt van and a keepsake slow down selling pieces of plaid poop. Poop keepsakes, I mean. Not plaid excrement. Despite the fact that I'm certain there's most likely a hole on the lookout for that.

There was additionally a bagpipe player who appeared to stash in light of the approaching precipitation. We halted close to him and pulled on our best in class waterproof cycling gear – the trusty canister liners. He proposed to play us a tune, regardless of us letting him know that we didn't bring any cash to the table. His name was Sandy and he drove from Glasgow consistently to play his bagpipes in that specific spot.

'Hae ye nae got legitimate waterproofs?' he asked, when he saw what we were wearing.

'No, tragically not. Simply canister liners,' said Ben.

'Yoo would do well to ride vigilant in those. Two individuals ur killed regularly on these roods. Yoo'll be gonnae home in a feckin' body bag.'

As we left the lay-by the climate shut in totally. An invulnerable cover of haze had fallen onto the mountainside, casings us in its moist, cold tissue. Our course book depicted this piece of the street as follows...

'On a fine summer's day this is a delightful ride... Be that as it may, when it's cloudy, wet and breezy the banks close in, and a headwind can make this part extreme going.'

This was most certainly a misrepresentation of the truth. The bagpipe player's words were tormenting me.

'Two individuals ur killed regularly on these roods. Yoo'll be gonnae home in a feckin' body sack,' I said without holding back, in my awful Scottish inflection. It sounded more Jamaican.

'I know. What the heck did he need to say that for? However, much obliged, Sandy, for horrifying us,' said Ben.

'He presumably had a point. Take a gander at us! We were unable to be all the more perilously dressed on the off chance that we attempted. Possibly we should push just a tad, just until the haze clears.'

'That sounds great to me. I disdain imparting a street to these moronic mentors and motorbikes anyway.'

There was almost no space to securely stroll on the edge of the street, so we wheeled our bicycles along the skirt which was amazingly boggy and uneven.

After with regards to 30 minutes we could make out what gave off an impression of being a bunch of traffic-signals through the fog. The lofty mountain street was being fixed and was down to one path. The traffic was sifted subsequently, and approaching traffic had to stand by at the lights. A worker ventured out from his lodge when he saw us approaching.

'Are you going to Glencoe?' he inquired. Ben looked to me, as he never known where we were going.

'Indeed, we are,' I said.

'I can't release you down that way, though it pains me to mention it. The perceivability is really awful and it would be dangerous.'

'alright, a walk in the park. We'll simply push our bicycles down then, at that point, assuming that is ok?'

'No, I'm grieved. I can't allow you to do that by the same token. The street is excessively tight and vehicles wouldn't have the option to see you, regardless of whether you were walking.'

'What would we be able to do then?'

'Assuming you stay nearby for ten minutes, I'll give you a lift down the mountain in the van.'

'Splendid. Much obliged mate,' said Ben excitedly.

'Sorry to be abnormal,' I said, 'However we're cycling from Land's End to John O'Groats and, I know this sounds frivolous, yet on the off chance that we got a lift with you then I would feel like we've cheated as we haven't actually cycled the entire way.'

'Gracious, George, quit being such a fanatic. It's two or three miles, and we don't actually have any decision,' said Ben.

'No, no, he's right,' said the worker. 'I can see that it would feel like cheating to get a lift. This is what I'll do. I'll radio down to the folks at the base, and in brief we'll stop the traffic in the two ways while you cycle down. Allow me just to proceed to get you two or three high-vis vests as well, for good measure. You look strange like that. Simply hand them to the folks at the base when you get there.'

'THIS IS AMAZING!' I yelled, as we plummeted down the mountain with the way to ourselves.

'No doubt, yet it would have been considerably more astonishing toward the rear of a warm van,' said Ben.

'Would you not have felt awful doing that?'

'No. Not at all. Despite the fact that, it is cool them shutting a whole mountain for us.'

'If by some stroke of good luck they could close the following 200 miles of street for us, too.'

It just required a couple of moments to arrive at the base, yet currently the traffic was upheld at the lights as should have been obvious. We turned in our vests to the man in the lodge and cycled off, trailed by the glare of many disappointed motorists.

During our plummet, I recalled that The Falcon's brakes were totally defective in the wet. The last time we had cycled in wet climate was in Dumfries and I had wound up sliding into the rear of a vehicle. I had some way or another failed to remember this reality, and carried on as though they would fix themselves.

On those tricky streets, my powerlessness to stop might have brought about me taking a diversion more than one of the numerous slopes. The breeze, fog and downpour were constant, and it was a test just to keep the bicycles out and about. That, and the additional danger of the threatening traffic, made cycling on this stretch of street especially dangerous.

'This is moronic,' said Ben, 'we should simply walk again.'

'Fine by me,' I said, getting off in a brief moment. It was 4pm and I had become marginally worried that we wouldn't come to any civilisation before dark.

'How far is it until the closest town or town?' asked Ben.

'A couple of more miles… likely,' I reacted vaguely.

Every inch of our bodies was drenched, and interestingly on the excursion, we began to feel the virus. Even when the weather had been cold before, we had maintained a good body temperature whilst cycling. Strolling had permitted our dissemination and pulses to dial back and our bodies were enduring at the

hands of the climate. I quickly lamented being so decrying towards the three sets of gloves referenced in our manual's example unit list. Only one sets of gloves would have made a major difference.

We walked for several miles with no sense of our surroundings at all. The haze was extremely thick that we were unable to try and see the opposite roadside, not to mention what lay in front of us. Then, at that point, arising out of the mist, a sign appeared.

Glencoe Visitor Centre

It resembled a desert garden in the desert. Just without the sand, unquestionably without the sun, and with parcels more rain.

'Please be open, please be open, please be open,' we repeated, as we walked up the long drive to the visitor centre. There wasn't a thing specifically that we thought the guest place could accomplish for us to facilitate our circumstance, however being inside and warm was generally that we desired.

It was open.

'They have a bistro!' said Ben. 'I keep thinking about whether they'll warm our microwave suppers up for us.' It was almost 5pm and we hadn't eaten since breakfast.

The kitchen was being monitored by a man named Paul, a smiley, whiskery refined man with enormous glasses. He was wearing an identification that said 'Guest Center Manager', so he seemed like the acceptable individual to inquire. We recounted to him our story, and he grinned and gestured away enthusiastically.

'Indeed, that is not an issue to warm up your suppers,' he said. 'You both seem as though you could do with a hot cocoa, too.'

It truly was the best hot cocoa I have at any point tasted; thick, excessively sweet hot cocoa, finished off with cream, marshmallows and a piece. I think you likely need to go through hours strolling in the breeze and downpour, dressed distinctly in some shorts and a canister sack to completely see the value in it, yet it's most certainly worth inspecting, in case you are ever in the area.

The Londis microwaveable spaghetti Bolognese wasn't really awful either. Again, I think our delight in this was incompletely due to the circumstances.

'I don't think I've at any point felt as hopeless as I did thirty minutes prior,' said Ben after a while.

'Indeed, it was really horrid,' I said. 'However, basically we're dry now and it's not far to go today.'

'That is the issue. Today isn't the finish of the bicycle ride. We've actually got many miles to go until John O'Groats and I simply need it to be over.'

'Are you hating it at all?'

'No. It's repulsive. I continue to figure how I could be at home sitting on the couch, drinking tea at whatever point I like, going to the film, going to the bar. The main thing getting me through this is realizing that every day implies we're one more day closer to finishing.'

'Simply envision the pride we'll feel when we've finished.'

'I used to imagine that, however presently I don't see the point. I mean is it truly worth all the effort?'

'I'm having a good time. Obviously I'm anticipating getting done, as well, yet I'm truly partaking in every day. Today has been horrendous, as a matter of fact, yet a large portion of it has been great. In addition, we've been to the film and bar, and drank a lot of tea since we've been on the road.'

Ben gave an enormous murmur. He had shown snapshots of disappointment previously, yet this was the primary genuine indication of disheartening. I trusted that it didn't be anything that a spot to rest and a difference in climate couldn't fix.

We remained in the bistro however long we could, yet Paul at last urged us to leave as he was quitting for the day. We put in no time flat attempting to dry our garments under the hand-dryers in the latrine, and afterward overcame it back outside.

It was all the while coming down outside, yet the haze was clearing and the sun was battling to get through the mists. Ben looked completely discouraged as he pulled the all around wet container liner over his head and moved on board The Horse. Wrong, that last sentence would sound very strange.

'Cheer up, mate. It's declining the entire way to Glencoe,' I said. 'No doubt right. I've heard that one before.'

'It is, I guarantee you. It's several miles.' 'Is that where we will remain tonight?'

'It's dependent upon you. We can attempt to track down some place there, or it's one more 15 miles along the banks of a loch to Fort William, which is a lot greater. It'll be level all the way.'

'We'll see. I'll tell you when we get to Glencoe.'

Ben accelerated like a man had, and we arrived at Glencoe quickly. 'What would you like to do, Ben? This is Glencoe. We can stop here if you like.'

'No. We should continue onward. The further we go, the nearer we get to getting done.' This was a first. Things were plainly more awful than I thought.

The A82 crosses Loch Leven soon after the town of Ballachulish and afterward follows the edge of Loch Linnhe the entire way to Fort William. The street was still unbelievably occupied, however the cycling was simple and the perspectives were striking.

Fort William is the biggest town in the Highlands with 10,000 occupants (I expect they have adjusted that figure to the closest thousand). The city of Inverness is simply the just bigger settlement.

Fort William depicts itself as 'the Outdoor Capital of the UK,' *because of the tremendous number of travelers who utilize the town as a base for ascending*, climbing and mountain trekking in the encompassing mountains. Notwithstanding its overall loftiness in Highland terms, the town place is moderately humble and the central avenue had an unmistakable absence of high-road chains, which made for a greeting change.

We asked an old woman who was remaining in a shop entryway assuming that she knew about anyplace modest to stay.

'Ye coods attempt th' Bank Street Lodge. It's mostly up towards Glen Nevis.' 'Mostly UP BEN NEVIS?' I yelled, subsequent to mishearing her. 'Ack noooo. Up towards Glen Nevis. It's nae far.'

The Bank Street Lodge sits on a lofty side-street, not a long way from the focal point of Fort William. The gathering was staffed by a straightforward woman in her sixties.

'Sae ye need somewhaur tae rest an' yoo'll dae a few positions consequently?' she said, like it was a solicitation she had heard often previously. 'Yoo'll hae tae hang oan hide a moment while ah telephone th' owner.'

'I have some small jimmies haur who need tae await at th' stop tonecht hide free... Ye clarify it tae 'er,' she said, pushing the telephone towards me.

'Errrr... hi... indeed... errr... my companion and I are searching for some place to remain this evening, free of charge, as a feature of a test that we're doing. We're glad to do any unspecialized temp jobs that you want doing; cleaning, washing, improving... ' I said. 'Also this is a cause bicycle ride, is it?' asked the expressive woman on the opposite finish of the phone.

'Well no, not actually. We going from Land's End to John O'Groats without going through any cash and we're attempting to demonstrate how pleasant individuals of Britain are.'

She gave a weak laugh.

'And you have made it the whole way to Fort William from Land's End without spending any money?'

'Yes.'

'Well, I wouldn't have any desire to destroy it for you now. I'm certain we can figure something out for you. Pass me back to Tootie and I'll stop for a moment to talk with her.'

'Uh huh... Alright... ay... Alright... ha... uh huh,' said Tootie, as she proceeded with the discussion with the owner.

We watched on, attempting to work out the thing they were talking about.

'alright,' said Tootie, in the wake of hanging up the telephone, 'Ah can lit ye rest in a bunk in one of th' dorm rooms. Consequently, she would like ye tae wipe out uir dryin' room which is under th' buildin', an' reasonable up aw th' fag butts frae in th' front ay th' lodging. Diz 'at soond wonder rite?'

'Sounds like an extraordinary arrangement. Much thanks to you,' I said.

Tootie showed us to a decent room with two arrangements of lofts. It was empty, and she said it was improbable that she would have to put any other person in with us.

We gathered a can, dustpan, mop, fabrics, canister sacks and several brushes, and Tootie showed us to the drying room, which was situated in an underground vehicle leave region. It was utilized by clients and staff to hang wet climbing gear and to store ski hardware.

We went through with regards to an hour eliminating the mats, clearing it out, stowing up junk and giving it an overall clean. It then took another 20 minutes to pick up hundreds of cigarette butts that lined the road outside the hostel entrance. I have an inclination that a high-extent of these were Tootie's.

During the cleaning we got conversing with a gourmet expert who worked in an opulent eatery directly in the distance from the inn. He was interested to hear about our experience and was quick to help us out.

'I can't propose to take care of you this evening, I'm apprehensive, in light of the fact that we're so occupied, however I'll make you up a stuffed lunch toward the beginning of the day in case you extravagant it.' We hadn't asked him for anything, and as of now the next day's lunch was taken consideration of.

'What will we do about food this evening?' asked Ben when we were back in our room.

'We've actually got those Londis fish pasta bakes.'

'Ughh, I don't figure I can confront one of those. I extravagant fish and chips.'

'You make me snicker. We have two totally fair microwave dinners, yet you actually need to go out and attempt and blag fish and chips.'

'Definitely, what's up with that?'

'Nothing. I would like fried fish and French fries, as well. We should go.'

Twenty minutes after the fact we were once again at the lodging with two segments of haddock and chips. We had lucked out at a focus point on the central avenue. The administrator wasn't in, and the young lady behind the counter given north of two fish dinners with next to no hesitation.

We ate in the mutual parlor region where the main others were three youthful Chinese understudies who were completely submerged in manuals about Scotland.

After we had completed supper, Ben chose – for no known explanation – to make a scrabble set out of a few pieces of paper, which he attacked heaps of individual letters. Ben had consistently considered himself to be a specialist scrabble player because of the measure of time he spent playing the game on set during his acting positions. This isn't an aftereffect of him having an especially wide jargon, yet basically on the grounds that he had retained all of the conceivable two letter words.

He was chafing to play against. At a certain point he basically added the letter 'X' to score 50 focuses with the word 'Xi' in two ways. I needed to endure an hour of his egotistical face as he heaped on the focuses with a progression of two letter words that he had no clue to the importance of. Xi is the fourteenth letter of the Greek letters in order, on the off chance that you were wondering.

Ben then got talking to the Chinese students. They were in Scotland as a component of a multi month visit through Europe. The discussion before long turned into an inside and out conversation about the benefits and impediments of socialism in current China. I didn't have the information or mental eagerness to partake, so lurked off to bed and passed on them to it.

Ben modelling state-of-the-art waterproof clothing

Paul, Glencoe Visitor Centre

Sandy, the bagpipe player

Benmore Lodge, Crianlarich

Fixing The Falcon, Craonachan

Day 17 – The hunt for Nessie

Fort William to Beauly – 63 miles

After the mercilessness of the earlier day's cycling I rested for nine hours in a row. Ben's rest was to some degree more limited after his extensive late-night socialism instructional exercise with the Chinese students.

Breakfast, then again, was not one of my generally paramount; a Londis fish pasta prepare cooked in the inn's microwave. They were at that point two days past their utilization by date, yet we didn't have the heart to toss them out, or the craving to take them both with us. In transit out, Tootie – who appeared to be on a 24-hour shift – gave us the pressed snacks that the gourmet specialist had guaranteed us.

The A82 was a lot more amicable once the mist had cleared. The bank-holidaymakers were all still snoozing, thus the street was nearly deserted.

A couple of miles north of Fort William we passed a sign for the Nevis Range, which is one of Scotland's primary ski regions. Seeing as we were passing, we chose to bring in and investigate. We lamented this choice immediately, when we understood that it was really a mile-long tough join away from the fundamental road.

I had consistently been extremely wary with regards to Scottish ski resorts. I envisioned them being little slopes with several flimsy drag-lifts shipping individuals the 15 meters to the highest point of the incline. At the Nevis Range I was stunned to see a few chairlifts, and a genuine gondola. Not the 'only one Cornetto' type that you find in Venice, however a legitimate trolley that extended up the mountain to the furthest extent that we could see.

In the colder time of year, it conveys many skiers and snowboarders, and in the late spring it transports climbers and mountain-bikers to the top.

'We should check whether we can get a let loose excursion the mountain. It very well may be enjoyable to look at the view,' I suggested.

'What might be the point in that?' asked Ben.

'I don't have the foggiest idea. I just idea it would be great to attempt to do these things while we're here. It's far-fetched we'll be going through here again whenever soon.'

'Yet what the goal in going up a dumb mountain in an inept streetcar?' 'I bet everything are splendid from up there. You'd get to see all the mountains and lochs.'

'We've seen only grisly mountains and moronic lochs for the last few days. I think I've seen enough of them, frankly. Additionally, take a gander at the sky. It will hurl it down soon and we'll have burned through heaps of time pissing about up a moronic mountain.'

'I thought part about the place of this excursion was to do fun things en route, too?'

'Better believe it, FUN being the usable word. There's nothing FUN about going up a major slope for no reason.'

'For what reason are you in an awful mind-set today?'

'I'm not. I would prefer to simply get cycling. I need to get to John O'Groats.'

I wasn't that fretted over going up the mountain either, truth be told, yet I was getting a charge out of aggravating Ben, so chose to proceed. The ticket office was shut, and a sign with the opening times showed that we had ten minutes to stand by, which made Ben considerably more furious.

Once it had opened we disclosed to the woman in the ticket office that we were expecting a free gondola trip to completely see the value in Scotland, and other such bollocks.

We were approached to pause and two exceptionally alluring women before long moved toward us and presented themselves as Katrina and Sarah from the advertising department.

'We'd love to have the option to permit you up the gondola for nothing, yet taking a gander at the condition of your bicycles I don't figure it would be a smart thought to cycle down the mountain,' said Katrina.

'Goodness sorry, you misconstrued,' I stifled. 'These bicycles aren't even adequate to come streets, not to mention a mountain. We simply needed to go up the gondola, have a brief glance at the view and afterward return IN the gondola.'

'alright. That is a consolation. Totally, it's certainly worth doing. The landscape at the top is astounding. Particularly on a sunny morning like this,' said Katrina.

'We have several these Ski Scotland shirts for you, as well,' added Sarah.

'I ridiculous LOVE Scotland,' said Ben as we boarded the gondola. It's stunning the distinction that a free shirt and several attractive young ladies can make.

'Poop, this thing is quick,' said Ben snidely, as the gondola set off up the mountain. 'It resembles being on Nemesis at Alton Towers.'

'It's a streetcar, not a rollercoaster, you idiot.'

'Goodness! Check out the perspectives! They resemble sooooo stunning. Look there's some grass. What's more there's a slope. This is the greatest day of my life.'

'Quit being a dick. We're not at the top yet.'

'Really, I concede that this is cool. I've never been up a streetcar. It's obviously superior to I was expecting,' he said, nearly sincerely.

We were the main individuals up the gondola after it opened, which implied that we had a totally pristine view. An interwoven green rug extended as should have been obvious. That was an allegory for what the woods and fields resembled from a higher place, coincidentally, not some Scottish sewing experiment.

The scene was intruded on exclusively by the numerous lochs, and the town of Fort William down to our left.

'Glad you came up here?' I asked.

'It's okay, I assume. Anything beats cycling.'

We needed to remain and absorb the perspectives for longer, however we had spots to go, and individuals to meet. Additionally, it is bleeding cold and blustery on the highest point of a mountain in some satiny shorts and a t-shirt.

We backtracked the street back to the A82 and afterward followed it uphill to Spean Bridge, where we halted momentarily at the Commando Memorial; a bronze sculpture to recognize the tip top commando unit who prepared nearby during the Second World War. We then descended to the shores of Loch Lochy – surely the most excellently named loch in Scotland.

Like Loch Ness, Loch Lochy additionally has its own legendary animal living underneath its surface. She goes by Lizzie. There have been many detailed sightings throughout the long term, yet Lizzie has consistently been dominated by the legend of her elder sibling Nessie simply up the road.

We halted for a rest at the Bridge of Oich, and I was frustrated to find that the region wasn't a home base for hooded adolescents, as the name suggested. Indeed it was a delightful cantilevered engineered overpass, worked in 1854 and planned by James Dredge, don't you know?

It was 1pm, so we unloaded our lunch. The student recollections returned flooding as we tore open the transporter sack to see what the gourmet specialist had given us.

'Yeahhhh,' said Ben. 'Past cook. This is a legitimate pressed lunch. Ham and cheddar sandwiches, a yogurt, an apple, fun-size Mars Bar, Dairylea Triangle and a container of natural product juice. Perfect.'

We acquired a tin opener from a close by bistro and afterward enhanced our
lunch with the virus prepared beans that we had been given in
Patna.

We halted at a bar close to Fort Augustus to fill our water containers, and Ben went to discard our lunch wrappings in a close by wheelie bin.

'There's an entire pack of bananas and an unused portion of bread in that canister,' said Ben when he returned.

'Truly? Do they look ok?'

'No doubt, they look totally fine. Will I proceed to take them?'

'Certainly. Maybe you ought to ask in that shop, for good measure, as the window watches out onto the canisters. It very well may be somewhat odd in case they saw you searching through their dustbin.' Ben skirted back across the street and entered the shop. He arose a couple of moments later with four yoghurts.

'Those women were well beautiful,' he yelled from across the street. 'They said we could have these yoghurts as they go off today.' He ventured into the canister to recover the bread and bananas, and skirted back across the road.

The bananas were marginally swollen however in any case fine, and the bread had just barely arrived at its best before date. We ate a banana and yogurt sandwich there and afterward (attempt one, under the steady gaze of you judge me) and saved the rest for later.

Loch Ness had vowed to be one more feature of our outing. Tragically, it didn't exactly satisfy our expectations.

The A82 (indeed, still that equivalent grisly street), sits genuinely high up the slope and not along the shores of the loch as we had anticipated. The perspectives are likewise genuinely confined due to a boundary of vegetation, divider, fence or field. It was somewhat underwhelming

Just then, we saw a disturbance of the surface and out rose a giant serpent like creature. Its enormous body undulated out of the water behind it, as it skimmed easily through the loch. It probably been around 30 feet in length, and I'm genuinely sure it grinned not long before it lowered again into the deeps.

I might have made that last passage up. Such is the popularity and legend of the Loch Ness Monster, however, that each visit to Loch Ness is probably going to be a failure. Even for the most sceptical unbeliever, there must still be that small element of excitement on seeing the Loch for the first time, that maybe, just maybe, a mysterious creature might poke its head out of the murky water right in front of your eyes. Then the realisation hits you that there is no monster, and it's just a lake. Furthermore a genuinely mediocre lake at that.

The one exemption along its shores is the eminent Urquhart Castle. The mind blowing ruins sit on a rough outcrop by Loch Ness. Notwithstanding its ruinous state, it stays an amazing sight and the palace has had an interesting history. It isn't known precisely when it was assembled, yet records show a palace on the site from 1230, with a fortification already involving the spot from as ahead of schedule as the sixth century.

The palace turned into a significant fortress in many fights and has changed hands a few times, as the Scots struggled for freedom. It is presently claimed by Historic Scotland, and the main things that are battled about these days are the postcards in the gift shop.

We had a walk around the site and one more search for Nessie, from one of the survey regions, prior to rejoining our dearest companion the A82, which we had been following for more than 130 hopeless miles.

The lovely town of Drumnadrochit – which I actually don't have the foggiest idea how to articulate – sits 66% of the way along the loch, at where we at last left the A82 and traveled north.

Drumnadrochit is the most well known place of interest for Loch Ness and flaunts several adversary Loch Ness galleries. One of them – Loch Ness 2000 – has a goliath fiberglass Nessie in the vehicle leave. We needed to stop. With a name like Loch Ness 2000 it vowed to be an exhibition hall of the future.

The gift shop was monitored by a silver-haired woman, yet was generally vacant. Absolutely everything for sale was Nessie shaped, had 'Nessie' written all over it or was tartan. Some were every one of the three. The woman didn't actually comprehend the idea of our bicycle ride, however consented to allow us to examine the show free of charge.

It truly was perhaps the most bizarre gallery I have at any point been to. Furthermore this is coming from somebody who has visited The Pencil Museum in Keswick. Albeit apparently a super durable show, all of the 'Entry', 'Exit' and 'Latrine' signs were composed on pieces of paper, in pen, and sellotaped to the entryways like they had been made the other day. Maybe this is the manner by which the galleries of things to come will look.

The actual display comprised of a diverse blend of outlined photographs of OFFICIAL sightings, documentation that PROVED Nessie's presence and a half hour video highlighting EXPERTS affirming that Nessie did UNDOUBTEDLY exist. Different researchers likewise gave logical PROOF that the beast was certifiable. I was even more an adherent to the Loch Ness Monster before I visited the historical center, than I was afterwards.

We ate another banana sandwich as we roosted on the divider in the vehicle leave. It was 6.30pm and we discussed throwing in the towel, however we (I) chose to attempt to arrive at the somewhat bigger town of Beauly before dark.

We left Drumnadrochit on the A831 prior to winding down onto the A833. The following three miles were probably the hardest of the whole outing. The street climbed steeply and The Falcon's absence of low pinion wheels created some issues. Even in its lowest gear it required a huge amount of force to complete one rotation of the pedals. Still up in the air not to be beaten by the slope, so persisted. Ben, then again, with his interminable number of cog wheels, chosen to get off when he got a quick look at the hill.

'Bollocks to this. I can't be tried to cycle up,' he said.

'You failure,' I gasped. 'I... will... not... be... beaten... by... a... slope.' I made it the whole way to the top ceaselessly, yet Ben had beaten me by a few minutes and he had strolled the whole way.

'You're a particularly difficult imbecile,' he said. 'All around good done. What have you demonstrated by doing that? You were more slow than me and you'll be multiple times more knackered.'

'It's a... it's a... great... sense... of... accomplishment,' I said, falling onto the skirt to attempt to facilitate the aggravation in my thighs.

'Do you have a pride?' 'None at all.

Just pain.'

We were compensated with a simple nine mile plunge, past fields of curious Highland cows, down into Beauly. On the edges of town we called into Lovat Bridge Camping and Caravan site, yet the woman who ran the spot – notwithstanding being exceptionally charming – couldn't help us out.

It was practically dim when we arrived at Beauly, and we got two dismissals from B&Bs on the central avenue in speedy succession.

The amazing looking Lovat Arms Hotel overwhelms the central avenue, and we realized we were risking a lot when we entered. After a long visit with the agreeable chief, he informed us that they had no rooms accessible, however assuming we had the option to find elsewhere around to remain, we could return for a free dinner that evening. This was very nearly a preferred prize over some place to sleep.

We talked to a mentor driver who was stopped up external the front of the lodging. He was remaining in Beauly short-term as a feature of a mentor visit and was minding the transport before supper with his gathering of oldies.

'Any possibility we could rest on the mentor this evening?' Ben recommended. 'We wouldn't filthy the seats or anything. We'd simply rest in the aisle.'

'Are you genuine?' he inquired. 'You're that frantic you would rest on the bus?'

'Completely.'

He thought for a moment.

'Well, I guess you could. I can't see an issue with that. I've quite recently got to fly into the lodging to get the keys. Back in a minute.'

'Pleasant one,' I said to Ben. 'You've blagged us a bus.'

'It'll resemble we're the Famous Five or something like that. Just there's simply both of us, and we don't have a dog.'

'Errr, better believe it, and I don't think the Famous Five at any point
    dozed on a transport, either.
Otherwise it's very much like that.'
    'I'm truly grieved, folks,' said the mentor driver when he returned. 'I've
had a consider it and I'm not going to have the option to allow you to rest on
the mentor, I'm afraid.'
    'Goodness, alright,' I said dejectedly. 'Would i be able to inquire as to why
you changed your mind?'
    'It's for protection reasons, though it pains me to say so. I recollected that
I'm not covered for individuals remaining on the transport for the time being.
If it somehow managed to burst into flames or something I would be held
responsible.'
    'We vow not to light any fires,' said Ben.
    'It's as yet a no, though it pains me to say so. Please accept my apologies
that I can't help you out.'

We attempted at another B&B simply off the central avenue, yet were
obligingly denied. Further down the central avenue we arrived at the
Caledonian Hotel; a somewhat pitiful looking inn/bar. The lights were off,
yet the flight of stairs was lit and we could hear the clamor of a TV from
higher up. Expecting that the gathering was higher up, we advanced up and
opened the entryway. A canine started woofing hysterically and a woman,
who was sat on the couch in obscurity, yelled at it to be quiet.
    'Excuse me, we're truly sorry to upset you,' I said hesitantly.
    'Och jesus christ ye terrified th' life out ay me. Ok didne hear ye come in.
Ah pondered whit Rufus was barkin' at.'
    Ben and I both had an abrupt surge of frenzy that we had strolled into
somebody's front room. The woman was perched on a major couch in
obscurity, sitting in front of the TV with a canine on her lap. It's not the
typical set up for an inn reception.
    'I'm truly grieved,' I said, 'we didn't intend to panic you. Is this the
gathering for the hotel?'
    'Och yes, ye could say 'at. Are ye lookin' hide a
room?' 'Indeed, well sort of.'
    'IAIN!' she hollered. 'Will ye get around here please. We have customers.'
    Iain risen up out of one more bar at the rear of the room drying a 16
ounces glass with a tea towel. He was a monster of a man; no less than six
foot tall, with a bar property manager's body. He was in his sixties, had a
white mustache and patches of wavy white hair on the sides of his head.
    'How would i be able to help both of you noble men?' he asked, in a voice
undeniably more delicate than his appearance proposed. He grinned as we

clarified our challenge.

'I'm certain we can figure you out with a room. We're not very bustling this evening. Indeed, you're the main individuals here. I'll get Cathy to show you to a room.'

The room was totally entrancing. It would have looked extremely rich 'once upon a time' – maybe the mid 1970s. Everything from the flower print backdrop to the bed blankets, the rug to the radio/morning timer seemed as though it was unaltered in numerous many years. I cherished it. It seemed like we were remaining in a museum.

After a speedy shower and change into our new Sunday Best – the Ski Scotland shirts – we strolled back up to the Lovat Arms Hotel. The director appeared to be somewhat astounded to see us back, yet was glad to respect his statement and thought that we are a seat in the café – concealed in the corner stowed away from the eyes of the good paying guests.

It was an astonishing dinner; steak pie with tasty lumps of meat, thick sauce, a light puff cake cover and stout chips. But the highlight for me was the vegetables. Carrots and peas have never tasted so great. Not that they were especially unique carrots and peas; simply that vegetables of any kind had been practically missing from our eating regimens since we started.

If a nutritionist had dissected what we ate during the bicycle ride, I think they presumably would have inferred that we ought not be alive, not to mention fit enough to cycle. I read some place that beige food is terrible for you. Nearly all that we ate was a shade of beige; bread, pasta prepares, chips, pasties and bananas. At any rate, all I'm saying is that peas and carrots taste incredible assuming you just eat beige nourishment for 17 days in advance. Give it a try.

The Caledonian Hotel was buzzin' when we returned. That is to say, that there was someone else in the bar. She was by all accounts a normal as she was sat on a bar stool and somewhere down in discussion with Cathy and Iain.

'Thanks again for allowing us to remain,' I said as we beat the lawyer exam on our way
to our room.

'Aren't you going to remain and go along with us for a beverage?' asked Iain. 'However, we… '

'Ah don't stress over that, I'll get you both a brew,' he said.

Two hours, four pints and two 'nightcaps' later, we were currently at the bar. The woman – Susan, I think her name was, as my memory of that evening is marginally dim – was a long-lasting inhabitant of the campground we had called at before. Since her marriage finished, she leased a manufactured house at the site, worked in a production line during the day and savored the Caledonian in the evening. They were generally extraordinary organization, and Ben and I were caused to feel very welcome.

I looked into the Caledonian Hotel on the web after our outing, and was lurched to peruse the surveys. Out of 18 surveys, 12 of them evaluated it 'awful'. Here is one such review:

'This lodging is without question the most exceedingly awful inn on the planet. It scents of flat brew and cigarettes when you stroll in the entryway. The staff are discourteous and similarly as rancid. Keep away from this damnation opening no matter what. You would genuinely be better dozing in your car!'

The Caledonian was, indeed, one of the most amicable and most exceptional inns I have at any point remained in. If you want a modern, featureless hotel, then the Caledonian is certainly not for you. If, however, you fancy a slightly different experience, where usual hotel policies don't apply, then I would wholeheartedly recommend it.

Katrina, Nevis Range

At the top of the gondola, Nevis Range

Nevis Range gondola

Loch Ness 2000, Drumnadrochit

A82, near Loch Ness

Urquhart Castle

Day 18 – Whisky tastings and llama farms

Beauly to Berriedale – 79 miles

The nearer we got to John O'Groats, the more prominent the feeling of excitement we woke with every morning. For most of the excursion, our first considerations on waking would be of gentle dread and expectation of the day that lay ahead. These musings turned more towards energy, as we felt the end goal getting closer.

Iain provided us with a tasty bowl of porridge for breakfast and we gained an outdated quiche from one of the close by shops prior to setting off.

Just in the wake of leaving Beauly the course turned right and we climbed the street up to an edge. The sky was dark to the extent the skyline, and we could see the cloudiness of heavy downpour somewhere far off in front of us. The climate divine beings were our ally, on the grounds that for the following 20 miles a gigantic tailwind moved us, and the mists, so we luckily never crossed paths.

We joined the A9 and crossed Cromarty Firth by means of the Cromarty span – worked in 1982, span truth fans – and afterward redirected onto minor streets through the towns of Evanton and Alness. We passed close by delightful evergreen timberlands with the street still straight from a battering by the rain.

After Alness, the street followed the coast along Cromarty Firth for a long time. The terrain was perfectly flat, and the wind so strong that even when we stopped pedalling it had the force to propel us along. We proceeded similar to the town of Milton where we turned inland once more. Here we had a choice to either follow the A9 to Tain, or take the 'more limited course,' as I portrayed it to Ben.

'Most certainly the more limited course. That is an easy decision,' he said, taking the trap. I had failed to make reference to him that the more limited course was essentially hillier.

'This is damnation,' he said, as we gasped up a street through thick forest. 'I bet everything street was dead flat.'

'No. It's similarly just about as uneven as this,' I lied, 'however with significantly more traffic.'

We then, at that point, had a pleasant long downhill into the town of Tain. We didn't stop, as we had a seriously engaging objective as a top priority two or three miles further on; the Glenmorangie whisky distillery.

I have never been a devotee of whisky. Truth be told, I would even go similarly as saying

that I disdain the stuff. It generally appeared to be the beverage of decision towards the finish of a long savoring meeting my late teenagers. From that point onward, the smallest taste returns me to the sensation of needing to heave my guts out. In any case, when in Scotland…

Glenmorangie has been the smash hit single-malt in Scotland beginning around 1983. Around 10 million containers are created every year. Not these are intoxicated in Scotland, be that as it may. Two or three containers are sent elsewhere.

The actual refinery is a wonderful old structure sitting simply off the A9 on the banks of the Dornoch Firth. We concealed our bicycles in a shrubbery in the vehicle leave, and strolled down to the refinery. The woman in the gift shop clarified that they ran hourly voyages through the refinery and the basements, trailed by a tasting meeting. On this event she was glad to forgo the confirmation expense, on the premise that we appeared to be 'two or three nice guys'.

'The following visit doesn't begin for an additional 30 minutes, so perhaps you might want to participate with the tasting meeting for the visit that has quite recently gotten done,' she suggested.

We sat in a room with around ten others – for the most part Americans – and attempted a progression of various whiskies that were depicted with terms, for example, hearty, oaky, green and cerealy.

'What does the delayed flavor impression of this one help you to remember?' said the woman. 'Upchuck,' I said under my breath.

'Caramel,' said Ben.

'Precisely,' she said. 'It has distinct caramel feelings, and traces of woodchip and oak.'

'You brown nose,' I said to Ben. 'Do you truly like this stuff?'

'No doubt, I love it. Don't you?'

'No. It's rank.'

'Certain individuals like to have a drop of water with theirs,' she then, at that point, said, passing around a container of water.

'Do you have any Coke?' I asked, just half tongue in cheek. The room howled uncontrollably, and I obliged it like I was a comic virtuoso, rather than a whisky pagan. 'Ha, whisky and Coke,' I chuckled. 'As if!'

To be reasonable for Glenmorangie, their whisky was most certainly the most un-hostile that I had at any point tasted. I would not go similarly as saying that I appreciated it, however it didn't make me gag and I figured out how to complete every one of the three shots.

'Do we truly need to go on the visit?' murmured Ben. 'I bet it will be truly exhausting. I simply needed to do the tasting.'

'No doubt, it would be discourteous assuming that we left at this point. We should do the visit. It very well may be fun.'

We met the other visit bunch – once more, generally Americans – at the assigned spot with their aide Sandra.

The visit was really intriguing and certainly worth doing. We were directed through every one of the various phases of whisky creation, which, albeit apparently mind boggling, still utilize the very essential cycles that have been utilized for many years.

The refinery appeared as though something out of a science fiction movie, with monster cauldrons (I feel that is the specialized name) of maturing 'stuff'. The scents that radiated around the room were totally overwhelming, yet not unpleasant.

At one point, Sandra opened the incubate on top of one of the cauldrons and we were told to put our head inside and take a legitimate sniff. Ben went first and put his whole head in and breathed in profoundly. He gave a boisterous hack into the cauldron and arose wheezing for air with his eyes streaming.

'Wow. I wasn't anticipating that,' he spluttered.

'It absolutely clears your sinuses, doesn't it?' said Sandra. 'Who's next? There's no compelling reason to place your head in to the extent Ben did.'

I was following up, and, in the wake of duplicating Ben, my eyes were streaming and I was hacking and spluttering as well. It was the manner by which I envision grunting a line of wasabi would feel. The remainder of the gathering ruled against having a go.

This specific bunch of Glenmorangie single malt is best kept away from. It contains hints of our spit.

The feature of the visit was a visit to the basements, wherein huge number of barrels are piled up until they are fit to be packaged. Every single element of the process is considered an influencing factor on the product, such as the natural spring water that is used from the nearby spring, to the type and age of the wooden barrels, to the sea air and the temperature. I felt remorseful that I had considered demolishing all of this with a sprinkle of Coke.

'alright, presently you would all be able to come and participate in a tasting of a portion of our whiskies,' said Sandra toward the finish of the tour.

'Much obliged, however we previously did one preceding this visit,'
I murmured to her. 'Good for you. You should come and do another
one.'

We properly obliged. It would have been discourteous not to. In addition, we had both become entranced by concentrating on the various individuals in the gathering. They were an exceptionally peculiar pack. One specific chap took notes on a little scratch pad the whole way round, and afterward posed

Sandra unmistakable inquiries toward the end, alluding back in his journal to how Glenmorangie was distinctive to different refineries he had been to. His better half couldn't have looked more discouraged the whole time.

We got conversing with Bruce and Anne – a couple from Vermont, USA. They also were whisky fans, yet not so no-nonsense as the freaky scratch pad guy.

'I've been to Vermont,' I said, to attempt to dazzle

them. 'Truly? Where did you go?' said Bruce.

'Errr, the Ben and Jerry's manufacturing plant,' I said.

'Definitely, Ben and Jerry's is about the main thing that carries individuals to Vermont.'

We endured one more tasting meeting, and consulted with Bruce and Anne about their excursion. They were going through three weeks in Scotland, climbing, eating and drinking.

'This is our location,' said Anne, 'in the event that you are ever in Vermont again, ensure you stop by.'

Sandra, the aide, then, at that point, given Ben and me an uncommon container of Truffle Oak Reserve single malt whisky – one of just 800 jugs produced.

'What's this for?' asked Ben. 'We don't merit this'

'Yes you do. It's our token of altruism. You can either appreciate it during your excursion, or save it to celebrate with afterwards.'

'That is so sort of you. We better not have any more today any other way we'll never come to John O'Groats,' I said.

My backpack was totally full, and there was no room in Ben's pack as it actually contained the total cookout set he had conveyed since Cornwall. After a touch of exertion, we figured out how to tie the significant boxed jug of whisky to the rear of The Horse, and we wobbled off with heavier bicycles and lighter heads.

I don't know whether it was the whisky or the climate, however the following not many miles were unquestionably difficult. We crossed the Dornoch Bridge which rides the Dornoch Firth, and the breeze had turned significantly and was currently blowing against us, just as opposite the left. This implied that in addition to the fact that we had to battle against it just to push ourselves ahead, yet we likewise needed to incline toward it to try not to be blown under the wheels of the numerous passing

verbalized lorries.

We pushed our bicycles for a huge segment of the scaffold since we didn't need our outing to reach an unexpected conclusion so near the completion, and furthermore in light of the fact that it rushed to stroll as cycle.

I'm certain Dornoch Firth would be exceptionally wonderful on a decent day, however the breeze had transformed it into a wild, scaring waterway and we were happy to arrive at the opposite side. If the name 'Dornoch' sounds recognizable to you, it is likely on the grounds that it is the area of Skibo Castle where Madonna and Guy Ritchie wedded in 2000.

We proceeded with uphill for some time prior to dropping to a boulevard across Loch Fleet, which structures part of a 19,000 section of land untamed life preservation region that is a well known spot for birdwatchers.

The town of Golspie (populace 1650) was a hurling city contrasted with a large portion of the spots we had gone as the day progressed. Places such as Evelix, Poles and Culmaily looked significant on the map, but often boasted one house, and sometimes not even that. Golspie even had a shop.

The whisky had blurred our brains and we had overlooked food. It was almost 5pm and we hadn't eaten anything since our porridge at the Caledonian.

The youthful clerk of the shop – a Scottish-conceived Asian young lady – provided us with a lot of bananas, which would have seen us through the remainder of the day assuming it had come to it. In that remote piece of Scotland, we didn't have the foggiest idea when we would eat again.

It was too soon for us to set up camp in Golspie, as we would have been left with more than 70 miles to finish on the last day. Just past the town we passed the tremendous looking Dunrobin Castle. I say 'breathtaking' on the grounds that I have quite recently seen pictures of it on the web. However, i don't recall having the option to see a lot of it from the street. Our course book said that it is 'certainly worth a stop', however I didn't peruse this until we were a few miles beyond.

The breeze had subsided and the downpour mists were carefully hidden, which left us with some wonderful cycling for the remainder of the day. Fuelled by the bananas we gained great headway, spinning one more 20 miles through the town of Brora and on to the town of Helmsdale.

It was 6.30pm when we arrived at Helmsdale, and we needed to choose whether to punch out or push onto the following town of Berriedale, another ten miles further on.

'I figure we should attempt to get to Berriedale today. It'll be 10 miles that we don't need to do tomorrow,' I said.

'I realized you planned to say that,' said Ben. 'In any case, what occurs assuming that we can't find anyplace in Berry Vale?'

'Berriedale.'

'Whatever. What occurs assuming we can't find anyplace there? Shouldn't we search for some place here first? This spot looks genuinely huge. There are B&Bs, a bar. I figure we could find some place easily.'

'We likely would, however I'm certain we'll track down some place in Berriedale, as well. It looks as large as this spot on the map.'

'Ten miles, you say?'

'Definitely. The other thing is there is a huge slope for the following 4 ½ miles, which would imply that assuming we remained here we would need to do that first thing tomorrow.'

'Yet in case we do it now, it implies that we need to do it NOW! In any case it's crap.'

'However in case we completely finish currently, then, at that point, we'll have only 43 miles left tomorrow, and it will all be genuinely level and easy.'

'Fine! Assuming that it quiets you down, we should completely finish. In any case, on the off chance that we end up destitute this evening then, at that point, I'm going to fucking kill you.'

The slope was just as tiresome as our course book recommended, and Ben groaned just as much as I suspected he would. We abandoned the coast as we crept gradually up into the slopes. By 'crept' I imply that we cycled gradually. Things had not got that bad.

The drop into the town of Berriedale was one of the steepest we encountered on the whole outing. Those doing the course from north to south would have this to handle on their first day.

Just before we arrived at the town, I figured out how to grind to a halt utilizing my feet in the rock of a lay-by. Ben shrieked to an end behind me.

'What did you stop for?' he asked.

'Did you see the doors to that house back
there?' 'No. What was uncommon about them?'

'I don't know. I was unable to see the real house, yet it looked very important.'

'So what?' asked Ben.

'Well, it's our final evening. Perhaps we should attempt to remain some place truly special?'

'I like your thinking.'

The sign on the gateway to Langwell House was modest enough – there was nothing to indicate that it was a hotel or guest house – but there was something about the driveway that stretched out of sight into the woods that gave a hint that it was more than just an average semi, and it made us need to discover more.

We pushed our bicycles down the lush carport. I don't know why, but rather it felt more pleasant to walk, as opposed to cycling down somebody's drive. We turned a corner hoping to see the house before us, however rather the drive proceeded. The road then emerged from the woods and was suddenly clinging to the side of a deep valley, with a river flowing peacefully at the bottom.

'What the heck is this spot?' asked Ben.

'It resembles we've wound up in Narnia or something.' 'Is it just me, or is everything a tad creepy?'

'I'm happy you said that. I'm crapping myself.'

There was no proof of human residence anyplace. Brief we had been on the edges of a town, and the following we had wandered into a different universe. We got on our bicycles. Not on the grounds that we were terrified, you see, but since we had been strolling for ten minutes and still not came to the house.

The drive proceeded for what felt like a few miles and we in the end saw the house; a genuinely unassuming structure, thinking about its area. It was an excellent white farmhouse sat in a great spot on the slope, with sees extending across the lush valley and out to sea.

We started to stroll up towards the house when we heard the thunder of a motor, and a quad bicycle came screaming down the track towards us. A man wearing armed force cover pants, a wax coat and a level cap moved off and afterward went after his shotgun from the rear of the quad.

A colossal Alsatian ran salivating and yapping down from the house and remained alongside him.

'Can ah help ye?' he said with an irate glare. Being gone up against in no place by a man with a firearm, and a canine with an evident desire for blood, was not the most inviting of good tidings I had ever had.

'I'm truly sorry to trouble you,' I said. 'We've ventured to every part of the length of Great Britain without spending a solitary penny. All that we own has been

gained en route including the entirety of our food and convenience. This evening is our final evening, and we saw this spot and figured it would be fitting to end our excursion some place truly special.'

The man's face stayed as harsh as in the past, he actually hung on close to the shotgun.

'Yes,' proceeded with Ben. 'Would there be any possibility whatsoever of us dozing here this evening? We're glad to accomplish some work in return.'

He paused.

'Nae. That willnae be possible.'
'Gracious, alright,' said Ben. 'Are you
the proprietor?' 'Nae, aam th'
gamekeeper.'
'Would it be feasible to address the
proprietor?' 'Nae. That willnae be possible.'
'We're somewhat of somewhat abandoned,' added Ben. 'It's practically
dull and we're in no place and we have no place to stay.'

'Ah cannae help ye,' said the man.

'Would it not be imaginable to have a speedy talk with the proprietor?
Perhaps they have a toilet we could snooze?' I said, starting to sound
somewhat frantic.

'Nae. I'm gonnae hae tae ask ye tae leave now.' With that, we got back on
our bicycles and followed the long carport back to Berriedale. The
gamekeeper showed up behind us on his quad for the last area, and shadowed
us to ensure that we left the property.

Berriedale was not even close as large as I had guaranteed Ben. Truth be
told, the term 'town' would be extremely liberal. It was 8.30pm and totally
dim. We thumped on the entryway of the house with lights on.
Notwithstanding a vehicle being left outside and the gleaming of a TV
noticeable through the draperies there was no answer.

'Should we thump once more?' asked Ben.

'I don't think so. It's somewhat late and they clearly don't have any desire
to reply.' 'How about we attempt the following house then.'
'I figure we should continue
onward.' 'What?'

'I try to avoid thumping on individuals' entryways late in the evening like
this. It feels wrong.'

'Indeed, it's not bleeding ideal, however we don't actually have a lot of
decision, isn't that right? Assuming you had quit being so obstinate and
searched for some place in that last

place then we wouldn't have this issue.' 'Well
knowing the past is something magnificent
isn't it?'

'So is foreknowledge, and it was really clear this planned to occur.' 'Okay,
I'm grieved. You're correct. In any case, basically we have that large slope
out of

the way, and it's not a lot further to John O'Groats.'

'Indeed, but rather that doesn't resolve the little issue of not having
anyplace to remain tonight.'

'Alright, we should continue onward and see what happens.'

Cycling was impossible. We had no type of lighting at all, and just a solitary Tony-the-tiger reflector on The Falcon's front wheel to protect us. The busy, unlit A9 meant that even walking was dangerous. We strolled along the edge of the street and moved onto the skirt each time a vehicle passed.

'What occurs on the off chance that we don't find anyplace?' asked Ben as we blundered around a precarious uphill bend in transit out of Berriedale.

'Then we continue to walk. It's the final evening. It doesn't actually make any difference in case we don't get any rest. It simply implies that when it draws light we'll be even nearer to John O'Groats.'

'And you'd be glad to walk all night?'

'Indeed, assuming it came to it,' I lied, frantically wanting to track down some place to sleep.

After several miles, we arrived at a cabin which was set away from the principle street. There was a sign external that said:

Kingspark Llama Farm
Bed and Breakfast

But then, at that point, underneath that, another sign, with two words that made our hearts sink:

No Vacancy

'I will ask in any case,' said Ben. 'Basically they'll have the option to let us know what there is in front of us and how far away.'

The entryway was opened by a grinning, silver haired man, with a dim mustache and a level cap.

'Goodbye. How might I help you?' he said, in a thick West Country highlight, which was somewhat astounding thinking about that we were under 50 miles from the highest point of Scotland.

'Hi. We're truly sorry to upset you this late, yet we're somewhat abandoned and we are searching for some place to remain this evening,' said Ben.

'We saw that you have no opportunities, yet contemplated whether you have any asylum whatsoever or on the other hand in case you was aware of anyplace close by that could possibly help?' I added. 'Well we're really shut right now for restoration. That is why according to the sign No Vacancy. Why you are abandoned out here?'

His name was Brian, and we let him know how we came to be abandoned close to home. He gestured along excitedly, and chuckled at different focuses including our visit to Langwell House right down the road.

'They are an unusual pack down at Langwell House. I'll listen for a minute, both of you stand by there and I'll proceed to have a word with my significant other Mary. I will not be a minute.'

'Mary says that it would be too hard to even think about figuring you out with a bed this evening, yet you are free to rest in the polytunnel,' said Brian when he returned. 'There's heaps of feed in there and I don't figure it will be too cold tonight.'

'That sounds astonishing. Much obliged to you. We're sorry again for upsetting you.' 'Not in any way. Come in and have a fast cup of tea before I show you to your

lodgings.'

We were driven through to the parlor and Mary showed up a couple of moments later with a plate of tea.

'I've concluded I can't make them rest in the polytunnel when we have this multitude of void rooms,' she said, sounding very flustered.

'We're glad to rest out there,' said Ben.

'We'll I'm not. It wouldn't be correct. Please accept my apologies, I'm somewhat worried by every one of the redesigns, and I've been somewhat sick recently.'

'Indeed, obviously. We totally comprehend. We feel downright terrible simply turning up like this.'

'I'll proceed to make up a bed for you both,' she said and vanished out of the entryway, before we got an opportunity to dissent further. We despised being a weight to individuals, and had attempted to stay away from it at each phase of the excursion. It was late, they had a sign saying 'no opportunity', yet they were giving us a room since they felt a feeling of responsibility and it didn't appear right.

'Brian, we would genuinely be a lot more joyful to rest in your polytunnel. We feel downright terrible simply turning up this way and we disdain being a weight on individuals,' I said.

'No, no, it's fine. Mary wouldn't fret,' said Brian nonchalantly.

'I know, yet it's obviously not a happy time. This excursion is about experience and to be straightforward a polytunnel would be more invigorating for our last night.'

Brian thought for a moment.

'That's right, I guess I can see the value in that. I invested some energy in the paratroopers and I can see what you're saying.'

'We would genuinely be such a great deal more joyful in case we didn't occupy one of your spaces,' said Ben.

Brian went to address Mary and after a ton of dissenting, Mary at last accepted.

Brian drove us out to the polytunnel, which – on the off chance that you are pondering – is essentially a nursery made with stick film rather than glass.

'There are a couple of openings in the rooftop, yet it won't rain this evening,' said Brian. 'You'll be fine. You can make a bed with the roughage, and I've presumably got an extra cover some place that I can give you. What might be said about supper? Have you eaten at all?'

'No, however could we ask you another blessing?' said

Ben. 'Of course.'

'We got this quiche,' said Ben, recovering the outdated quiche that we'd procured from the shop in Beauly. 'Might we actually destroy it in your microwave?'

'No issue by any means. I'll proceed to figure that out for you.'

He returned a couple of moments later with two plates of quiche, and an invited backup of heated beans.

There was something extremely beautiful with regards to lying on the feed, underneath the polythene rooftop. This was the means by which we had gone through our first evening, on the roughage close to the bull in Harry Mann's animal dwellingplace. During the 18 days in the middle of we had rested in an opulent inn, a waterway boat, an understudy house, a bar, a tent in a vehicle leave, a contract killer's living room, an older woman's extra room, an inn, a bunk house, a homestead house, our own independent level, our own home, and presently we were back on the feed. We had gone full circle.

Out of every one of the various kinds of convenience, our two evenings on the feed were without a doubt our generally agreeable. Next time you hear the nativity story, don't feel frustrated about Mary and Joseph; they had it exceptionally fortunate indeed.

Iain, Caledonian Inn, Beauly

Cathy, Caledonian Inn, Beauly

Golspie Beach

Day 19 – The finish line

Berriedale to John O'Groats – 43 miles

Brian had been off-base with regards to the downpour. It pissed it as the night progressed, and the rooftop released like a strainer. But it wasn't cold, and the sound of rain on a polytunnel is very hypnotic and we both slept like babies; waking up crying every hour with wet pants.

Barring any serious issues, it was to be our last day's cycling. Under 50 miles lay among us and John O'Groats.

'Mary is making you a cook,' said Brian when we went to bid farewell, 'and you're not escaping this one.'

'Goodness okay then, at that point. Assuming that you demand. It smells stunning,' said Ben.

We talked to Brian and Mary over breakfast, and asked them how two Bristolians had wound up in North-East Scotland running a B&B and a llama farm.

'It simply kind of occurred,' said Brian nonchalantly. 'We loved the region here in Caithness and chose to move here a couple of years prior. We got the llamas since we heard they adjust well to the environment, and the rest is history.'

'Would we be able to view your llamas before we go?' I inquired. 'Obviously. You will assist me with taking care of them after this.'

We completed our morning meal then, at that point, followed Brian into the field behind his home. We passed a bunch of aviaries lodging a few enormous parrots.

'Those simply kind of occurred, as well,' said Brian.

We took care of the five amicable and messy looking llamas – or 'normal looking' as Brian liked to portray them – and had a meander around the remainder of the farm.

We then, at that point, followed Brian over a fence and two or three hundred meters across another field. We arrived at a snooker-table estimated substantial stage, on which sat a round metal turret like you would find on a tank.

'This came as somewhat of an amazement to me after we purchased the spot. I didn't realize it existed,' he said as he unscrewed the huge metal cover of the turret.

'What is it?' I asked.

'It's an old conflict fortification. Come and bring a look.'

We moved down the stepping stool into the haziness and Brian lit a light. The room was the size of a little single room with seats covering each wall and racks for provisions. There were many items scattered about from 'back in the day' such as tins, pots, cans and a half-finished bottle of whisky stashed on one of the shelves; although this was possibly Brian's. Why the wild of Caithness was at any point considered in danger during the conflict, I am not sure.

'This is a phenomenal spot, Brian,' said Ben.

'Indeed, isn't it just? I regularly descend here for a couple of hours to escape from the spouse,' he said with a wink.

We got back to the house to gather our things and bid farewell to Mary. They had both been unimaginably liberal notwithstanding us turning up close to home late around evening time during an especially troublesome time. Our final evening was not the luxurious villa that we had expected, yet it was surely one of our generally pleasant and memorable.

The course among Berriedale and John O'Groats was genuinely ordinary. Brian had provided us with a rundown of spots that we MUST see while we were nearby: Dunbeath Castle, Laidhay Croft Museum, Hill O' Many Stanes, and an unearthed Iron Age town. Notwithstanding our best expectations, when we were out and about, we had an exclusively keen interest in the completion line.
'Wasn't that the mood killer for Hill O' Many Stanes?' I called to Ben half-heartedly.
'Gracious bollocks to that,' answered Ben. 'We're almost at John O'Groats. Furthermore at any rate, the English for that deciphers as 'slope of bunches of stones'. I've seen a lot of those previously, thank you very much.'

We halted momentarily in Wick to fill our water bottles at a gas station – with water, not petroleum – and afterward set off on the last 15 miles to John O'Groats. During these last couple of miles we passed many End to Enders heading the other way, all new legged with glad grins and no thought of what lay in front of them. We gave each gathering a best of luck wave and traded brief cheers of help as we passed. It is just on these methodology streets into John O'Groats and Land's End that you are probably going to chance upon opposite End to Enders. The complicated organization of British streets is with the end goal that there is no specific leaned toward course, as cyclists, sprinters and walkers explore their direction from one finish of Britain to the other.

We arrived at the edges of John O'Groats soon after 1pm, having covered the 43 miles from Berriedale in three hours. We stopped briefly and
peered not too far off towards the harbour.
'This is it, Ben,' I said. 'Only two or three hundred
meters to go.' 'Thank fuck for that,' said Ben.
'Do we cross the end goal clasping hands or what?'
'Damnation no! We should simply cycle across it like we have for the last thousand miles.'
As we freewheeled down the slope towards the well known sign, I felt an abrupt swell of feeling that got me totally off guard. I had never questioned

that we would finish the excursion, yet I was out of nowhere hit with the acknowledgment of what we had achieved.

We had cycled between the two most far off focuses in Great Britain in 18.5 days. This was an accomplishment in itself, however we had begun our excursion at the foot of England in a couple of undies, and that's it. There we were, under three weeks after the fact, at the highest point of Scotland, completely dressed, with bicycles, having tracked down some place to remain each night and nourishment for virtually our dinners as a whole. I felt monstrously proud.

The real end goal lies, haphazardly, in the lodging's vehicle park, and we crossed it courageously watched by a welcome party of none.

'You're not crying are you?' said Ben critically, as we ground to a halt.

'No. As though! It should simply be the breeze,' I said, and I admired see his eyes

gushing, as well. I gave him a major

embrace. 'You enormous

gaylord,' he said.

We had been given an 'official' End to End card from Jemma at Land's End that we needed to get stepped in the John O'Groats inn to demonstrate that we had made it. In spite of the fact that, I'm not exactly certain who we expected to demonstrate this to.

The lodging bar was vacant separated from the barman, who was inclining toward the bar while watching a TV across the room.

'Hi. Is this where we get the Land's End to John O'Groats authentication thing stepped?' I asked.

'Can do,' he said, not taking his eyes off the TV.

'Extraordinary, much appreciated,' I said, sliding the piece of paper along the bar to him. 'We've just cycled the whole way from Land's End without spending any money and we had to blag all of our clothes and food and accommodation and we stayed in a stable with a bull and with a hitman and in a posh hotel and in a polytunnel and in a canal boat and we had to work for lots of our meals and we didn't even have a bike pump and then this one time we got a

cut and afterward we had to...'

'There you go,' he interfered, stepping the card and passing it back to me, still without turning away his look from the TV.

To us, we were the most gutsy individuals to have at any point ventured foot into the John O'Groats Hotel. To the barman, we were only the most recent in the long queue of individuals finishing the outing, regularly, similar to us, with their own 'odd' take on it. He had seen everything previously, and he didn't care a whole lot. He simply needed his shift to complete with the goal that he could return home. I cherished him for this, and it was practically desirable over a messy hello from an over-excited welcome party. It unquestionably brought us right down to earth.

My body was depleted of all life, however my psyche was alive and dashing at considerations of what we had accomplished and of the things that we had experienced.

I had fallen profoundly enamored with Great Britain. I subtly consistently had been, however I was as of now not hesitant to let it be known. As a country, we don't give ourselves enough credit. We are, as indicated by open discernment, a nation loaded with ASBOs, underage consumers, severe, presumptuous moaners and pregnant young people. Indeed, we have our concerns, however it genuinely is an awesome spot to live. England is a long way from broken; it simply needs a touch of adoration and affection.

At each phase of our excursion we were overpowered by the liberality and graciousness of individuals that we met. Complete outsiders made a special effort to offer us food, convenience, garments, bicycles, headings, lager or discussion. England is a blend of societies, races and characters, and this varied blend of characters ought to be embraced and celebrated.

And it's not simply individuals; Great Britain is incredibly lovely, as well. We anticipated that Cornwall should be pretty, and we realized the Scottish Highlands would be fabulous, yet it was the pieces in the middle of that amazed us. There was not an inch of the 1000 miles that didn't have an allure. Even Runcorn had a certain charm. These days, with modest flights and the channel burrow, it is so natural to vanish to some distant land, instead of investigating all of the magnificence right on your doorstep.

This excursion was never about cash. I would rather not lecture you about industrialism or society's fixation on cash – I'm certain you have your own viewpoints on that. Going without cash was basically a method for putting us helpless before everyone around us, and permit us the chance to meet individuals, see puts, and have encounters that we would not in any case have had.

It did, nonetheless, show us the unlimited chances that are available to us, even without cash. It costs nothing to get out and investigate your neighborhood town. It costs nothing to burn or stroll through the lovely British open country. It costs nothing to pause and converse with individuals. It costs nothing to swim in the ocean or a lake, or to visit large numbers of Britain's most amazing sights. It costs nothing to request help. It costs nothing to make new companions, and it costs nothing to grin and have a good time. It took this experience to assist me with understanding that Great Britain is without a doubt a Free Country.

It is astonishing what undertakings you can have when you venture outside your front entryway. Get out there. Investigate yourself. You will not be baffled, I promise.

It is guaranteed that cycling can prompt ineptitude. This idea had been niggling away in my brain all through the three weeks that I spent sat on The Falcon, with a seat produced using the hardest, most ball-annihilating material known to man. Nonetheless, precisely nine months subsequent to returning home, my better half brought forth our child little girl, and, with that, an entirely different experience began.

Brian and Mary, Kingspark Llama Farm, Barrisdale

Sam feeding the llamas

A parrot, Kingspark Llama Farm

A llama, Kingspark Llama Farm

The final stretch to John O'Groats

Almost there

If you might want to see a greater amount of the photographs from the excursion, catch wind of future activities, or basically need to say 'greetings' then kindly stay in contact through the links
below.

facebook.com/GeorgeMahood

twitter.com/georgemahood

instagram.com/georgemahood

george@georgemahood.com

I have a site as well, yet there is truly very little to see there.
If you join to my bulletin you will be among quick to hear about any new releases
http://www.georgemahood.com/contactgeorge
Signed paperback copies of all my books are available here:
http://www.georgemahood.com/shop/

If you enjoyed reading Free Country, I would be extremely grateful if you could leave a quick review on Amazon (the link will take you directly to the page). As an independently published writer, your audits and proposals to companions are fundamental for me to assist with getting the news out about the book.

Thank you such a huge amount for reading.
You are OFFICIALLY an extremely decent person.

OPERATION IRONMAN:
One Man's Four Month Journey from Hospital Bed to Ironman Triathlon

Operation Ironman follows George Mahood's moving and engaging excursion from a medical clinic bed to an Ironman marathon. After significant medical procedure to eliminate a spinal string cancer, George set himself a definitive test –

a 2.4 mile swim,

a 112 mile bicycle

ride, and a 26.2 mile
run,
all to be finished inside 16 hours.

He was unable to swim in excess of a length of front creep, he had never ridden an appropriate street bicycle, he had not run farther than 10k in year and a half… and he had never worn Lycra.

He had four months to plan.

Could he do it?

Operation Ironman is accessible now on Amazon.

HOW NOT TO GET MARRIED:

Confessions of a Wedding Photographer

Before turning into a creator, George Mahood went through 10 years filling in as a wedding photographic artist, covering north of 250 weddings. In his facetious diary, he lifts the cover on the business and the customs and patterns related with the advanced wedding.

Sometimes disputable, frequently adroit, yet continually interesting, George Mahood offers some commonsense counsel to those arranging their own wedding, sharing accounts of the weddings he shot just as his own marriage, while revealing some insight into the job of the wedding photographic artist and what it resembles to record the main day in these couples' lives.

How Not to Get Married is available on Amazon.

Acknowledgements

Firstly, I might want to say thanks to Ben for participating in this test with me. I might have portrayed him all through this book just like a whinging, youthful moaner – which is totally precise – yet he was additionally immensely engaging, loaded with energy and splendid organization. His vast energy and mind helped keep my inspiration step up all through and I can't imagine any other person I would prefer to have finished the excursion with.

Huge on account of Mark and Victoria as far as it matters for them in this undertaking and I trust that all of their diligent effort is rewarded.

Special thanks should likewise go to Rachel for her adoration, backing… and evidence reading.

And at long last, and above all, I might want to thank the many incredibly kind and liberal individuals that helped us en route. Regardless of whether this was with food, garments, bicycles, convenience, headings, discussion or lager, we are unbelievably thankful as far as concerns them in demonstrating how splendid individuals of Britain are. Without these individuals, this experience would just not have been possible.

BIG LOVE to every one
of you. George

www.facebook.com/georgemahood
www.twitter.com/georgemahood
www.instagram.com/georgemahood
www.georgemahood.com